Woman and the Priesthood

Woman and the Priesthood

by Rodney Turner

Published by
Deseret Book Company, Salt Lake City, 1975

Lithographed by

DESERET PRESS

in the United States of America

To my mother, the pioneer of my faith.

PREFACE

Woman And The Priesthood is a reaffirmation of certain basic ideals pertaining to those eternal relationships which exist between God, man and woman. Never has there been a greater need to consider these ideals in their wholeness and interrelatedness, for never have they been subjected to greater distortion and fragmentation. As the world hurtles toward its certain destruction, it spins off bits and pieces of truth. Fragmented truth is the raw material out of which error, the mother of moral and spiritual confusion, is made. She has a large and ever-increasing posterity.

The current assault on personal morality and the institution of marriage originates in Satan's campaign to destroy the family of God. If our common enemy is to be thwarted in his efforts, the Lord's people must be armed with an understanding of and a commitment to those principles which never change. Failing to do so will enable Satan to breach the walls of both Church and home, producing casualties far greater than any yet suffered.

There can be no illusions, no blind optimism. Life in this fallen world is made up of lights and shadows in varying proportions depending upon the individual. Each of us is a portrait done in colors mixed in part by our own hand and in part by circumstance and the hands of others. I have tried to present as honest and, therefore, as balanced a view of the sensitive themes treated in this book as my own understanding would allow. This has necessitated the juxtaposition of things as I believe they are with things as I believe they should be. Reality is most clearly perceived in the light of valid ideals.

Consequently, I have emphasized broad principles rather than detailed specifics. In doing so, the chief frame of reference is the word of the Lord as taught by his prophets, both ancient and modern. No apology is made for this approach since I am convinced that temporal and eternal salvation is attainable only when revealed truth is given preeminence over the rationalizations of men, however well intentioned.

Woman And The Priesthood is not and does not purport to be an authoritative statement on any of the doctrines of The Church of Jesus Christ of Latter-day Saints. The opinions stated herein are my own, being a distillation of more than twenty years of teaching, counseling and personal experience. Let them stand or fall on their own merit. That they are subject to challenge goes without saying. However, every effort has been made to assure doctrinal accuracy and inferential validity. Still, the whole truth escapes us, being possessed by God alone.

Humility enjoins tolerance upon us all—as is suggested by the following remarks of Brigham Young concerning the doctrine of sanctification:

> Were the former and Latter-day Saints, with their Apostles, Prophets, Seers, and Revelators collected together to discuss this matter, I am led to think there would be found a great variety in their views and feelings upon this subject, without direct revelation from the Lord. It is as much my right to differ from other men, as it is theirs to differ from me, in points of doctrine and principle, when our minds cannot at once arrive at the same conclusion. I feel it sometimes very difficult indeed to word my thoughts as they exist in my own mind, which, I presume, is the grand cause of many apparent differences in sentiment which may exist among the Saints.[1]

May I caution the reader against the unwarranted assumption that the writer is "as good as his word." For me, as with most of mankind, the ideal is yet to become an unblemished reality. I have not written from the lofty peaks of moral and spiritual perfection, but from the "low valley" and "plain road" of human fallibility.

A generation of Latter-day Saints is coming which, because they are pure in heart, will be privileged to establish a modern "City of Holiness" and to enter the literal presence of Jesus Christ, the God of Israel. It is to them and to

---

[1] Journal of Discourses Vol. II, p. 123. Hereafter this source will be abbreviated JD followed by the appropriate volume and page number.

their parents, teachers and guides that this work is hopefully
directed.

Rodney Turner

Provo, Utah
June 6, 1972

CONTENTS

The Family of Man

*For this cause I bow my knees unto
the Father of our Lord Jesus Christ.
Of whom the whole family in
heaven and earth is named.*[1]

Man is a citizen of the eternal universe and the highest
order of intelligence found therein. All other species of life
are lesser than and subservient to him. And man, in all of
his gradations, is, in turn, subject to the patriarchal rule of
Elohim, the Man of Holiness, the supreme exemplar of the
race.[2] His family lives in the vast reaches of space in states
ranging from organized intelligence to resurrected immortality. Therefore, those who seek man's origin on this small
planet, do so in vain. This earth is but one of God's latest
creations, organized for the purpose of providing some of
his children with bodies of flesh and bone as well as a dwelling place where they can undergo the experiences of mortality.

[1]Ephesians 3:14, 15.
[2]Moses 7:35; Abraham 3:19.

2   In testifying of the risen Christ, Joseph Smith and Sidney Rigdon declared: "That by him, and through him, and of him, *the worlds* are and were created, and *the inhabitants thereof* are begotten sons and daughters unto God."[3] Similar testimonies to the ubiquity of man were given by Moses[4] and Enoch[5] and Abraham.[6] Man is the living witness of the divine Father's nature, existence and unceasing efforts to bring to pass the immortality and eternal life of his begotten sons and daughters.[7]

The celestial residence of this Most High God is the birthplace of the entire human family.[8] William Wordsworth, with poetic insight, wrote:

> Our Birth is but a sleep and a forgetting:
> The soul that rises with us, our life's Star,
> Hath had elsewhere its setting,
> And cometh from afar:
> Not in entire forgetfulness,
> And not in utter nakedness,
> But trailing clouds of glory do we come
> From God, who is our home. . . .[9]

Divine revelation through the Prophet Joseph Smith made it possible for the Latter-day Saint poetess, Eliza R. Snow, to expand on Wordsworth's thought.

> O my Father, thou that dwellest In the high and glorious place,
> When shall I *regain* thy presence, and again behold thy face?
> In thy holy habitation, Did my spirit once reside?
> In my *first primeval childhood*, Was I nurtured near thy side? . . .

---

[3]*Doctrine and Covenants* 76:24. Hereafter this work will be designated D&C, followed by the appropriate section and verse number. (Italics by the writer.) Hereafter all italics will be by the writer, except when otherwise indicated.

[4]See Moses 1:27-39.

[5]Moses 7:29-31.

[6]Abraham 3.

[7]Moses 1:33, 38, 39.

[8]See D&C 76:23, 24, Moses 3:4-7, Job 38:7.

[9]William Wordsworth, "Ode on Intimations of Immortality From Recollections of Early Childhood."

I had learned to call thee Father, Through thy Spirit from on high;
But until the key of knowledge Was restored, I knew not why.
In the heavens are parents single? No; the thought makes reason
   stare!
Truth is reason, truth eternal Tells me I've a mother there. . . .[10]

Declared Elder Melvin J. Ballard:

No matter to what heights God has attained or may attain, he does
not stand alone; for side by side with him, in all her glory, a glory like
unto his, stands a companion, the Mother of his children. For as we have
a Father in heaven, so also we have a Mother there, a glorified, exalted,
ennobled Mother. That is a startling doctrine, I recognize, to some folk,
and yet we ought to be governed by reason in giving consideration
to this doctrine which is a revelation from God. . . . Motherhood is eternal with Godhood, and there is no such thing as eternal or endless life
without the eternal and endless continuation of motherhood.[11]

The doctrine that mortals were first begotten in spirit by
a heavenly mother is shocking to those who have assumed
that the expression "Father in heaven" was mere metaphor.
They are victims of the pagan-Christian notion that God's
being is altogether dissimilar from that of man's. This is
scripturally unsupportable and theologically incorrect. The
physical being of man testifies to the physical being of God.
Each is an affirmation—not a negation—of the other. We do
not refer to deity as *he* simply to avoid reference to him as
it. He is a *he.* The pronoun, he, would be logically meaningless (having no referent in fact) were there not some appropriate counterpart to God which established his heness—
that something is termed, *she.* We cannot define anything that
is not relatable to something else. This is precisely why
Christian theologians maintain that he, God, is incomprehensible and indefinable. Christ, however, maintained that it was
life eternal "to know thee the only true God." How can
we *know* an incomprehensible deity? There are men and
there are women; there are fathers and there are mothers.

---

[10]Hymns, Church of Jesus Christ of Latter-day Saints, p. 139.
   [11]Hinckley, Briant S. *Sermons and Missionary Experiences of Melvin J. Ballard.*
pp. 205, 206.

4   God does not produce his children by spontaneous generation from inert matter or by some sort of cloning from his
own body. All life forms have their own respective progeni-
tors in accordance with the law of biogenesis.[12]

The origin of man *is* the destiny of man. Thus, insofar
as dwelling with God is concerned, his worthy sons and
daughters do not go to heaven—they *return* to heaven. In
doing so they join that divine dynasty of fathers, mothers,
sons, and daughters which constitutes the family of God in
immortal glory.[13] Although they are holy beings, their majesty
is not cold and impersonal, they do not reign in passionless
splendor. To the contrary, as resurrected men and women,
they know life in its perfection—in its fulness. Words stand
mute before the joy of their lives. We speak of happiness,
delight, ecstacy—but how little we know of them! How brief
and mitigated are our encounters with them! Mortals cannot
experience the infinite richness, the indescribable wonder
which characterizes the lives of those who qualify for mem-
bership in the exalted family of Man.[14]

This family begins and ends in eternity. Indeed, from
the divine perspective, mortality is but a segment of eternal
time.[15] Compartmentalizing the spiritual and the temporal
is characteristic of finite man, not God. Time, space and
matter are everlasting. The Lord draws no distinction between his spiritual and his temporal creations.[16] All that he
does partakes of his own nature and is, therefore, eternal.
Then too, by definition, the universe consists of *one* reality.
A supernatural (metaphysical) order of existence is a
figment of the imagination. Things spiritual and things temporal co-exist on a single continuum of matter, much as
wave lengths of radiant energy appear as progressively

[12]*Teachings of the Prophet Joseph Smith*, ed., Joseph Fielding Smith, (Salt Lake
City, 1938), p. 373. Hereafter this source will be abbreviated TJS followed by the appropriate page number.

[13]D&C 132:19, 20.

[14]D&C 101:36; See also I Corinthians 2:9; I Peter 1:8; Moses 1:5.

[15]TJS, p. 371.

[16]See D&C 29:31-34.

darker hues on a light spectrum. All that exists anywhere throughout the eternities—whether temporal or spiritual, organic or inorganic, from the person of God to the most minute micro-organism or particle of matter—is to be found on that continuum.[17]

Therefore, earth-life is not something wholly distinct from life in heaven; it is an inexact replication of it. We learned of marriage, family and home in our "first estate." It was there that the foundation of human society was laid. Upon that foundation the Lord built the first home on this earth. Marriage and the family were not the chance inventions of primitive men (the opinions of social anthropologists notwithstanding); they are creations of God.[18] Their roots are in heaven; their branches touch the earth. They figure prominently in our happiest contemplations. When skillfully woven into a tapestry of righteousness and truth, they abide forever. Life's fabric never becomes worn, its colors never fade, its threads never break.

Unfortunately, there is one who seeks to destroy this tapestry before it can be completed. He does everything possible to pervert and defile the natures of men and women, together with those divine institutions which are based upon those natures. He seeks nothing less than the overthrow of the home; his attacks on personal morality and the marriage relationship are but means to that end. Just as Lucifer sought to win the Father's family in heaven, so does he now seek to rob God of his family on earth. Satan is a home-wrecker without peer. His efforts in this respect began almost as soon as man and woman were placed in the garden. However, he was thwarted by love—Adam's love for his Father and for Eve, and the Father's love for his children. Love remains the single most potent defense we have against the forces of evil.

---

[17]See D&C 131:7, 8; 93:33.
[18]See Abraham 3:26.

6 Winds of Change

Indeed, our world is dying for the want of love. Its death throes are a catalogue of the sins of man. They are on every hand: shouted from the housetops, flaunted before our eyes—shamelessly, defiantly. Prophecy is proving only too reliable. All things are in commotion, men's hearts do fail them as they cry "peace, peace" but find no peace—either within their nations, their families or themselves.[19] We are being swept along in an ever-swifter tide of changing events of such complexity as to defy the talents of our presumably best minds. All around we see the flotsam—the debris—of broken homes, broken lives and broken hearts. Theories are advanced, vast sums expended, programs multiply, and panaceas pronounced—still conditions worsen. The finger of accusation is pointed first here, then there, at this, at that—but solutions are not forthcoming. We drug ourselves with drugs, alcohol, sex, money, possessions, pleasures, status, power, things—even hatred—but we are not healed. Perhaps the problem is racism—we will fight for our rights. Perhaps the problem is poverty—we will demand wealth. Perhaps the problem is war—we will riot for peace. Perhaps the problem is masculine oppression—we will espouse female equality. Yes, the problem is easily identifiable: it is huge, ubiquitous and invidious—and it is always someone else's fault.

Has modern man encountered some irresistable force for social disorganization? Has the so-called knowledge explosion blown us from our ancient moorings and precipitated us into a new order of things which requires the abandonment or radical modification of our basic ideals and institutions? Specifically, is the family as we have known it—like some pre-historic animal—doomed to extinction? A growing host of contemporary thinkers believe so. They feel that the technological revolution has triggered a series of cultural explosions in virtually all aspects of life which will inevitably

---

[19]Jeremiah 6:14; Luke 21:9; D&C 45:26.

affect the nature of all human relationships. They believe that
a new age is upon us; one calling for a rethinking of our
priorities and values. For them the past is irrelevant and the
present is but prologue to things to come. Many who espouse
such sentiments are also prepared to declare the concept of
god a vestigial remain from that past and write "super-
annuated" across the ten commandments.

With the demise of moral absolutes, they argue, human
relationships can be more meaningfully redefined. Lives may
touch more lightly, less permanently than before. Sexual love
can be less restricted so that men and women may interact
with less self-consciousness, more openly, more spontaneously.
Our allegiances can be nobler, less selfish because they will
be directed toward the good of *all* mankind. Everyone can
be everyone else's keeper. No need for narrow loyalties to
a particular family, religion, or nation; mankind should be
our only loyalty, we should be bound by no other. Since all
are equal, there is no place for intolerance or talk of differences—there are none. So go the views of modern social
hedonists. However, we cannot redefine—much less annul—
God's laws. Sin is sin whether it travels by camel-back or jet
propulsion. Every age has claimed to be the exception to the
rule for which there is no exception. Material progress is no
excuse for surrendering divine principles. The world desper-
ately needs to preserve the ideals of chastity, marriage, and
the family. The more complex, remote and artificial the
general culture, the more imperative it becomes to perpetuate
the home and those foundation principles upon which it
rests.

Undeniably, the achievements of science and technology
have wrought profound modifications in the material circumstances of life on this planet, but they do not necessitate the surrender of our traditional moral values and social
patterns. And it is folly to blame our deteriorating social
and moral climate on them. Material progress is not the vil-
lain in the piece; society's ills long antedated the industrial
revolution or the atomic age. Actually, our altered material

8 situation has served more to expose our ills than to create them.

The problem does not lie in what man knows, or has, or confronts, but in his inability to successfully cope with changing circumstances. Is every ship sunk in a gale? The storm which swallows up one vessel sees another safely on its way. It is one thing to say that we are threatened by the winds of change, it is another to say that those winds make shipwreck inescapable. Such obvious evils as immorality, suicide, alcoholism, drug addiction, divorce, desertion, crime, delinquency and civil strife are not the inevitable fruits of modern life. Rather, they are but proofs that we have abandoned those principles designed to bless and sustain mankind irrespective of any external conditions encountered.

Further, it is fruitless to ask whether changes in the general society have produced the deteriorating position of the home, or whether the deterioration of the home has led to these changes. It is futile to debate sub-causes and sub-effects. What we must determine is the *first cause,* the beginning of beginnings. Not to do so is to become enmeshed in symptoms of symptoms. This is precisely what we have done. The result is confusion and impotence. It is much like a canoe floating inexorably toward a cataract while its oc-cupants argue over who was at fault for losing a paddle. One says, "It slipped from my hand because you pushed me." The other replies, "But you threw me off balance." The first rejoins, "Yes, but you tipped the canoe when you reached for your cap." And so on to final disaster. Urbanization, industrialization, shifting economic patterns, universal educa-tion, geographic mobility, the threat of nuclear destruction, a burgeoning population, the emancipation of women, or-ganized religion's diminishing significance, and the emergence of a hedonistic moral code—all of these popular suspects have contributed to our ills and compounded our problems, but no one—nor any combination of them—constitutes the primal cause of social disorganization.

Loss of the True God

That cause is spiritual rather than temporal in nature, being nothing less than man's false conception of God. The Prophet Joseph Smith said, "It is the first principle of the Gospel to know for a certainty the character of God, and to know that we may converse with him as one man converses with another. . . ."[20] All correct religious principles stem from that one central truth. When it is obscured or lost, the lives and institutions of men are characterized by relative weakness, instability and decay. Theology is to religion what a tree is to its fruits; bad theology produces bad religion. If we err in our understanding of God and his kingdom, we will err in our understanding of man and his institutions. In nothing is the harvest of a given religious philosophy more clearly perceived than in its impact on the basic structure of society. If marriage is dishonored, if the family is divided, if the home is unstable, it is because those spiritual laws which produce social stability and progress have not been obeyed. The failure to do so may be due to either ignorance or sloth, but the consequences are the same. To the extent that anyone lives in accordance with those laws their homes will be places of marital peace and happiness. However, in the absence of true religion—the gospel of Jesus Christ in its fulness—there is a structural weakness in the best of marriages and familial arrangements that makes for fracturing and disorganization under conditions of severe stress. Such conditions are upon us now. Even knowledge *about* the revealed Gospel of Jesus Christ is not enough today. Unless that knowledge is internalized, its sustaining power remains untapped. True religion cannot be worn, it must be absorbed. The world cannot practice true religion while it worships a false, non-existent god. True religion involves correct knowledge of the "only true God, and Jesus Christ, whom thou hast sent."[21] The world was robbed of that God many centuries ago.

---

[20]TJS, p. 345.
[21]John 17:3.

10   He first revealed himself to man in the Garden of Eden where God walked and talked with Adam and Eve. They knew by direct observation that they were in the literal, physical image of Deity. Man did not theorize God into existence or rationalize a kinship to him—our first parents *experienced* this knowledge.[22] Thereafter, they taught it to their family, and it became the common legacy of mankind. However, the passage of time saw men pervert this truth by turning to Satan-inspired gods of wood and stone. Heavenly bodies, the phenomena of nature and various forms of animal life were assigned divine attributes.[23] The created became the creator.

But then, as civilized man discovered more and more about the natural order of things, he repudiated his primitive gods in favor of a more esoteric deity. God was dematerialized into an essence of mind by the Greek philosophers who exalted him to transcendent eternality—the "Nous of the Cosmos." He became Aristotle's self-thinking thinker and unmoved mover—an ineffable omnipresence. Satan, the great extremist, had led mankind from one absurdity to another! Both well-served his purposes: the literal, material, anthropomorphic nature of God had been negated. However, heaven sent another witness of the truth into the world: the Only Begotten Son of the Father took upon himself a body of flesh and bone and testified that he was the perfect representation of the Father.[24] The very presence of Jesus Christ was a living reconfirmation of the fatherhood of God, and therefore, of the reality of his heavenly family. And when the Son of the Man of Holiness ascended "to my Father, and your Father; and to my God, and your God," his material body of flesh and bone was *inseparably* connected to his spirit body for all eternity.[25]

In birth and in death, Jesus demonstrated in the most objective way possible not only the materiality of God's own

---

[22]See Joseph Smith, Lectures on Faith, Lecture 2.
[23]See Romans 1:18-25; Acts 17:22-31.
[24]See John 14:7-10; Colossians 1:14, 15; Hebrews 1:3.
[25]See John 20:17; Luke 24:36-43; Acts 1:9-11; Alma 12:45; D&C 88:27, 28:93:33.

being, but the literalness of his fatherhood as well. Jesus was not speaking metaphorically in calling him Father; he was witnessing to a fundamental reality. He was literally sired by the Father both in spirit and in flesh.[26] Jesus, Adam and Moses—as well as others—perceived by personal experience, the anthropomorphic nature of God and, therefore, the theomorphic nature of man. But again, all too soon, this priceless truth was repudiated—pearls had been cast before swine. The Christian Neo-Platonists of the post-apostolic period were repelled by the notion of a material god; the concept was too exoteric for these rational sophisticates, being incompatible with their philosophic preconceptions. Not wishing to abandon Christianity entirely, they clumsily super-imposed an esoteric definition of god on the plain declarations of scripture. God was defined in their Christian creeds as he had been described in their pagan classrooms. To this extent, the Nicean and Athanasian creeds might have been written by Plato himself. Jesus, the revelation of the Father, had seemingly lived, died and been resurrected in vain; his witness was set aside in favor of the uninspired rationalizations of spiritually blind philosophers.

In destroying the truth about God, the advocates of philosophy's deity robbed mankind of the truth about itself. Plato triumphed over Paul who had testified, "For this cause I bow my knees unto the Father of our Lord Jesus Christ, of whom the whole *family in heaven and earth* is named."[27] Christian apologists cut the golden link between the Father's family in heaven and his family on earth. In doing so, they made man less than an orphan in the universe—he was rendered a mere creature, an animal, devoid of any inherent divinity or reason for existing other than to glorify some amorphous cosmic mind. The teachings of Jesus Christ were replaced with the doctrines of devils.[28]

---

[26]Romans 8:29; Colossians 1:15; John 3:16.

[27]Ephesians 2:14, 15.

[28]Now the god of traditional Christianity is being discredited by the discoveries of science. Gentile philosophers who knew nothing of the "only true and living God" fabricated a colossal error which cannot survive the test of time. No man by reasoning alone can find out God. He was first revealed to the gentiles by such prophets as the apostle Paul. See Acts 17:18-31; Ephesians 2:11-19; 3:1-8.

12   Once more, idols arose—this time, invisible idols—idols of the mind. The divine foundation of marriage and the family was again destroyed. How could they be more than mere temporal institutions designed for man's mortal condition? God was without body, parts and passions—he had no materiality. Men and women could not, therefore, be his *literal* progeny; they were simply his creatures. True, man was endowed with certain moral and intellectual faculties which set him apart from other life forms, but he had no direct connection with that transcendent being which ruled the universe. Under the theological circumstances, any idea that men and women could establish eternal relationships patterned after God's own heavenly family was ludicrous.

Indeed, rather than marriage being a divine order, it was a lower state of existence—celibacy was far more god-like. Sex was a thing heaven tolerated; like man's very body, it was of the earth earthy. After all, had not the original sin of Adam and Eve been sexual in nature? Such were the teachings of post-apostolic Christian theologians. The great apostasy was underway. It was forseen by the Prophet Isaiah.

> The earth mourneth and fadeth away, the world languisheth and fadeth away, the haughty people of the earth do languish. The earth also is defiled under the inhabitants thereof; because they have transgressed the laws, changed the ordinance, broken the everlasting covenant. Therefore hath the curse devoured the earth, and they that dwell therein are desolate: therefore the inhabitants of the earth are burned, and few men left.[29]

Can men transgress laws, change ordinances or break covenants which they never had? And if the laws and ordinances of the Gospel of Jesus Christ—including marriage—are not the ones Isaiah had in mind, then to what is he referring? Certainly not to those pertaining to the Law of Moses, for Christ fulfilled that law himself.[30] Then too, the burning of the inhabitants of the earth is invariably

---

[29]Isaiah 24:4-6.
[30]See Matthew 5:17, 18. That Christ did fulfill the Law of Moses is the burden of Paul's letter to the Galatians.

associated in scripture with the world coming of the Son of Man in the last days.[31] No, Isaiah was plainly alluding to the paganization of the Church of Christ. This was confirmed by the Lord in a revelation given in 1831 in which the apostasy was cited as the reason for restoring the true Church.[32]

Is it any wonder that increasing numbers of professing Christians are prepared to abandon the old ship of matrimony for a more modern form of marital transportation? In the past, marriage faired comparatively well because the cultural elements were, in the main, friendly toward it. Today, however, these elements are in ferment; cultural storms are raging and the seas of change are heaving themselves beyond their bounds. Under these circumstances, false religion is incapable of safeguarding the home from serious threat. The sins of the Neo-Platonic fathers are being visited upon their children's children. False theology is the basic cause for the jeopardy in which marriage finds itself. False theology stripped the family of its divine nature and destiny. False theology weakened the foundation of the home, making it vulnerable to the tremors and earthquakes of modern civilization.

Modern marriage is in danger because modern marriage has no transcending reason for being. Children are no longer an economic asset. Large families are considered an evil by those who fear an expanding world population. Traditional mores are giving way to moral relativism, etc. etc. The theological and spiritual impoverishment of many churches is exposed by the feebleness of their counter-attack and the spineless manner in which they are acquiescing to some of the most outrageous proposals made by the basest elements of society. Ours is not the first civilization to discredit man's basic institutions; virtually every ancient society did so—now they are museum specimens.

Unfortunately, the trials of modern life are tending to disintegrate the very foundation of the Christian home. Sexual laxity among young

---

[31]See 2 Peter 3:10; Malachi 4:1.
[32]See D&C 1:14-16.

14   people, birth control and intemperance, are insidious, vicious enemies of the home. When family life disintegrates, the foundation and bulwark of human society is undermined.[33]

Those who are committed to the worship of the true God and who find in his literal fatherhood the key to life's meaning, will not be overcome by the world. The Church of Jesus Christ of Latter-day Saints is built upon the sure foundation of revealed knowledge concerning the family of Man. Neither it nor that family will be overthrown.

---

[33]President David O. McKay, "The Instructor" January 1958, p. 1.

II

Man and Woman

*So God created man in his own
image, in the image of God
created he him; male and female
created he them.*[1]

Man and woman originate in God.[2] Whatever their differences, the sexes are biologically, psychologically and spiritually bone of one another's bone and flesh of one another's flesh. They develop out of a shared beginning. Even as a fetus establishes its species before it reveals its gender, so are men and women human before they are masculine or feminine. Like branches of a tree, they emerge from a common trunk. In doing so, they remain together even as they grow apart in their individual quests for fulfillment.

---

[1]Genesis 1:27.

[2]The origin of the sexes has not been revealed. A nascent form of sexuality may have characterized each primal intelligence. In its fullness, maleness or femaleness was acquired as a genetic endowment from mankind's celestial parents. In asserting that sex is eternal, John A. Widtsoe wrote: "A wiser power than any on earth understands why a spirit in the far off beginning was male or female." *Priesthood and Church Government*, p. 90. Hereafter this work will be designated as PCG, followed by the appropriate page number. See TJS, pp. 352-55.

16 In growing apart, men and women do not develop traits and emotions which are wholly unique—much less antithetical—to one another.[3] Male and female qualities are found in both sexes in balanced, but not equal, proportions. As with hormones, those qualities which are dominant in one sex are designed to be recessive in the other. In this way, each sex is distinguished by its chief characteristics. This permits each to draw upon the virtues and strengths of its opposite member without any loss of self-identity and without any claim to moral exclusiveness.

Compassion is no more unique to women than is courage to men. Both sexes are designed to manifest all of the attributes of God, but each is to do so without doing violence to its own nature and calling. Both should sing the same song, but not the same part. For example, mother love stems from *being* a mother, not from being a father. While both sexes are to express the same basic emotions, they are to do so *as* men and *as* women. Jesus often manifested love, compassion and gentleness, but he did so in the context of his manhood. He did not become effeminate in order to effect a gentle demeanor. Nor will any true woman assume a masculine attitude in order to express courage, determination or any other presumedly masculine quality.

One's sexual nature determines one's eternal possibilities. Satan's efforts to nullify that nature is a direct consequence of his own awful plight. The Gods are men and women in the fullest and best sense of those terms. They graciously share their endowments with their faithful children. However, it is most unlikely that men and women had their sex arbitrarily imposed upon them. For while scripture states that God "made" man male and female insofar as *this* world is concerned, it does not explain the basis upon which any

---

[3]Human traits and emotions were manifest in man's first estate. While the *manner* in which they are now expressed may be somewhat a matter of learned behavior, the *inclination* to do so is not. Whatever our situation, to some extent we all express the common emotions of the race as it existed in the pre-mortal world and as it exists now.

given spirit is tabernacled in a male or female body.[4] But
regardless of when or how males and females came into being, the principle of agency must have played a part in anything God did; coercion is alien to his nature. Then too, the
arbitrary assignment of sex would have rendered him particularly vulnerable to criticism at the last judgment. Thus,
just as it is very likely that one's sex reflects one's own inate
predisposition or personal choice, so must the roles the sexes
play stem from their own inherent proclivities. What men
and women are should determine how they will act—not
vice versa.

Today, much in the fashion of Huxley's *Brave New
World,* men speak of controlling the genetic factors in the
unborn so as to produce various human types which will
meet society's pre-determined requirements. This is diabolical.
Man is more than a composite of protein molecules; he is
not meant to be manipulated, even by God—much less by
anyone else. God's humility protects us from the devil's
pride. Being far more humble than some of Satan's unwitting
allies, the Lord has never presumed to impose his will on
others; He has always respected man's independent co-
eternality. God's laws are framed to serve man as he is and
as he wills to be. Law is the servant, not the master, of mankind.[5] Men and women are not programmed with artificial
characteristics to serve the veiled purposes of some cosmic
scientist. The sexes are genuinely distinctive from one
another; only in denying their true natures do they become
false and artificial.

More than male gallantry lies behind the belief that,
in this fallen state, women as a group are more refined and
spiritually inclined than men. Said Brigham Young:

---

[4] Genesis 1:27, Matthew 19:4; Ether 3:14-16; Moses 3:1, 7, 9; Job 38:7. Joseph Smith
declared: "The organization of the spiritual and heavenly worlds, and of spiritual and
heavenly beings, was agreeable to the most perfect order and harmony: their limits and
bounds were fixed irrevocably, and *voluntarily subscribed to in their heavenly estate by
themselves,* and were by our first parents subscribed to upon the earth. Hence the importance of embracing and subscribing to principles of eternal truth by all men upon the earth
that expect eternal life." *History of The Church,* Vol. VI, p. 51.

[5] See TJS, p. 354.

18

The men are the lords of the earth, and they are more inclined to reject the Gospel than the women. The women are a great deal more inclined to believe the truth than the men; they comprehend it more quickly, and they are submissive and easy to teach. . . .[6]

Having observed several women leave a saloon, President Young asked:

What do you think of that, sisters? It is a disgrace to the name of lady. Is it any more a disgrace in woman than in man? Yes, because he is by nature coarser and more prone to such wickedness than she is. Woman is altogether of a finer nature, and has stronger moral inclinations; it is not natural for her to indulge in wickedness that man takes common delight in.[7]

It is this very difference between the fallen natures of men and women which is being undermined by contemporary social and moral trends. Women cannot change their attitudes and behavior without changing themselves. If women are not the gentler, the purer sex, it is because they have altered that nature with which the Creator endowed them in the beginning.

Not only should men and women manifest their shared human traits and emotions within their respective natures, it is also imperative that they honor those roles which are indigenous to those natures. Men must act the part of men —being sons, husbands, fathers, providers, agents of God in the world at large, and brothers to their brothers. Women must act the part of women—being daughters, wives, mothers, homemakers, teachers and guides of their children and sisters to their sisters. These are the core roles each is ordained to play. All other things are secondary to them. When men and women cannot or will not fulfill these roles, society is thrown off balance with resulting disorder and suffering.

Only through an harmonious blending of their natures can man and woman achieve perfection. Such a blending requires that they fulfill their foreordained callings. There can

---

[6]JD 14:120, See JD 12:194.
[7]JD 18:233.

be no warfare between them. Neither must deny or betray the virtues, rights and privileges of the other. Neither must impugn the uniqueness of the other. To weaken or repudiate the profoundly distinctive qualities of either sex is to pervert the original natures of both. This is death. Only as the sexes comprehend and magnify one another can manhood and womanhood be transformed into godhood.

> As unto the bow the cord is,
> So unto the man is woman:
> Though she bends him, she obeys him,
> Though she draws him, yet she follows,
> Useless each without the other![8]

The very beings of man and woman serve to delineate their proper roles and, therefore, to delimit the manner in which they are to exercise physical and moral agency. As with all other things, mankind has been placed in a kingdom of law appropriate to its nature, to which it is subject, and in which it must fill the measure of its creation.[9] When men and women attempt to ignore the appointed bounds of their habitation by violating the laws and breaking through the frontiers of that kingdom, the inevitable consequences are futility and sorrow.

Degrees of Glory

Regardless of what they were in the beginning, in mortality, neither men nor women are struck from a common mold. Like the stars in the heavens, they are of many different spiritual, moral and intellectual magnitudes. This diversity, together with man's essential complexity, accounts for the failure of the social sciences to achieve the validity and reliability possible in the physical sciences. While we refer to the *laws* of physics and chemistry, we are yet to

---

[8]Henry Wadsworth Longfellow, The Song of Hiawatha, *The Poems of Henry Wadsworth Longfellow*. Thomas Y. Crowell Co., 1901, p. 291.
[9]D&C 88:36-39; 93:30-32.

20 seriously apply that term to man's findings pertaining to his inner-most self. For this reason, human progress has been predominantly of a material order. Man continues to know more about his outer environment than his inner nature. He continues to obey those laws which serve his flesh with far more zeal than those which serve his spirit.

Yet the essence of man *is* his spirit—the seat of human individuality.[10] The variety of physical types and characteristics which distinguish one race, one ethnic group, or one individual from another, testify to similar spiritual differences among men and women. We brought many of these differences with us from our former estate. Although sinless at birth[11] and tabernacled in infant bodies, the spirits entering mortality are physically mature men and women possessing distinctive attributes, capacities and proclivities.[12] We do not spring into existence at the moment of conception, becoming as it were but chance recapitulations of our hereditary forebears. Human individuality is an eternal principle. We do not *become* individuals, we *are* individuals. We are not founded *in* mortality, we are added upon *by* mortality. Mortality modifies personality, it does not create it. And at death, we return to a spirit state, retaining those modified qualities which we formerly possessed.[13] The thread of life is never broken; it is characterized by an ongoing continuity from one phase of existence to another. Were this not the case, it would be meaningless to speak of the *eternal* nature of man.

In the beginning, all men and women were characterized by the positive attributes with which they were endowed by their divine parents. Thus each individual began organized existence with a natural-spiritual predisposition toward moral virtue. This is why Brigham Young maintained that the "natural man" (meaning the immortal spirit) is good.

---

[10]See D&C 93:33.
[11]See D&C 93:28; Abraham 3:22; Moroni 8:8.
[12]Ballard, *op. cit.*, p. 248, JD 11:305.
[13]See Alma 34:34; 40:11-14.

That which was, is, and will continue to endure is *more natural* than that which will pass away and be no more. The natural man is of God. We are the natural sons and daughters of our natural parents, and *spiritually we are the natural children of the Father* of light and natural heirs to his kingdom; and when we do an evil, we do it in opposition to the promptings of the Spirit of Truth that is within us. Man, the noblest work of God, was in his creation designed for an endless duration, for which the *love of all good was incorporated in his nature*. It was never designed that he should *naturally* do and love evil.[14]

However, God's "design" for his children is mitigated by the moral agency with which he has also endowed them. The power to be good is equally the power to be evil. So that while those women who yield themselves to the Spirit of the Lord will be modest and virtuous—*if* taught these principles—yet modesty and virtue are not characteristic of all women. This applies to every facet of human personality. Women do not necessarily manifest a love for virtue, goodness, marriage, motherhood and the things of God simply because they are women any more than men manifest a love for courage, honor, strength and fatherhood simply because they are men. The "natural" tendencies of which Brigham Young spoke have been negated in some men and women. The true woman is she who understands and seeks to perfect her eternal nature, while the false woman is she who, for whatever reason, has gone against it. Such generalizations are inevitably tainted with oversimplification, still, they are of value in arriving at a sense of the pattern of things. No harm is done so long as we do not fail to qualify them when considering a specific individual. With this understanding, we proceed to generalize.

Each of us is a living degree of glory. We range from those who are characterized by godly dispositions on down to those who are extremely "carnal, sensual and devilish." Broadly speaking, it may be said that the dominant spiritual coloration of each of us is either celestial, terrestrial, or telestial—which is to say, either holy, good, or wicked.[15]

---

[14]JD 9:305.

[15]See D&C 88:28-35. The fourth class, the mortal sons of perdition—being a unique group—are not pertinent to this discussion.

22   These basic spiritual temperaments are, of course, subject to
such modifying influences as one's hereditary endowment,
psycho-physical makeup, external environment and life experiences. Still, all things being equal, the chief determinant
of one's interests, attitudes, beliefs and behavior is the spirit's
own proclivities.

These proclivities are expressed through the human will
which is ordinarily capable of responding to all external
stimuli in its own unique way. And it is only when the spirit
is free to exercise its own will (mind) that its true character
can be ascertained. This is why moral agency is so vital to
the work of God.[16] However, one's spiritual status is not only
determined by the quality of the individual will and the extent to which the things of God are comprehended, it is
also determined by the degree to which one is responsive
to the spiritual powers of God. The more these powers
directly influence the individual's life, the closer one is to
God and, therefore, the greater one's present glory.

A telestial person is one who is more or less indifferent
to God and His laws and who, therefore, tends to resist his
Spirit. A terrestrial person is one who seeks to live according
to the light and knowledge possessed and who, therefore, is
relatively responsive to the influence of the Spirit. A celestial person is one who not only enjoys the Spirit, but who
has come unto Christ by entering into a valid covenant with
him, thereby receiving the higher endowment known as the
gift of the Holy Ghost.[17] Thus, one's degree of mortal glory
is determined by the extent to which he or she has become
spiritually one with God.[18]

---

[16]See D&C 101:78.

[17]See John 14:16, 17; 16:13; D&C 76:50-52, 71-79, 81-84; 84:44-46, 74; 88:6-13; 130:
21-23; 2 Nephi 31:12, 13; Moses 6:60, 61.

The Spirit of the Lord is God's universal influence which guides and sustains all
life. The gift of the Holy Ghost is the privilege of receiving specific instruction and support when needed from the third member of the Godhead.

[18]Presently, we are in a fluid (repentable) state which allows us to modify our
condition. The resurrection seals that glory upon us which we ultimately attain. See
D&C 76; 88:29-35; Alma 41.

The City of Men

The very attributes which characterize a woman of high spiritual endowment suggest that, for now, her essential mileu is the home rather than the world at large. Those who are continually subjected to the ravages of wind, rain, heat and cold are invariably weathered by them. Likewise, no woman can fully identify with the work-a-day world of men and escape unmarked. Men, with their generally less refined natures, do not; how can women hope to do so? Modern urban life is often soul-desensitizing. The dull routine, the unremitting pressures, the ceaseless competitiveness, the constant jostling with alien personalities, the daily necessity of reestablishing one's worth—these are the elements which batter away at the basic personalities of many men and women today.

One has only to recall the bone-weary demeanor of subway riders in New York, the strained expression on the faces of most pedestrians in any city, or the frustration of home-bound workers on the car-clogged freeways of the land to know that we have paid a high price for twentieth century civilization. Consider how most people spend their leisure time. Modern man never exposes his basic unhappiness more clearly than when he is pretending to amuse himself. How joyless are his pleasures!

The urbanization of human life has taken a toll in human identity. As men become alienated from the earth which gave them life, so do they become alienated from themselves. Self-rejection, anxiety, loneliness—how frequently we hear such terms today! It is significant that Cain became a fugitive and a vagabond only after he had defiled the earth with his brother's blood. It was then that the earth turned against him, forcing him to wander for survival. And it was because he had become a wanderer, exiled from the land, that he built the first city on this planet.[19] Without God, the city and all that it represents is a curse. It allows wicked men to

---

[19]See Moses 5:42.

24   establish concentrations of mutual contamination where evil can feed upon itself while hiding in the anonymity of its own mass.

When women willingly join men in their "city," when they willingly forsake the home, they, too, become fugitives and vagabonds in the earth—fugitives from their own natures, vagabonds in a masculine world. For it is in willingly becoming "city dwellers" that they compromise those qualities and attitudes which are the hallmark of the true woman. They do this, not by their physical presence in the city, but by their emotional commitment to it. The Savior declared: "where your treasure is, there will your heart be also."[20]

It is in putting their hearts upon the "treasures" of the city that they become spiritually impoverished. Their destitute condition is exposed by a certain brittle facade which, although similar to that of many males, is nevertheless more offensive because it is a contradiction of the feminine character. In its extreme form, this acquired masculinity emerges as a third sex—being neither truly male nor female. That women can take on something of the male temperament is undeniable. Indeed, if obliged to live and think like a man —facing the life situations of a man—there are few women who will not do so.[22]

The foregoing is equally applicable to men. At present, we can only guess at the impact of technology on the human personality. Men have moved indoors, away from the land, from the natural order of things into the artificial environment of the modern office, plant and store. It is in just these settings that the toll on the male character has been the greatest. The influx of millions of women into these same settings seems only to have accelerated the process of change for both sexes.

As was previously stated, however, these alterations in the human temperament are only symptomatic of the fact that the world has lost its way. Admittedly, this generation

[20]Matthew 6:21.
[22]See 1 Nephi 17:1, 2.

has had a radically different order of things imposed upon it, but men and women can cope with change without compromising their own identities when they are committed to righteous principles. Lacking those principles, and becoming conditioned to non-masculine and non-feminine roles—with all of their concomitant implications—men and women tend to think, talk, dress, and respond less and less *as* men and women. The recessive qualities inherent in each sex assume a kind of perverse dominance and, like some cancer of the emotions, destroy the very being they were meant to temper and enhance.

If women, by imitating the masculine way of life, assume male nuances, it is not unlikely that men, in duplicating the thought patterns and activities of women, will assume female attitudes and characteristics. This is precisely what is happening among some segments of society today. The two sexes are breaking away from their natural moorings and drifting toward each other.

Indeed, society has less and less need for men and women *as* men and women. Modern technology—both industrial and medical—has made it possible for the sexes to replace one another in virtually all enterprises between birth and death. Even government affirms the equality of the sexes. No distinction—whether in law, education, employment, economic rewards or civil and personal rights—are to be tolerated. In so far as human biology will allow, we are legislating a uni-sex society. Women are not being so much liberated as they are being absorbed into a neuter gender world of common humanity. Many are simply exchanging one form of bondage for another. When the novelty of their new surroundings has worn off, they will long for the good old days, forgetting that they, too, left much to be desired.

Admittedly, circumstances have forced many women to join the work-a-day world for sheer survival. From time immemorial, infant mortality, disease and war have created serious imbalances in the ratio of males to females. Many women have been obliged to live with little or no male sup-

26 port. Then there are those whose husbands are either unwilling or unable to provide for their families. Divorce and desertion are also major causes of the influx of wives and mothers into the labor force. Many of these women are victims of unrighteous social conditions. However, there are many others who are not justified in leaving their homes for outside employment. They—and often their husbands—are motivated by purely selfish factors. Dislike of childbearing and childrearing and/or the other duties associated with motherhood and homemaking, rejection of husband, an appetite for material luxuries, economic freedom, the desire to gratify some ambition, to exploit a presumed talent or to be part of that supposedly more exciting world beyond one's front gate—these are the chief reasons millions of women are turning to the "city of men." These women left home to embrace marriage, only to leave home to escape it.

Woman's Freedom

The false prophet has been joined by the false prophetess. Strident female voices now proclaim the emancipation of woman from her womanhood. No longer is she to be bound by the restrictions of her traditional role in society. No longer will she accept the male-imposed bondage her sex has known from time immemorial. She is free! This movement is but one manifestation of a general retreat from the old established order of things. Ours is the time of fulfillment of Isaiah's words, "As for my people, children are their oppressors and women rule over them."[23] The order of heaven is being turned upside down. Life is in commotion. The tides of change are moving swiftly, sweeping before them much that has been; it was inevitable that many women would be swept along by these tides. Mass education, industrialization, and the technological revolution have

---

[23]Isaiah 3:12.

profoundly influenced the lives of millions of females. They have become breadwinners in their own right. Money is freedom. The political and social emancipation of women is due more to their growing economic independence than to any other single factor. In this respect, they are not unlike children who, finding themselves gainfully employed, promptly demand greater freedom of action than they previously enjoyed. Males have abetted this trend, not only by creating the very conditions which allowed women to achieve economic independence, but by their own willingness—even eagerness—to have them become co-producers of material wealth.

Woman's historic calling as wife and mother is being minimized. As the family has diminished in size and importance, so has the role of mother and homemaker. Modern inventions have allowed for the semi-automation of the home. Technology has created time; many wives and husbands are inclined to hoard it for themselves. It is paradoxical that the conveniences of modern life have led to decreased, rather than increased, emphasis on the family. As it becomes easier to have children and care for the home, we are less and less inclined to do so. The reason for this is obvious: we no longer *need* children as we once did. Or perhaps we might say, the need for children *as children* has not been too widespread. Once they were an economic asset, now they are a liability. Now they must be desired for themselves, not for any economic contribution they might be able to make. Sadly, fewer and fewer men and women have this desire. Hearts are shrinking. The love of many grows cold. Having little love to give, they have little need for children upon whom to bestow it. Many reasons may be advanced for having small families—all very logical—but the truth is, nothing within our power really deters us from producing life but the want of love.

The radical feminist movement is anti-woman. Those who succumb to its blandishments are not freed, but enslaved. How many times have men been sold into servitude

28 with promises of freedom! Those who speak of liberating women are time-bound in their thinking. They define freedom in terms of the here and now. Temporal freedom. Mortal freedom. The freedom to be fulfilled as they *will* to be fulfilled. Selfish freedom. Ego-centric freedom. Knowing no world but this world, having no god but a false one, they are determined to drink life to its dregs. In all of this, they are but mimicking those they purport to repudiate. Like slaves, their overweening ambition is not to transcend their masters but to join them. Contrary to their charge, it is not the male ego, but the female nature which has rightly defined wifehood and motherhood as the noblest callings of womankind.

Extremists in the feminist movement utterly reject this viewpoint. The idea of losing their lives in a cause other than themselves is considered laughable. They do not agitate for the right to be women; they demand, instead, the right to be *persons*—meaning, the right to renounce their uniqueness and, therefore, their responsibilities as women. Certainly, one should be respected as a person, but this does not necessitate the denigration of those characteristics which make one a male or female person. We cannot dichotomize humanity and sexuality; the two are interwoven in every normal person. Nor is sexuality limited to sex activity anymore than piety is limited to prayer. Both terms are multifaceted. The sexual natures of man and woman encompass all of the emotions, powers and proclivities which serve both to unite and to distinguish the sexes. Consequently, those who refuse to accept the full implications of their sexuality do not obey those divine laws which direct and control that sexuality. It is no accident that many advocates of woman's "rights" also espouse the cause of complete sexual permissiveness.

In insisting upon the privilege of uncontrolled sexual activity, *as persons*, these deluded souls are reducing themselves to something less than complete human beings. Their attitude constitutes the shadow of the eternal reality which will follow. For paradoxically, their negation of those responsibilities which are associated with being a whole man or a whole woman will lead to God's negation of them *as whole persons.* Having denied the divine meaning of manhood and womanhood, they will be shorn of those attributes and powers which are the essence of these states of being. To that extent, the impersonal pronoun will apply; rather than being a he or a she, they will become an "it."[24] And that, presumably, is what they were agitating for all along.

While women are fully justified in denouncing male exploitation, to insist upon being accepted as neuter persons rather than female persons, is to expose themselves to even more pernicious forms of male exploitation in the future. They forget that woman's nature was meant to have a mollifying effect on man. For it was from her that he was to first learn the ways of tenderness and compassion, of sacrifice and devotion. Only by magnifying their roles as mothers, can women effectively temper their sons. When women reject their divine appointment and strike out in pursuit of some quasi-liberty patterned after the behavior of men, there is no one left to gentle their sons and prepare them to love and honor woman as she was meant to be loved and honored. Thus, an emotional vacuum is created in the hearts of men and women alike. Life for everyone becomes unbalanced, skewed in favor of the material and the rational as opposed to the spiritual and the emotional. Hearts become hardened. Lives are blighted. Minds destroyed. Bodies corrupted. Souls lost.

We must not forget that woman was given to man to be his "helpmeet"—not his competitor. God's pronouncements upon Adam and Eve subsequent to their transgression in Eden were meant to apply to the entire human race.[25] If men and women refuse to abide by the principles enunciated in those pronouncements, nothing can save them from personal and collective disaster. Indeed, to the degree that

---

[24]See JD 4:143.
[25]See Genesis 3:16-19.

30   we have deviated from them, we are evidencing the pathology of disorganization. Those who will not faithfully execute the will of God as revealed in the *first* judgment will inevitably face the consequences of their rebellion at the *last* judgment.

Men need liberating no less than women; the entire human race is in bondage to sin and error. The whole world needs to be liberated from its false conceptions of God, man, woman, love, marriage, sex, family, and life itself. Man's problems do not arise from his institutions, but from his ignorance of their true nature and purpose. It is a straight and narrow path that leads to true freedom. Few have been the times when mortals have enjoyed the liberty, the security, and the happiness for which they were organized. Only as men and women come to understand and to accept themselves for what they are, will they find the happiness they seek through becoming *what they were meant to be.*

The Time of Fulfillment

But it may be asked, "Were men meant to be nothing other than husbands and fathers? Were women meant to be nothing but wives and mothers? What of our own needs? Is there to be no self-identity as a person in one's own right? Can I not sing my own song, dream my own dream, express my own creative ability—can I not be fulfilled in the secret places of my own soul?" If "man is that he might have joy," if eternal life is to be more than an everlasting recapitulation of mortality, how could it be otherwise? Clearly, men and women are meant to be "free indeed." The enslaved farmer depicted in Edwin Markham's "The Blind Plowman," or the haggard seamstress of Thomas Hood's "Song of the Shirt" are not examples of the nobility of work. Rather, they make plain the fact that we are stripped of our essential humanity when we are reduced to the quest for bread alone. So too, our divine potential cannot be realized unless that inner core of self-hood is fulfilled along with all else. We are not only children of God, not only human beings, not only men and women—we are also eternal intelligences—self-existing personalities. Our heavenly Father wills the perfection of his sons and daughters in every dimension of their beings. A "fulness of joy" can come in no other way.

However, for many reasons, we cannot expect—much less demand—total self-fulfillment in mortality. Life has its priorities. First things must be done first because they *are* first things. Now is the time to lay the foundation for eternal life—not to live it. We cannot now be all that we would be or do all that we would do. Indeed, perfect happiness through total fulfillment is impossible in this life.[26] The Savior surrendered himself to the will of the Father "from the beginning."[27] In doing so, he muted his glory in order to minister to his brothers and sisters. How many gifted men and women have willingly sacrificed their desires and abilities for others! This is the essence of true discipleship. We cannot have an eye *single* to the glory of God if we insist upon self-fulfillment here and now. Paradoxically, genuine self-fulfillment can only be achieved as we voluntarily surrender it. We must lose our life before we can find it.

Then too, one's particular circumstances together with the impact of the agency of others on one's own agency precludes total fulfillment in mortality. This life is characterized by imbalances, by injustices. The wicked seem to prosper about as much—if not more—than the righteous. Virtue does not appear to triumph as often as we would like. The inequities of this world tempt us to covet the other man's health, freedom, wealth, talents and pleasures. We overvalue the things of time because we underestimate the things of eternity. The bird in hand continues to be more highly prized than the uncertain covey in the bush. Lacking faith in God and his promises, we put our trust in man—his arm and his possessions. Solomon had all that money and power could buy. He was glutted with success. Yet be-

---

[26]See D&C 101:36-38.
[27]3 Nephi 11:11.

32

ing so, he pronounced it all "vanity and vexation of spirit."[28] It was "vanity" because it could not be forever retained. It was "vexation of spirit" because it did not produce lasting happiness.

This does not mean that material possessions and self-realization are without enduring value; to the contrary, they are of everlasting worth. What it does mean is that there is a due time and a proper way to achieve them. Like God, himself, we must labor before we can rest. The basic needs of mankind must be satisfied before we can cater to our special interests as individuals. It is not, therefore, a matter of women being limited to their roles as wives and mothers. They can and should develop all of the dimensions of their being to the extent that their primary roles will permit.

However, if they are to do so without inadvertently stealing time, effort and devotion from the things that matter most, they must be convinced that nothing they may do outside of the home can begin to equal in lasting significance the things they can accomplish in the home. Lacking this conviction, many women commit little disloyalties against their families while carefully justifying themselves in doing so. Indeed, the ability to rationalize our failings is one talent with which we are all fully endowed at birth. The Savior's admonition to "seek ye first the kingdom of God, and his righteousness," applies with equal force to men and women. This commandment cannot be kept without self-denial. For most, this means setting aside some of life's ambitions, opportunities, and pleasures. For others it means surrendering life itself. Jesus did both.[29]

But that is all past. Today we sing, "Once a meek and lowly lamb, *now* the Lord, the great I AM." And so shall it be for every righteous man and woman. Faith in the Lord must include the hope that—whatever our present limitations —we will yet come into our own. Joseph Smith, who was

---

[28]Ecclesiastes 1:14.
[29]D&C 122:5-8.

also cut down in the prime of his manhood, assured the saints that nothing of genuine worth is really lost. "All your losses will be made up to you in the resurrection, provided you continue faithful. By the vision of the Almighty I have seen it."[30] And Brigham Young promised the Saints:

> I say again—"Seek ye first the kingdom of God and His righteousness," and in due time, no matter when, whether in this year or in the next, in this life or in the life to come, "all these things" (that appear so necessary to have in the world) "shall be added unto you." Everything that is in heaven, on the earth, and in the earth, everything the most fruitful mind can imagine, shall be yours, sooner or later.[31]

With such assurances, men and women can rejoice in being what they were meant to be and in doing all that God has called them to do.

---

[30]TJS, p. 296. See also JD 2:122, 125.
[31]JD 2:125.

III

In the Beginning

> . . . *We will go down, for there is*
> *space there, and we will take of these*
> *materials, and we will make an earth*
> *whereon these may dwell; And we will*
> *prove them herewith, to see if they*
> *will do all things whatsoever the Lord*
> *their God shall command them; . . .*[1]

God is the highest good; the *summum bonum* of life.[2]
His works testify to his perfection and are flawless when they
leave his hands. Summing up his labors in organizing the
earth, the Creator told Moses: "all things which I had made
were very good."[3] Life on this planet began in the heights
of excellence. The world was a place of light, life and truth.
Sin and death were unknown. Man was magnificent in form
and intelligence. He did not originate in chaotic darkness.
He did not evolve over eons of time out of ignorance and
bestiality. He did not stumble upon God and his laws—much

---

[1]Abraham 3:24, 25.
[2]See Matthew 19:17.
[3]Moses 2:31.

36 less fabricate them. They were revealed to man at the out-
set of his earthly soujourn. To be happy, it only remained
for him to obey those laws and to worship that God. This,
the race has not done.

Employing their God-given agency, men have rampaged
across the world defiling and defacing every lovely thing. In
this senseless enterprise, they have been fiercely abetted by
Satan, who contrived to lead the pillage and spur his dupes
on to ever more terrible assaults against heaven's rule. Suffice
to say, every ideal God has shared with man has been perverted by him.[4] The Lord taught Adam correct principles
pertaining to religion, government, society, the family and
general morality only to have his children—generation after
generation—wrest them into a thousand counterfeit forms.
In the main, the story of mankind has been the story of
paradise lost. But how was it in the beginning? Let us return to the Garden.

In the Garden

After organizing the earth and preparing the Garden of
Eden, the Most High placed Michael, who subsequently became known as Adam, in his new home.[5] Although he was a
perfect being, yet he was incomplete—for "man" is both
male and female.[6] Adam was but half of *man* therefore, he
was alone. But, as the Lord observed, it was "not good" for
him to remain so.[7] If man was to achieve eternal life and
"a fulness of joy" (which must be shared to be possessed),
he could not remain alone.

To be alone is to be without life-creating power, without
ultimate wholeness or the perfection of heaven. Those of a
divine temperament are frustrated until this condition is remedied. Spirit cannot be isolated from spirit without suffer-

---

[4]See JD 8:209.
[5]Genesis 2:7-15; D&C 27:11.
[6]See Moses 2:27; 6:9.
[7]*Ibid.*, 3:18.

ing some degree of death. The gods are not alone. They delight in sharing themselves with others. But what a miserable deity the Christian world has concocted for itself—one that is utterly transcendent, formless, sterile, void of materiality, having no companion and no peers—yet ruling in awful remoteness over a vast and uncomprehending universe.[8] Such a state would relegate the God of Heaven to the depths of hell! Jesus, the living revelation of the Father, gave the lie to this satanic doctrine. His life was one of constant interaction with others. Little children, publicans, sinners, pharisees —the high and the low—all knew (without knowing) what it was to walk and talk with God made flesh. He died so that no one need ever be alone or lonely again.

Of course, various members of the animal kingdom were also denizens of the Garden and they were doubtless interesting and amusing company, but they were not the god *kind*, the man *kind*.[9] They were lesser orders of life, totally distinct from man. Adam could not treat them as equals or become one with them. He was worthy of a companion whose attributes and powers were like his own. Nor would another male—a mere replica of himself—do, for he would still be alone. He needed the complement of his own being—a female. When he awakened from the sleep of forgetfulness put upon him by the gods, she stood before him. *Man* was complete.

Giving Woman Away

In the divine order, woman is given to man, not man to woman. Eve was brought to Adam to be his helpmate, he was not brought to her. Paul noted, "For the man is not of the woman; but the woman of the man. Neither was the man created for the woman; but the woman for the man."[10] At first glance, it might appear that woman is inferior to

---

[8]See JD 2:120.
[9]Moses 3:18-20.
[10]I Corinthians 11:8, 9.

38   man, that she exists only for his benefit. This is incorrect.
Man and woman are equal before the Lord. However, they
are not the same before him. Maleness and femaleness do
make for very real differences between the sexes. God respects these differences; his reactions to them are not arbitrary.
The respective callings of men and women simply reflect the
unique qualifications and temperaments of each. Indeed, as
was previously stated, their happiness depends upon their
acceptance and magnification of these intrinsic natural factors. The highest expression of godhood is achieved through
a perfect blending of the attributes of man and woman. How
could she be less than his equal?

The practice of giving men their wives stems from the
principle of stewardship and, ultimately, from the fact that
all organized life exists as such by the grace of God and is,
in effect, his possession. This does not mean that man is
merely God's puppet. Being co-eternal with deity, we have a
certain autonomy—free will. However, in aspiring to the
divine way of life, we voluntarily submitted to the divine
rule of law. It is, therefore, in God that "we live, and move,
and have our being."[11] He possesses us because we willed to
be possessed. "The earth is the Lord's, and the fulness thereof; the world, and they that dwell therein."[12] It is his
"property right" to give his daughters to whom he will. The
custom of the father of the bride "giving her away" origi-
nated in Eden. An examination of the scriptures, especially
the Old Testament, reveals many instances where wives were
given to men, by a father, another wife, a king, or a prophet.
For example, Laban gave his daughters Leah and Rachel
to Jacob, and they, in turn, gave Jacob their hand-maidens
as concubines. Pharaoh gave Asenath to Joseph. Jethro gave
his daughter Zipporah to Moses. Saul's daughter Michal was
given to David and later taken from him and given to
another. And so it goes. Even the Lord, in rebuking David
for taking Bathsheba, told him through Nathan the prophet:

---

[11]See Acts 17:28; D&C 88:13, 41; 93:29-33; TJS, pp. 352-355.
[12]Psalm 24:1.

"And I gave thee thy master's house, and thy master's wives into thy bosom, and gave thee the house of Israel and of Judah; and if that had been too little, I would moreover have given unto thee such and such things."[13]

The Doctrine and Covenants also attests to this principle.

Abraham received concubines, and they bore him children; and it was accounted unto him for righteousness, because *they were given unto him,* and he abode in my law; as Isaac also and Jacob did none other things than that which they were commanded; . . . as also many others of my servants, from the beginning of creation until this time; and in nothing did they sin save in those things which they received not of me. David's wives and concubines were *given unto him of me,* by the hand of Nathan, my servant, and others of the prophets who had the keys of this power; and in none of these things did he sin against me save in the case of Uriah and his wife; and, therefore he hath fallen from his exaltation, and received his portion; and he shall not inherit them out of the world, for *I gave them unto another,* saith the Lord.[14]

However, the giving of a wife should be done only with the willing consent of the woman herself. Any degree of coercion is devilish. God, who forces no man to heaven, will not justify the marriage of a female to anyone she does not freely accept. The story of Isaac and Rebekeh is a case in point.[15] Abraham, concerned lest Isaac marry a Cannanite, sought a wife for him from among their own people in Haran. After meeting Rebekeh, Abraham's trusted servant approached Bethuel, her father, in behalf of Isaac. Although her family agreed to the alliance, the final decision was left to Rebekeh, "Wilt thou go with this man?" and she said, "I will go."[16] Another intermediary was the angel Gabriel who, acting in behalf of the Father, presented Mary with the most sacred proposal any mortal woman has ever received. After explaining to the young virgin that she had found

---

[13]2 Samuel 12:8.
[14]D&C 132:37-39.
[15]See Genesis 24.
[16]*Ibid.,* 24:58.

40 favor with the Lord and was to be blessed above all women in bearing the very Son of God, she gave her consent saying, "Behold the handmaid of the Lord; be it unto me according to thy word."[17] Unfortunately, this principle has been frequently violated. Countless females have been bought, sold, used and destroyed at the whim of unfeeling fathers, husbands, masters, kings, conquerors, libertines, etc. No one has the right to force any woman either to marry or to remain married against her will. Free agency is a golden thread woven through every principle of life and salvation.

The Woman, Eve

The two immortals met as apparent strangers.[18] Whatever association they may have had in their previous estate was completely forgotten. Initially, the man did not refer to her as a specific person with a unique identity. However, he did recognize her as being of his species—the man kind—rather than merely another form of the animal kind. Unlike the brute creation, she was "taken out of man." For this reason he declared her to be "bone of my bones and flesh of my flesh," and assigned her a generic identity just as he had every other living creature. "She shall be called Woman."[19] Since the male determines the sex of the unborn child, woman is a product of man. And since the female brings forth the race, man is a product of woman. Each serves the other. Paul observed, "For as the woman is of the man, even so is the man also by the woman; but all things of God."[20]

How long Adam and the woman lived in the Garden before transgressing the law is unrevealed. Although they were husband and wife, the pre-fall period of their relation-

---

[17]I.V., Luke 1:26-28. Mary became, *in fact*, the wife of Joseph only after bringing forth her first born son. See Matthew 1:24, 25.

[18]They did not become mortal until after they fell. See 2 Nephi 2:22.

[19]See Genesis 2:20-23. Eve was no more made from the literal rib of Adam than he was literally moulded from the ground. Mankind are *procreated*, not created.

[20]1 Corinthians 11:12.

ship could hardly be characterized as a courtship—much less a marriage. Apparently, it was a time of deepening, but innocent association. Men and women should become friends before they become mates. What we can be to others depends upon what we have experienced with others. Adam and the woman not only experienced innocence in paradise together, but also temptation, transgression, fear and divine judgment. These things helped to forge an unbreakable bond of love and mutual concern between them. In Adam's eyes, she was no longer just Woman, she was his beloved wife. He named her Eve—the mother of all living.[21]

The significance of the woman being named Eve is heightened by the fact that it was done, not by God, but by her husband. Adam had been made lord of all creation—guardian over the entire earth and every living thing thereon. In connection with this appointment, he named all things. The right to name connotes the right to rule. In naming his wife, Adam became—by divine appointment—her steward. And in accepting that name, Eve acknowledged Adam's position and submitted herself to the righteous leadership of the holy priesthood. A similar commitment is inferred in those marriages where the woman *takes* upon herself the name the man *gives* her—his name.

Further, to name is to claim. In naming Eve, Adam claimed her for his own. Likewise, the only church Christ acknowledges as his own is the one which he personally—by direct revelation—has named and claimed: The Church of Jesus Christ of Latter-day Saints.[22] Only this church can be the "bride of Christ"—all others have *taken* his name in vain because he has not *given* them that name.[23] Further, those who merit the celestial kingdom receive a new name from the Lord—this name is the "keyword."[24] They are

---

[21]Genesis 3:20. Note that whereas the pre-mortal name of Adam is known, that of Eve is not.

[22]See D&C 115:3, 4; 1:30; 3 Nephi 27:8.

[23]See D&C 63:62; John 3:29; Matthew 9:15; 25:1-13; Ephesians 5:23-25; Revelation 21:9.

[24]See D&C 130:11.

42 claimed by the Father as his sons and daughters, for in receiving that name, they enter into a higher association with him.[25] So too, the naming of Eve marked the beginning of a new and profoundly significant relationship between earth's first husband and wife. Their marriage had been spiritually consummated. Man and woman were prepared for parenthood. They left the Garden together and entered that fallen world which awaited their coming. There were promises to keep.

The First Judgment

The judgment of God upon "Woman" as represented by Eve was:

> . . . I will greatly multiply thy sorrow and thy conception; in sorrow thou shalt bring forth children; and thy desire shall be to thy husband, and he shall rule over thee.[26]

This is the origin of the supposed "curse on woman." At first glance it might appear that God acted out of pique, that he arbitrarily determined to make woman suffer for daring to transgress his law. Such was not the case. It was, in reality, a revelation pertaining to woman's temporal calling as a wife and mother. Adam was forewarned of the inevitable consequences should he break the law.[27] He deliberately (but not willfully) transgressed it. Lehi tells us that "Adam fell that man might be."[28] Paul corroborates this view, "And Adam was not deceived, but the woman being deceived was in the transgression."[29] God, in personifying all truth and all law, functioned as the spokesman of truth and law. Cause led to effect: transgression resulted in

---

[25]Abraham, Sarah and Jacob are three examples of those whose names were changed after making higher covenants with God. See Genesis 17:1-5, 15-16; 32:24-28.

[26]Genesis 3:16.

[27]See *Ibid.*, 2:16, 17.

[28]See 2 Nephi 2:25.

[29]I Timothy 2:14.

the fall and the fall resulted in death—both spiritual (banishment from God's literal presence) and temporal (mortality).[30] The wages of sin is, inevitably, death.[31] In meeting with the fallen pair prior to their expulsion from the garden, the Lord simply made clear the implications of their new condition.

Relatively speaking, pain and sorrow are the natural concomitants of child-bearing and child-rearing for mortal women in a fallen world. Moreover, Adam's transgression affected all creation. His entire stewardship fell when he fell; the earth, vegetation and animal life became subject to change, decay and death.

> And unto Adam he said, Because thou hast harkened unto the voice of thy wife, and hast eaten of the tree, of which I commanded thee, saying, Thou shalt not eat of it: cursed is the ground for thy sake; in sorrow shalt thou eat of it all the days of thy life; Thorns also and thistles shall it bring forth to thee; and thou shalt eat the herb of the field; . . .[32]

The Lord's words appear harsh when viewed "through a glass darkly" by our carnal minds. The truth reveals them to be otherwise: the earth, having become a telestial kingdom, would, according to its appropriate natural law, produce vegetation in opposition to that indigenous to the garden. Man, faced with this opposition, would be obliged to labor for his sustenance. The virtually effortless life he had known in the garden was replaced by one of contrasts, contradictions and struggle. He would, indeed, "be as gods, knowing good and evil." That knowledge would be gained as those who had passed this way before had gained it: by experiencing truth (reality) in its various dimensions. Mortality was but one of them. Man was destined to know many "thorns and thistles" before his temporal day ended.

---

[30]See Moses 6:59.
[31]Romans 6:23.
[32]Genesis 3:17, 18.

44   **Woman's Second Steward**

God's dictum that man was to "rule over" woman has more often than not been misinterpreted and misapplied.[33] Some unconscionable males have sought religious sanction for their domination and abuse of woman-kind by appealing to scripture—Christian and otherwise. In most areas of the world in most periods of human history, the subordination and oppression of females has been justified—actually, dictated—on the grounds of manifest male superiority. Actually, the inequality of the sexes is a male myth fabricated to the specifications of the male ego. It has cost womankind dearly. Often viewed as little more than chattel, the vast majority of women have been denied any meaningful sense of identity or personal worth. We are reminded of the arrogant duke in Browning's "My Last Duchess." Irritated because his gentle wife did not exist for him alone and because she had a heart "too soon made glad" by the courtesies of others, her husband "gave commands; then all smiles ceased together." She had been a possession which could not be possessed. The duke, commenting on her portrait to the emissary of a count whose daughter he hoped to marry, dismissed his last duchess from mind by pointing to another of his properties: "Notice Neptune, though, taming a sea-horse, thought a rarity, which Claus of Innsbruck cast in bronze for me."[34]

Human beings are not things to be used and discarded by other human beings. How we are regarded by others influences our self-respect and, consequently, what we become. Held in low esteem—even contempt—some classes of women exist in cultural wastelands generation after generation. The derelictions of their menfolk are stoically endured; it is woman's lot. Because of the darkness of their lives, such women have long since lost all self-vision. And their

---

[33]To "rule over" simply means to lead, to guide and, in effect, to be responsible for woman's welfare. See JD 9:195.

[34]Robert Browning, "My Last Duchess."

menfolk—trapped in that same darkness—suffered a like fate; they became blind leaders of the blind.

Of course, the overall treatment of women varies from culture to culture and group to group. However, it is safe to say that, with but a very few exceptions, women have never been shown the respect, protection, guidance or love they both needed and deserved. They are the betrayed sex. Unfortunately many modern women are compounding their plight by betraying themselves in new and more damaging ways. Still, the cause of womankind is just. If they are to plead it effectively, they must understand what their true cause is, what God willed for them in the beginning, and why he said, "thy desire shall be to thy husband, and he shall rule over thee."

In the beginning, man and woman enjoyed the immediate presence of God. They were spiritually alive, therefore they had no need of a Savior or a mediator. Although married, they had not yet forsaken "father and mother;" they were, so to speak, still living at home. And they had no conscious intention of leaving that home, there being no reason to do so. Nor did man seek to impose his will on woman. Each looked upon the other as an equal, a peer. Indeed, they related to one another more as brother and sister than as husband and wife. Theirs was still a marriage in name only. Initially, it was to God that they turned for love and instruction, not to one another.

This apparently idyllic arrangement ended with Lucifer's successful beguilement of Woman. She was, for all her physical maturity, like a little girl who, lacking experience, succumbs to the blandishments of a would-be molester. Hers was not the knowing, sophisticated sin of a worldly person. It was more the seduction of an innocent, trusting child. Note that the stated reasons for her disobedience reflect her feminine nature: the fruit was good for food (tasty), pleasant to the eyes (beautiful), and would make her wise (curiosity).[35] Doubtless, the last rationalization was the decid-

---

[35]See Moses 4:12.

46   ing factor—feminine curiosity being what it is. Adam, having greater understanding, was impervious to such appeals. He was not beguiled; he partook "that man might be."[36] The apostle Paul cited this distinction between the two as justi- fication for women keeping silent in church. He may have felt that they had already caused enough trouble.[37]

Be that as it may, their transgression made them spiri- tually contaminated. Since no unclean thing can dwell in the presence of God,[38] He could not permit his intimate associa- tion with his errant children to continue. Divine law required that they be driven from the Garden of Eden. They had to leave home. However, the Lord did not love them one whit less for their disobedience. He had no intention of abandon- ing them to some unknown fate. Communication with the man would be maintained by God's own voice and by an- gelic messengers. The guidance and protection the Lord had afforded his daughter was also to continue. However, inas- much as he could no longer be her immediate head, God appointed the man to act in his stead and "rule over" Woman.[39] This assignment was, in fact, given to Adam in connection with the keys and powers of the priesthood pre- viously bestowed upon him as sovereign lord over the earth and all things thereon.[40]

The Order of Heaven

It is an irrevocable law that every thing must be bound by and subject to a law higher than itself. The gods in eternity are subject to other gods above them. There is no such thing as a headless god.[41] The treason of Lucifer was

---

[36]2 Nephi 2:25.

[37]See I Timothy 2:11-14.

[38]See Moses 6:57; 3 Nephi 27:19.

[39]Rule should not be interpreted as tyrannical dictation, but as guidance and responsibility. As Brigham Young said "When I say rule, I do not mean with an iron hand, but merely to take the lead—to lead them in the path I wish them to walk in." JD 9:195.

[40]Genesis 1:28. see TJS, p. 157.

[41]See TJS, pp. 371-373. The "Most High God" may not be a specific deity at all. The term may be applicable to any one who attains unto the fulness of the Father's glory. Such a being would thus become the most high God to his own dominions. See D&C 93:19, 20; Ephesians 3:14-19.

motivated by his desire to be independent of all authority—a law unto himself. Therefore, he fell from law into lawlessness, into chaos. All who would defy their bounds and limitations, becoming answerable to no one, partake of his spirit and are potential candidates for his fate. Thus, the order of heaven requires that every soul have a head, a steward over him or her. Every steward is, therefore, someone else's stewardship. No one is "headless." Exalted men and women rule over their own posterity (not the posterity of others) throughout all eternal time.

This is not according to present customs, for now when a young man reaches the age of twenty-one years he is free from his parents, and considers that he is no longer under the necessity of being controlled by his father. That is according to our customs, and the laws of our country. It is a very good law and adapted to the imperfections that now exist; but it will not be so in the eternal worlds. There will never be any such thing there as being from under their father's rule, no matter whether twenty-one or twenty-one thousand years of age, it will make no difference, they will still be subject to the laws of their Patriarch or Father, and they must observe and obey them throughout all eternity.[42]

This order *of* heaven is a major reason for the order *in* heaven. Each honors his steward and his stewardship.

A similar arrangement should exist among the saints on earth. Said Paul, "But I would have you know, that the head of every man is Christ; and the head of the woman is the man; and the head of Christ is God."[43] Such a relationship can only apply to those who are members of the body of Christ—the true Church. Among the saints, a woman is justified in binding herself to her husband's law when he, in turn, is bound to Christ. However, such is not the case in the world at large where Christ is not acknowledged as "the head of every man." It follows, therefore, that husbands in worldly marriages have no divine right to exercise dominion over their wives. Ironically, those who insist that marriage should

---

[42]Orson Pratt, JD 15:319, 320.

[43]I Corinthians 11:3. Children have no stewardship (they are *not* their brother's keeper) unless "set apart" by their parents to oversee their brothers and sisters on a temporary basis. See Ephesians 6:1-4.

48   be a partnership between equals in which the wife enjoys autonomy along with her husband are correct—but not for the reasons they advance. Worldly marriages are between peers. Neither is justified in imposing his or her authority on the other because neither has any legitimate authority to impose beyond that granted by human law. By the same token, no man-made church has a divine right to speak for God or to impose its will upon others in his name. Historically, many churches, like many husbands, have exercised dominion either by employing threat, brute force or civil power. It is no mere coincidence that the traditional authority of both husbands and churches is being challenged today.

Paul's statement was not a generalization, nor was it timebound; it also applied to the eternal order of things. It is an allusion to the new and everlasting covenant of marriage within the new and everlasting covenant of the gospel. Under the patriarchal order of marriage, the father—the patriarch, the high priest in the home—holds the keys of the priesthood for his family.[44] He presides. His position in the home is similar to that of a bishop over a ward, a president over a stake, the prophet over the Church or God over the universe. Baptism is a pledge of allegiance to the kingdom of God by which anyone becomes a citizen thereof. Ordination to the priesthood makes a man an officer of that kingdom and commits him to specific service under the authority of Christ. Likewise, in being sealed to a worthy husband, a woman commits herself to the law or guidance of her husband. Thus an unbroken chain of stewards and stewardships extends back into the eternities. Everyone has a secure and honorable place in the family organization. Everyone has a steward and a stewardship. Everyone finds happiness and fulfillment under the law.

Woman, being the "weaker vessel," should be under the constant protection and guidance of the priesthood.[45]

---

[44]A temple marriage or sealing is tantamount to the patriarchal order, being the gateway to it.

[45]See I Peter 3:7.

Ideally, her father is her first guide and protector. He, in 49
turn, gives her to her husband who becomes her second
steward. Should she become orphaned or widowed, the male
leader of the family should assume responsibility for her welfare. If there is no one available or qualified to do so, then
the organized priesthood as represented by her bishop or
some other responsible officer of the Church should, with
her consent, become her guardian.[46] Since most women have
neither the physical strength nor the social and economic
independence of men, they both require and are entitled to
such consideration.

However, woman is not the "weaker vessel" when it
comes to spirituality, intelligence, emotional stability and
sheer physical endurance. Indeed, females tend to live longer
and to face the stresses of life better than males. Woman's
dependence stems largely from her role as a childbearer
and, consequently, from her need to be sustained and pro-
tected in her motherhood. Caring for her children imposes
restrictions upon her; thus her "weakness" lies more in her
calling, than in her nature. Said President Joseph F. Smith:

> There are people fond of saying that women are the weaker ves-
> sels. I don't believe it. Physically, they may be; but spiritually, morally,
> religiously and in faith, what man can match a woman who is really con-
> vinced? Daniel had faith to sustain him in the lion's den, but women
> have seen their sons torn limb from limb, and endured every torture
> satanic cruelty could invent, because they believed. They are always
> more willing to make sacrifices, and are the peers of men in stability,
> godliness, morality and faith.[47]

Being especially threatened by change, women tend to
be the preservers and the proponents of the status quo. They
are conservative by nature because they have so much of
genuine value to conserve. They are creators. It is against
their nature to jeopardize or to destroy things as they are.
Therefore, they are inclined to restrain the often hasty, ill-

---

[46]See I Timothy 5:3-16.

[47]Joseph F. Smith, *Gospel Doctrine*, 7th Ed. p. 352. See CR, October 5, 1947, p. 152.

50 advised actions of the male whose vaunted ability to meet critical situations with calm reason is grossly exaggerated. Humans are much more creatures of reflex action and unintelligent habit than we care to admit. It is said that the world is yet to produce an authentic female philosopher. This is to woman's credit. She has sustained life while the philosophers philosophized, kings plotted, generals waged battle and soldiers died. War and immorality are fellow players in the game of murder. She has been the pawn of both. Time and again she has picked up the broken pieces and mended her world as best she could. She has replenished the earth every time the four horsemen have ravaged the land. She has maintained the continuity and the perpetuity of the race. In doing so, more often than not she has been at the mercy of men with little understanding or compassion. The principle of stewardship, of the strong safe-guarding the weak, has been woefully absent in most human societies.

Note that initially man's stewardship over woman was founded upon divine authority and personal worthiness, not usurpation or brute strength. Woman was justified in acknowledging him as her steward. In doing so, she did not disavow her Heavenly Father. God commands our love and obedience above everyone else; we never outgrow him. If a clear choice must be made between God and mate, it should be made in God's favor.[48] Fortunately, Eve did not have to make such a choice, she and her husband were one in their devotion to the Lord. This is as it should always be. The ideal is for parents, husbands and wives to be united in all things under God. Each relationship then strengthens and reinforces every other one.

However, since mortals are not always united, the guiding principle is that we honor our immediate steward unless doing so would mean sustaining that person in unrighteousness. We owe no one our allegiance when they are out of harmony with God and the moral law.

---

[48]See Luke 14:26; Matthew 10:33-38; Mark 12:28-31.

It is not my general practice to counsel the sisters to disobey their husbands, but my counsel is—*obey your husbands;* and I am sanguine and most emphatic on that subject. But I never counselled a woman to follow her husband to the devil.[49]

All things being equal, as long as a woman is under her father's roof she owes him her chief loyalty. When she marries, that loyalty passes to her husband. A woman should not attempt to have two stewards, two heads, anymore than a man should attempt to serve two gods. "No man can serve two masters"—especially when they are in clear opposition to one another.

True, we can give equal allegiance to the three members of the Godhead because a flawless unity exists among them. They act in concert. Human differences and imperfections, however, make it essential that we have but one immediate temporal steward. Double-minded men and women are unstable in many ways; they are prone to guile, duplicity and hypocrisy.[50] A woman cannot have an eye single to both her husband and someone else. A two-headed woman is a monstrosity. Her husband is her rightful head as long as he is worthy to be so and/or as long as she elects to remain with him. Many marriages have been threatened—even ruined—when loyalty to parents or families took precedence over loyalty to mate. Husband and wife are to *cleave* to one another, not to their relatives however fine.

"And as you keep nothing from each other, so, on the contrary, preserve the privacies of your house, marriage state, and heart, from father, mother, brother, sister, aunt, and from all the world. You two, with God's help, build your own quiet world. Every third or fourth one you draw into it with you will form a party, and stand between you two. That should never be. Promise this to each other. Remember the vow at each temptation. You will find your account in it. Your souls will grow, as it were, to each other, and at last will become as one. Ah, if many a pair had, on their marriage-day, known the secret, how many a marriage were happier than, alas, they are!"[51]

---

[49]Brigham Young, JD 1:77. (Italics original)

[50]James 1:8.

[51]Quoted by David O. McKay, Conference Report, April 1952, p. 87. Hereafter this source will be abbreviated CR followed by the appropriate date and page number.

52   Mediation of the Priesthood

While the Lord was the immediate steward of Adam and Eve, each had direct communication with the other. It was a triangular association with God at the apex.

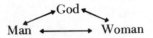

However, the Fall altered this arrangement; it became linear. God remained at the apex but the man stood between him and the woman.

Now there was a mediator between herself and her Father. Face to face communication was ended. The Lord told Moses, "So I drove out the man, and I placed at the east of the Garden of Eden, cherubim and a flaming sword, which turned every way to keep the way of the tree of life."[52] Years passed. The dispossessed couple were grand-parents before the Lord, speaking to them from the direction of the garden, (for they "saw him not; for they were shut out from his presence"[53]) instructed them to begin offering up blood sacrifice. Finally, "after many days," Adam was taught the plan of salvation via the three-fold instrumentality of an angelic being, the Holy Ghost, and the voice of God.[54]

Immediately following Adam's conversion and spiritual rebirth, he taught the Gospel of Jesus Christ to his wife: "And Eve, his wife, heard all these things and was glad, . . ."[55] The joyful parents then made a futile attempt to share the message with their children. The manner in which saving knowledge passed from God to man (the priesthood), from man to woman, and from parents to children in the days of

[52]Moses 4:31.
[53]See Moses 5:4.
[54]See Moses 5:6-10; 6:51-68.
[55]See Moses 5:11.

Adam established the pattern by which that knowledge has   53
been transmitted ever since. No authoritative gospel dispensation has been vouchsafed to mankind in any other way.

Since Jesus Christ is the mediator of the new and everlasting covenant, all eternal things must be done in his
name. However, in his absence he has authorized the Holy
Melchizedek Priesthood to represent him among men.[56]
It functions as a mediator for the mediator. Just as it is true
that no one can come unto the Father but by Christ,[57] so it
is true that no one can come unto Christ but by the Melchizedek Priesthood. "He that receiveth you receiveth me,
and he that receiveth me receiveth him that sent me."[58]
In accepting the rule of Adam, Eve was, in fact, honoring
her Father and preparing herself to return to his presence.
So it is with everyone who comes under the wings of the
Holy Priesthood.

Our modern prophets have emphasized repeatedly the
necessity of yielding obedience to one's file leader. This principle cannot operate at one level of heavenly government
while being inoperative at another. Heber C. Kimball asked:
"Is it not right for all men to be obedient to their superiors.
And if so, is it not right for women and children to abide
the same principle?"[59] The law is no respector of persons. In
truth, no woman of understanding wants to be headless:

> The female sex have been deceived so long, and been trodden
> under foot of man so long, that a spirit has come upon them, and they
> want a place, and a name, and a head; for the man is the head of the
> woman, to lead her into the celestial kingdom of our Father and God.[60]

Child to Adult

The Fall signaled a coming of age for Adam and Eve.
Although they met on earth as full grown adults, it appears

---

[56]Moses 6:52; D&C 18:23-25.
[57]See D&C 132:12.
[58]Matthew 10:40; See also D&C 84:35-37.
[59]Heber C. Kimball, JD 3:270. See 4:82, 128; 10:310.
[60]Brigham Young, JD 11:271.

54   that they did not experience conscious sexuality until after
becoming mortal. It was then that they left the ways of
childhood forever. In this respect, their pre-Fall attitude toward their bodies corresponds to that of any very young child.
For like such a child, their nakedness did not cause them
any embarrassment. In our culture, this condition is quickly
remedied as the child is "socialized." He soon learns that
nakedness is "naughty." The natural order of things must
yield to the discipline of propriety. Puberty brings increased
awareness by exposing the heterosexual side of adulthood.

And so initially, "they were both naked, the man and
his wife, and were *not ashamed.*"[61] But upon eating the forbidden fruit, their organisms underwent a radical modification.[62] Blood, the sign of death, replaced the spirit element
which had formerly coursed through the veins.[63] The two immortals had fallen to mortality. It was shortly thereafter that
they first experienced self-consciousness. "And the eyes of
them both were opened, and *they knew* that they were
naked. And they sewed fig-leaves together and made themselves aprons."[64] This act was prompted by a new understanding of the significance of their anatomical differences.
While they had always known that those differences existed,
like little children, they had both been indifferent to them
and ignorant of *why* they existed. In covering themselves,
Adam and Eve acknowledged the sacred—not shameful—
character of their life-producing powers.

But if there was no shame attached to their nakedness,
why did they "hide themselves from the presence of the
Lord God amongst the trees of the garden"? And why did
Adam say, "I was *afraid,* because I beheld that I was naked,
and I hid myself?"[65] The answer lies in the Lord's response,
"Who *told thee* that thou wast naked?" In other words, who

---

[61]Genesis 2:25.
[62]The forbidden fruit was just that—fruit. The idea that the original sin was sexual
in character is utterly false. How could it have been when the pair were married?
[63]See Smith, Joseph Fielding, *Man—His Origin and Destiny,* pp. 362-64.
[64]Genesis 3:7.
[65]Moses 4:14-16.

had told them that it was shameful to be naked? Indeed, who did *tell* the innocent pair of their impropriety? Who *socialized* them? Obviously, not God, his very question exonerates him. Then it must have been someone else, someone who also had contact with Adam and Eve. That someone was Satan, himself—the great *accuser*.[66]

It was the father of lies who introduced sex education into the world. In doing so, as with too many modern "educators," he emphasized the purely physical dimension of the matter. He was not concerned with its spiritual foundations. He did not teach the innocents of the beauty and the wonder of their divine endowment. Rather, his objective was to shame them by making profane what was intrinsically the most sacred of powers. How young people are taught about themselves and their relationship to those of the complimentary sex makes all of the difference. Far more of today's instructions in this area are inspired by the devil than naive parents and teachers realize. By their fruits we know them. In response to Satan's malicious revelation, Adam and his wife improvised coverings for their nakedness. Indeed, there was far greater reason to shield themselves from the evil eyes of Satan and his associates, than from God or one another. It is so today.

In this instance, as in all other efforts by Satan to frustrate the Lord, his hidden purposes were achieved. Eve was a child-woman no longer. She was prepared to fill the measure of her creation. Thus, she had a new need in life, one that her Father could not meet. For this reason the Almighty decreed, "Therefore shall a man leave his father and his mother, and shall cleave unto his wife: and they shall be one flesh."[67] It was *because* they were male and female that they were to leave their parents and establish their own home. Otherwise, there was no justification for becoming "one flesh" since they would have been unable to procreate.

---

[66]In Hebrew, the very word, Satan, means accuser. See Revelation 12:10.

[67] Genesis 2:24. To become "one flesh" with one's own sex or with some order of animal life is perversion and abomination. See Romans 1:26, 27, 32; 1 Corinthians 6:9, 10.

56   In establishing their own home and family, Adam and Eve were going on to perfection. Paul said, "When I was a child I spake as a child, I understood as a child, I thought as a child; but when I became a man, I put away childish things."[68] It was time for our first parents to do the same. While we rejoice in the ways of little children, those same ways are grotesque in older persons. So too, the continuance of Adam and Eve's child-like existence would have meant that "they would have had no children; wherefore they would have remained in a state of innocence, having no joy, for they knew no misery; doing no good, for they knew no sin."[69] Had that immature condition been perpetuated (as most Christian theologians would have it) Eden would have become a kind of heavenly hell. We are on earth for the purpose of avoiding just such a fate. The Father sends his children away from home so that they can return as mature men and women. In doing so, he does not suffer that poignant sense of loss which comes to those who see their little children growing away from them one by one. There is no last child, no fading sight and sound of little ones for him. Heavenly parents rejoice in the knowledge that even as some of their offspring are passing on to adulthood, other bright faces are taking their places.

Desires to Husband

Although God pronounced a curse upon the serpent for its part in the transgression of Woman, a similar anathema was not pronounced against her. In spite of this, woman's position vis a vis man, together with her emotional dependence upon him, has been spoken of as a curse.

True there is a curse upon the woman that is not upon the man, namely, that "her whole affections shall be towards her husband," and what is next? "He shall rule over you."[70]

---

[68]I Corinthians 13:11.
[69]See 2 Nephi 2:23.
[70]Brigham Young, JD 4:57. See 9:195.

In elaborating on this point, Brigham Young said:

> I do not know what the Lord could have put upon women worse than he did upon Mother Eve, where he told her: "Thy desire shall be to thy husband." Continually wanting the husband. . . . I do not know that the Lord could have put upon women anything worse than this, I do not blame them for having these feelings. I would be glad if it were otherwise. Says a woman of faith and knowledge, "I will make the best of it; it is a law that man shall rule over me; his word is my law, and I must obey him; he must rule over me; this is upon me and I will submit to it," and by so doing she has promises that others do not have.[71]

While the Lord did not refer to his judgment upon Woman as a curse, still President Young was essentially correct in maintaining that, in a manner peculiar to themselves, normal women are emotionally dependent upon men. Wrote Lord Byron: "Man's love is of man's life a part; it is woman's whole existence." In more extended lines he said:

> Alas! the love of women! it is known to be a lovely, and fearful thing; for all of theirs upon that die is thrown: and if 'tis lost, life has no more to bring to them but mockeries of the past alone.[72]

Female liberationists would doubtless respond, "Spoken like a true male chauvinist!" They would argue that the traditional manner in which females have been socialized and controlled inevitably rendered them more emotionally dependent upon men than they should have been. Thus, they regard this dependence as a learned behavior. However, the Lord has indicated that it is both reflective of woman's temperament and essential to her role in the plan of salvation. Jesus said, "For where your treasure is, there will your heart be also."[73] It is very likely that as more women place increasing value on those interests and opportunities which lie

---

[71]JD 16:167.
[72]The New Dictionary of Thoughts, a Cyclopedia of Quotations, com. by. Tryon Edwards, D. D., Standard Book Company, 1961, p. 369.
[73] Matthew 6:21.

58   outside of the home, Byron's assessment of the female nature will become less and less valid as a generalization. If men can lay up treasures on earth rather than in heaven, women can place their affections on the world rather than on their husbands and families.

Although woman's organization and circumstance was such that she could center her life in her husband and her home, she is not compelled to do so. Her agency is equal to that of man; she can obey or disobey as she chooses. But, like man, while she is free to make the choice, she is not free to determine the consequences of her decision. As Brigham Young noted:

> Many are disposed through their own wickedness "to do as I damned please," and they are damned. The volition of the creature is free, to do good or to do evil; but we are responsible to God for our acts, as man is responsible to man if he breaks the laws which man enacts. When we boast of our independence to act, it would be well for us to remember that we are bounded by these limits; if we transcend them and violate the laws of God and man, we shall sooner or later be made to suffer the penalty, without any reference to our choice whether we are willing to suffer that penalty or not. Hence, true independence and freedom can only exist in doing right.[74]

The obligation to submit to the leadership of fallen man after having enjoyed the personal guidance of God is, undeniably, a descending. Yet, doing so will be the means of woman's very exaltation. If woman is "cursed" with love for man, man is likewise "cursed" with love for woman. To love is not to be cursed unless it is done at the price of righteousness and truth. The woman who is married to a worthy husband does not regard herself as being cursed. She is happy because she is needed, fulfilled and loved. The cursed woman is not an Eve, a Sarah, an Emma Smith, or any other woman wedded to a godly man. The cursed woman is she who is bound in her emotions to a man who is, himself, a slave of the world, the flesh and the devil.

---

[74]JD 11:254.

If Adam was to "rule over" his wife, it was imperative that her affections be centered in him and him alone. That such could be the case, was assured by Woman's very nature. Therefore, God's words constituted a prophetic commandment, "Thy desires shall be to thy husband." It was meant to be so. If Eve was to respond to her husband's leadership as she had responded to her Father's, Adam would have to care for her and she for him. Indeed, without understanding and mutual affection, honoring the commandment to multiply would have been little more than an act between animals. The instinct to reproduce was implanted in all living things, but only in man was it to be fulfilled in a setting of spiritual oneness. This is the tie which binds mate to mate and parent to child. This, together with that unique intelligence which humans possess, transforms them into fathers and mothers in the highest sense of these terms. For the less the intelligence of the reproducing life forms, the less applicable are these terms to them. Love, light and truth find their ultimate expression in man. It is in the context of these three principles that the commandment to multiply was given. They lift the relationship of husband and wife above the animal plane of instinctual response or mere heartless submission to a divine fiat.

The Latter-day Saints regard the intercourse of the sexes both in time and in eternity, as regulated by sacred law given by our Father in heaven who has organized us male and female for a wise purpose in himself, and that purpose is made manifest in the first great command given to our first parents, namely, to multiply and replenish the earth. And the saying to the woman after her transgression as written in the book of Genesis, that her desires should be towards her husband and he should rule over her—the desires planted in the breast of the woman tending to draw to the opposite sex culminating in a union, is a wise dispensation of Providence for the accomplishing of the great end in view to encourage and stimulate them to multiply and replenish the earth, and take upon themselves the care, labors, anxieties and responsibilities attending the rearing of families.[75]

---

[75]Erastus Snow, JD 23:225, 226.

60   Mutual affection makes the burdens of parenthood less burdensome. It is the chief preventative of boredom and the very spirit of heavenly government. For the rule of God is designed to be a rule of love for both the ruler and the ruled. No matter how virtuous and sincere all concerned might be, if they are devoid of affection for one another, the relationship—although proper—will lack warmth and spontaneity. To honor one's leader with lips and hands when the heart is far from him makes for a burdensome and imperfect allegiance. Duty to God, husband, wife, family, country, etc., is noble in principle. However, in the absence of genuine affection, it is usually characterized by the hard, hollow ring of sounding brass and tinkling cymbals. An emotionally—starved marriage has just that ring. One's duty may be done only because it is one's duty. Indeed, feelings of guilt at not loving one's mate (or one's God) may motivate us to almost obsessive, Pharisaic activity. The overly-solicitous mate, the too-perfect homemaker, the too-dedicated churchgoer, the too-precise keeper of commandments, etc.—all may hide a divided heart beneath the frenzy of "doing their duty." The frantic perfectionist in marriage or religion is weighed in the balances and found wanting in love. For love, like the Spirit of God, is as the invisible wind—blowing where it will.[76] It is free, light, and refreshing. It brings those rains which soften the heart, enlighten the mind, and nourish the soul. Contrast the flexible, life-giving spirit of Jesus with the rigid, mortifying character of his antagonists. Those women who truly love their husbands—like those saints who truly love their Savior—find the yoke easy and the burden light.[77]

Fortunate, indeed, is the woman who has found a worthy, compatible, bearer of the priesthood to be her companion. No, woman's curse is not that she is called upon to accept the righteous leadership of the priesthood, but that she is denied the opportunity of doing so. Man, not God, has put this curse upon her by his own failure to rise to

---

[76]See John 3:8.
[77]See Matthew 11:28-30.

his divine potential. The pains of a woman with self-under-
standing and spiritual sensitivity do not stem from being
a female, but from being unfulfilled. She is the dove that
left the ark only to find "no rest for the sole of her foot."[78]
She has a heart and mind to give but no one to receive it.
She is as one who sought the true God in a land of idols,
who sat by the rivers of Babylon weeping for a lost Zion.
Such a woman may or may not be married. In either case
she is conscious of a void in her life marked by loneliness
and discontent.

Such a woman's needs *as a woman* cannot be met by
turning to Christ. He is the Bridegroom of the Church as a
body, not of its individual members, male or female. Woman
is alone until she marries and becomes one flesh with her
husband. She cannot become one flesh with God. Nor can
that aloneness be overcome through some mystical union
with her Savior. Such pathetic efforts at sublimating pent-
up needs only produce a sickness in the soul which opens
one up to even more of the devil's machinations. Like must
cleave to like. We come to Christ for salvation—not as men
or women—but as sinners. "There is neither Jew nor Greek,
there is neither bond nor free, there is neither male nor female: for ye are all one in Christ Jesus."[79] Woman does not
need man as man to obtain a place in the kingdom of God.
However, she does need man if she is to be fulfilled as a woman and obtain eternal life.

What havoc Satan has wrought in the lives of thousands upon thousands of well-meaning women who have
been duped into believing themselves the brides of Christ,
even to the point of wearing wedding bands and assuming
life-long vows of celibacy. Would God give contradictory
universal commandments? Would he command woman to put
her heart upon man and cleave to him in marriage only to
have her renounce her womanhood in favor of a supposedly
higher calling? Where in all the Bible is there a hint of such

---

[78]See Genesis 8:8.
[79]Galatians 3:28.

62   a thing other than in Paul's recommendation—which he clearly labeled as his opinion, not God's will—to the Corinthian saints?[80] Even in that instance, the apostle's suggestion stemmed from his feelings about then-existing conditions. If Paul believed that the end of the world (or the age) was near, his recommendations rested upon a false assumption since, quite clearly, the world is still very much with us. If, on the other hand, Paul was not alluding to the end of the world but to the end of that particular gospel dispensation, his words reflect a passing situation. Being, admittedly, only personal opinion, they cannot rightly be employed in defending a doctrine alien and anti-thetical to the clear commandment of God.

Then too, Paul's words provide little aid and comfort to the Catholic position that Christ's church has been on the earth since the time of the apostles. For what did Paul mean by referring to "the present distress" or writing that "the time is short" and that "the fashion of this world passeth away"?[81] If he was speaking temporally, the very existence of the world and the Catholic church belie his notions. If, however, he was alluding to things spiritual, his words are evidence of the very apostasy that negates the claims to authority of the greatest exponent of celibacy in the Christian world! Nowhere does Jesus suggest that celibacy was to be preferred over marriage. The Matthean passage employed by proponents of celibacy is misinterpreted.[82] It is not to celibacy but to his entire statement on marriage that Jesus referred in saying, "He that is able to receive it let him receive it."[83] The Savior's own mother, the holiest of mortal women, did not practice celibacy. Both Matthew and Mark are explicit in pointing out that she was the mother of at least four sons and two daughters in addition

---

[80]See 1 Corinthians 7.

[81]See 1 Corinthians 7:26-31.

[82]See Matthew 19:9-12.

[83]Matthew 19:12. See also Inspired Revision and modern versions for clearer rendering.

to Jesus.[84] No woman who understands her divinely ordained role in mortality will deliberately choose the celibate life. She will, like Jephthah's daughter, "bewail her virginity" until the hour of her death.[85]

The carnally minded woman, oblivious to the deeper aspects of her own being, does not appreciate such sentiments. If she thinks of her plight at all, it is largely in terms of those physical burdens and material limitations she encounters day by day. For her, success is a matter of life's luxuries, small vanities, triumphs and satisfactions. She neither expects nor desires more than flesh and the unaided human spirit have to offer. Like her male counterpart she is without God in the world. And like the publican, she loves those who love her—but only within the restricted limits of her own spiritual capacity.

She is the most unfortunate of women. She is self-cursed in that she is content to be co-owner of things as they are. The Lord is more ambitious for her than she is for herself. He wills to free her from all imperfection—including fallen man and his fallen world. Sadly, this is the last freedom most humans ever seek. Nevertheless, such freedom is attainable through Christ.[86] Those women who do not choose the Lord's freedom will still be freed from all physical and emotional bondage to men. For in rejecting the Gospel of Jesus Christ, they disqualify themselves for eternal marriage. Therefore, in the resurrection, they will become forever *alone*. They will be independent of man, *as man,* in every way. As servants of the Lord, they will have the opportunity to develop their own talents and to pursue their own lawful interests without the "burdens" of wifehood and motherhood.[87]

On the other hand, the woman who is faithful to all of the laws and ordinances of the Gospel is delivered from "the curse" in another way. She will be freed, not by rejecting the rule of her "Adam," but by sustaining him in his office and

---

[84]See Matthew 13:55-56; Mark 6:3.
[85]See Judges 11:37, 38.
[86]See John 8:31-36.
[87]D&C 132:16, 17; 76:109-112.

64   calling. She will be freed, not by ceasing to love her husband, but by being delivered from the temporal limitations
of that love.[88] She is delivered from her bondage to fallen
man through a mutual metamorphosis: he becomes like unto
God, her first steward, even as she is transformed into a
heavenly wife and mother.[89] Like Father, like son; like
Mother, like daughter. The cycle is complete.

> What we experience here, is but a school
> Wherein the ruled will be prepared to rule.
> The secret and the key, the spring, the soul
> Of rule—of government, is *self control.*

> Clothed with the beauties purity reflects
> Th' acknowledg'd glory of the other sex,
> From life's crude dross and rubbish, will come forth,
> By weight of character—by strength of worth;
> And thro' obedience, Woman will obtain
> The *power of reigning, and the right to reign.*[90]

---

[88]Speaking of that future time when women are delivered from "the curse," George Q. Cannon asked: "Will she cease to love man? No, it is not necessary for her to cease to love." JD 13:207.

[89]See JD 15:132.

[90]Eliza R. Snow. From, "Woman."

IV

A Marriage In The Lord

Nevertheless neither is the man without the woman, neither the woman without the man, in the Lord.[1]

A divine ideal exists for every principle of truth. We approach that ideal only to the extent that we allow ourselves to be led by the Spirit of the Lord. God gives us the principle and we make of it what we will. Consequently, every marital enterprise inevitably mirrors the spiritual predispositions of the parties to it. Marriage, too, has its degrees of glory. It would be as fallacious to assume that all marriages are either good or bad as it would be to maintain that all governments are either democratic or despotic. The *principle* of marriage, like that of government, is of God; however, it does not follow that any given marriage—or government—is necessarily godly. Free agency makes for relativity in human affairs. We can plot the beliefs, conduct

---

[1] 1 Corinthians 11:11.

66   and institutions of men on continuums stretching from one extreme to the other. This enables us to evaluate all things by contrast and comparison. It will be helpful to consider a few basic deviations from the true order of marriage before attempting to describe a marriage in the Lord.

Worldly Marriages

Telestial Marriage

The natural man or woman is "an enemy to God" because he or she is devoid of any real concern for or commitment to his will.[2] Their spiritual condition is succinctly described by the prophet Alma.

> And now, my son, all men that are in a state of nature, or I would say, in a carnal state, are in the gall of bitterness and in the bonds of iniquity; they are without God in the world, and *they have gone contrary to the nature of God;* therefore, they are in a state contrary to the nature of happiness.[3]

Yet happiness is their objective and they live to obtain it in the here and now. Such men and women manifest a Ptolemaic disposition in a Copernican universe. Whether they are artists, entertainers, scientists, intellectuals, businessmen, hedonists, or what-have-you, everyone and everything else is subsidiary to their interests. Self-indulgence dominates the natural man syndrome.

Their reasons for marrying are many: an unhappy home life, boredom, money, career advantages, social status, etc. But whatever the reason, it is central to themselves. Theirs is a thing-oriented, utilitarian outlook on life. Marriage is valued only to the extent that it caters to their wants. They need a mate *to do something for them:* "feed me, house me, clothe me, satisfy me, make me happy." While they may profess love for their companion, it is usually peripheral to

---

[2]Mosiah 3:19.
[3]Alma 41:11.

their own fulfillment. It is a dross-filled, self-serving emotion at best and a manipulative device at worst.

Heartbreak is almost always the lot of the husband or wife who is genuinely devoted to such a mate. The woman who puts her heart upon this type of man is to be pitied. Her very devotion dooms her to a shallow, futile existence. Yet she may live only to please the man in her life. Right or wrong, he is her god—her magnificent, but unworthy, obsession. Improvidence, drunkenness, brutality, infidelity— nothing can free her from her human bondage. She is a natural woman bound to and, therefore, the slave of a natural man.

Yet, time takes the measure of such marriages and when their original purpose has either been satisfied, frustrated or replaced with new interests and desires, they are—one way or another—repudiated. As with so many other things today, telestial marriages have a built-in, planned, obsolescence. Many are not designed to be more than a throw-away relationship—a paper towel, to be used and then tossed aside. The sophisticated exponents of such unions know them for what they are and contract them with no thought of permanency. In theatrical parlance, they sign for the run-of-the-play in full expectation of a limited engagement. The more naive participants in such marriages are not so crass in their assessment. Because they beguile themselves into believing that the marriage will do more for them than it possibly can, they expect it to last as a viable relationship longer than it will. Needless to say, children are almost always an unwanted by-product of such marriages and are more often than not the innocent victims of parental immaturity and selfishness. Although telestial marriages—like telestial beings, are quite variant in manifestation, godlessness is common to them all.[4] Their numbers are increasing at an alarming rate.

---

[4] D&C 76:98-106.

68   **Terrestrial Marriage**

Just as terrestrial people are morally and spiritually superior to telestial people, so are terrestrial marriages superior to telestial marriages in terms of quality, satisfactions, and longevity. Terrestrial people are honorable people; they establish honorable marriages—good marriages. The love they express for one another, although imperfect, is genuine. Loyalty and fidelity to one's mate is the rule. Indeed, the deep and lasting devotion of Robert and Elizabeth Browning for one another typifies this aspect of terrestrial marriage. Ordinarily, children figure prominently in these marriages. They are welcomed and cherished. Consequently, Terrestrial marriages are characterized by strong familial ties. While religion is usually a prominent aspect of such unions, there are exceptions. Shared interests of a non-religious type may serve both to vitalize and to sustain the relationship. What is important is that there are meaningful interdependencies and commonalities. The chief ingredients in a terrestrial marriage are respect for moral law, love, genuine compatability, and similar values and goals.

The conscious need for religion is partly a matter of one's upbringing and partly one's own spiritual proclivities. Since all are not equal in these factors, all do not have the same felt need for religion. Most people today do not include it in their definition of marital happiness.

However, a marriage of the highest quality cannot exist in the absence of sincere religious commitment. Without some conscious faith in things spiritual, a terrestrial marriage comes perilously close to becoming a telestial one. Any marriage is vulnerable to the extent that it is oriented to the things of this world. Only those men and women who are strongly motivated to live by the finest ethical and religious principles enjoy any valid security in their temporal unions. In this respect, those whose lives are Christ-centered are the most secure of all. Although terrestrial marriages may be very happy and rewarding, they are still inferior to the

divine ideal. They cannot achieve perfection, nor can they   69
endure beyond their mortal hour.

Modern Marriage

In emphasizing the virtual equality of the sexes, the so-called modern marriage is something of a reaction against the Victorian marriages of the nineteenth century. Today, marriage is emphasized as a "partnership" in which the husband and wife each hold fifty percent of the voting stock. Both are president of the company. Being a two-headed affair, the modern marriage is, in actuality, headless. Because both preside, neither leads. It is pure democracy. Such marriages are based upon false sociological theories as well as a fatal misunderstanding of the implications of the psychophysical differences between the sexes. These differences should dictate the valid roles of husbands and wives. In largely ignoring these differences, the modern marriage is essentially a contractual agreement between consenting adults in which they specify the limitations of their obligations to one another both qualitatively and quantitatively. It is understood that each is free to pursue his or her own destiny even though they share certain phases of their lives with one another. The wife has the same rights, privileges and opportunities possessed by the husband. In so far as circumstances will permit, each can do all that the other does and become all that the other becomes.

This type of marriage is encouraged by modern contraceptive methods which serve to produce an even greater sense of equality between the sexes by virtually freeing the female from unwanted pregnancy. The legalization of abortion is an additional equalizing factor. Now, the female can also enjoy sex for its own sake without the old fears marring the experience and without the risk of limiting her possibilities for self-expression. She can sow without the necessity of reaping.

70   Sadly, the more women imitate the ways of men, the less feminine they become. Modern marriage is a fraud, a sham, a lie. It will degenerate into something less than what it is even now. Actually, it has already begun to do so as legal marriage is replaced with "arrangements" that are even less binding than traditional common law marriages. Just how happy are modern marriages? The point is debatable, yet appearances suggest that there are a good many frustrated wives who sense a lack in their lives. "What is wrong? Why am I so miserable, so upset? Why do I feel incomplete, unsatisfied? What is missing?" The answer can be seen in their mirror: they haven't got a head. The piper will be paid but, unfortunately, little children and abandoned women will pay the most. When it comes to the wages of its sins, the modern marriage is not a fifty-fifty partnership.

Victorian Marriage

If modern marriage is sentimentalized democracy, Victorian marriage was stern autocracy. Whereas the modern marriage leaves the wife without a guide, the Victorian marriage subjected her to a tyrant. Both are extremes. Both are worldly in origin and unacceptable to the Lord. When maintained in the name of religion the Victorian marriage was a pharisaic charade. How grey, how austere, how full of pointless sacrifice it could be! In the Victorian scheme of things, a wife was much more the servant than the helpmeet. She was duty-bound to love, honor and obey her husband simply because he was her husband. His word was law; she was expected to be as submissive to it as the children she bore him.

Sex was an indelicate matter virtuous women tolerated in order to produce children for the master of the house. It was unclean, unfeminine, unfeeling. Yet, prostitution was a hypocritical fact of life in that staid society which required a husband to be a gentleman with his wife but allowed him

to play the libertine with lesser females.[5] This double standard continues today in many parts of the world where
prostitutes and mistresses are quietly accepted as a matter
of course.

The feelings of his children toward their stern parent
were often a commingling of fear, hatred, and respect. He
was the living embodiment of the awesome god so dear to
the hell-fire sermons of evangelical preachers in every generation. Rigid controls produce duplicity in the ruled. In any
situation where one is denied any real personal freedom, there
is an inclination to obtain by guile what should be obtained
by honest interaction. The idea that women must employ
devious methods to obtain their rights stems from the fact
that they have generally been the oppressed sex. The Victorian wife, being no exception, was likewise obliged to
"stoop to conquer" her autocratic husband. The spirit of
Victorian marriage motivates the popular notion that wives
can best manipulate their husbands by being guileful and
coquettish.

It should be understood that while the term, Victorian
marriage, is descriptive of a type of marital relationship popu-
larly identified with the prim rule of queen Victoria, it has
always existed. While there is a definite sameness about
most marriages in any given cultural setting, there are exceptions. In a simplistic society such as is found among
savage tribes, such exceptions are rare. But as a society becomes more complex, these exceptions increase. Variations
on the authoritarian marriage still dominate the marital scene
throughout most of the world. However, industrialization is
rendering the Victorian-style husband more and more of an
anachronism in the technologically advanced nations where
wives are becoming skilled wage earners. Those who achieve
economic independence are seldom slow to demand personal
sovereignty as well. Despotism can only rule where it controls the necessities of life. The dominating husband no

---

[5]See JD 20:201.

72 longer does so; he is a victim of the very thing which has been the traditional source of his authority: material wealth.

Priesthood is power and authority. Satan endeavors to get men to abuse it. He is abetted in his efforts by human nature, for as the Prophet Joseph Smith observed:

> We have learned by sad experience that it is the nature and disposition of almost all men, as soon as they get a little authority, as they suppose, they will immediately begin to exercise unrighteous dominion.[6]

The tyranny Victorian men exercised over their wives and children becomes an even greater abomination when practiced under the guise of the priesthood. Such despotism is antithetical to everything Jesus, the Great High Priest, represented. Unhappily, due regard for a woman's feelings and desires has not always been shown by some holders of the priesthood. This was perhaps more the case in the past than today. Said President Young: "Men, as a general thing, do not know the dispositions of their wives and children, nor how to govern and control them; and it is certainly a pretty close, intricate, point."[7] Such ignorance caused the love of more than one pioneer wife to grow cold toward her inconsiderate husband. She viewed him and his religion as so many dry bones in the valley of Jehoshaphat. Her only hope was that the resurrection would put some flesh on both.

Were the Lord to express himself on the marriages of this world, he well might say, "A plague on all of them." They are either too self-centered, too man-centered, too woman-centered, too child-centered, or too something else-centered. They are gentile. They are not God-centered. God the Father is the Great Patriarch of the human family. True marriage reflects his exalted station, being likewise patriarchal in nature. We now turn to it.

---

[6]D&C 121:39.
[7]JD 14:162.

A Marriage In The Lord 73

"Except the Lord build the house, they labor in vain that build it."[8] So wrote the psalmist, and so it is. Of himself, finite man is incapable of producing any lasting enterprise. All that he does is tainted by all that he is. The very word, "history", betrays his mortal limitations: he cannot hold on to the present, it is forever slipping through his fingers into the past. However, such is not the case with God. For him, there is no loss of time nor of the things which time has brought into being. He dwells in the sum of existence: "the past, the present, and the future were and are, with Him, one eternal now."[9] Being the very fountainhead of life, God must be a party to our human associations if they are to take on the character of everlasting things.[10] Apart from him, all is indeed "vanity and vexation of spirit."[11] Truly, they labor in vain who labor without the Lord.

And everything that is in the world, whether it be ordained of men, by thrones, or principalities, or powers, or things of name, whatsoever they may be, *that are not by me* or by my word, saith the Lord, shall be thrown down, and shall not remain after men are dead, neither in nor after the resurrection saith the Lord your God.[12]

Unless the Lord is a direct party to the marriage covenant, it is doomed. The seeds of its own death are brought to the union by its mortal participants.

Only "in the Lord" can it be said that man is not without the woman nor the woman without the man.[13] And, we might add, only "in the Lord" can it be said that the parent

[8]Psalm 127:1.
[9]TJS, p. 220.
[10]See D&C 88:13, 14.
[11]Ecclesiastes 1:14.
[12]D&C 132:13.
[13]See I Corinthians 11:11. Commenting on this passage, Orson Pratt said: "If a man be in the Lord he must not be without the woman and the woman must not be without the man." JD 14:243.

74   is not without the child nor the child without the parent. In the resurrection, those who are not one with the Lord are not one with anybody; they are alone. The degree to which we are able to establish a perfect union with the divine is the degree of our freedom, glory and joy. It is the degree to which we have overcome aloneness.

It is apparent, therefore, that marriage cannot be fully understood apart from God and godhood. And these are mysteries of which we know but little. Consequently, our perception of the subject of marriage is necessarily gained through a glass darkly.

But the whole subject of the marriage relation is not in my reach, nor in any other man's reach on this earth. It is without beginning of days or end of years; it is a hard matter to reach. We can tell some things with regard to it; it lays the foundation for worlds, for angels, and for the Gods; for intelligent beings to be crowned with glory, immortality, and eternal lives. In fact, it is the thread which runs from the beginning to the end of the holy Gospel of salvation—of the Gospel of the Son of God; it is from eternity to eternity. When the vision of the mind is opened, you can see a great portion of it, but you see it comparatively as a speaker sees the faces of a congregation. To look at, and talk to, each individual separately, and thinking to become fully acquainted with them, only to spend five minutes with each would consume too much time, it could not easily be done. So it is with the visions of eternity; we can see and understand, but it is difficult to tell.[14]

Being most aware of this limitation, we will proceed.

Celestial Status

Many souls will be saved in the celestial kingdom without eternal marriage.

In the celestial glory there are three heavens or degrees; And in order to obtain the highest, a man must enter into this order of the priesthood [meaning the new and everlasting covenant of marriage]; And if he does not, he cannot obtain it. *He may enter into the other,* but that is the end of his kingdom; he cannot have an increase.[15]

---

[14]Brigham Young, JD 2:90.
[15]D&C 131:1-4; see *Ibid.,* 132:17.

Therefore, pertaining to salvation in that kingdom, four basic possibilities exist for a given married couple (see chart): a) neither mate will gain it, b) one mate will gain it (without exaltation) while the other does not, c) both mates will gain it but without exaltation or d) both mates will gain exaltation in the celestial kingdom via the new and everlasting covenant of marriage.

Possible Celestial States

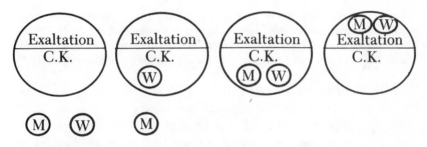

Obviously, a valid baptismal covenant with Christ is a necessary prerequisite to a valid eternal covenant with one's husband or wife. We can become one with our mate for eternity only because we have become one with the Lord for eternity.[16] We must enter the circle of his family before we can establish our own family. To do so we must be born again into that circle through our acceptance of the plan of salvation with its attendant principles and ordinances.[17] In other words, we must be saved in the celestial kingdom before we can be exalted therein.[18] A marriage in the Lord is, therefore, dependent upon personal salvation in the Lord.

Priesthood Powers

A marriage becomes eternal—which is to say divine—in nature when it is contracted under the law of God and

---

[16]See John 17:11, 21-23; D&C 93:20.
[17]See Moses 6:57, 62; 2 Nephi 31:9-21.
[18]See D&C 88:21, 22.

76 validated by the Holy Ghost through the instrumentality of the sealing powers of the priesthood as held by the presiding high priest of the Church.[19]

Referring to Heaven's view of marriage wherein man and woman become one flesh both in spirit and in body, Jesus commanded, "What therefore God hath joined together [via the sealing powers of the Holy Priesthood], let no man put asunder."[20] In point of fact, what God has joined together *cannot* be put asunder—insofar as eternity is concerned—by man.

> As I have said, there is no power that can separate a virtuous man and woman who have been united by the power of the Holy Priesthood; no power can do it; they must do it themselves if done at all. These ties that bind us together will endure through time and eternity.[21]

The authority to bind (or seal) is the authority to loose (or unseal). Lacking the former, we lack the latter as well. Jesus' promise to Peter of the keys of this binding—loosing authority was realized when Elijah the prophet bestowed that power upon the apostle during the episode on the mount of transfiguration.[22] In 1836, Elijah returned and granted the very same keys to Joseph Smith in fulfillment of Malachi's closing prophecy.[23]

> The Lord gives the President of the Church the keys of the kingdom; he has the right to bind on earth and in heaven; he has the right to loose on earth and in heaven. If circumstances warrant it, he may cancel the sealing and the Lord would sanction it.[24]

It has been assumed by some that the mere performance of a temple marriage guarantees eternal life and exaltation. Such is not the case. The blessings associated with the

---

[19]See D&C 132:7, 19.

[20]Matthew 19:6.

[21]George Q. Cannon, JD 26:253. See JD 1:58.

[22]Matthew 16:18, 19; 17:1-13.

[23]See Malachi 4:5, 6; D&C 2; 110:13-16.

[24]Joseph Fielding Smith, *Doctrines of Salvation*, Vol. II, pp. 84. Hereafter this work will be designated DS followed by the appropriate volume and page number.

various ordinances of the priesthood are predicated upon our obedience to all of the laws of God.[25]

There are many called Latter-day Saints who are anxious to obtain their endowments, washings, sealings and anointings, and baptisms for themselves and their dead, and who would think they were deprived of very great blessings if they could not have these privileges; and yet they act as though if they could only snatch these blessings from the hands of the servants of the Lord they would be all right, and they could do in other respects just as they please. They could neglect to pay their tithing and the observance of the commands of the Lord generally, and walk after their own vain imaginations all the days of their lives. What a fatal mistake is here! By your own works ye shall be judged, whether they be good or evil. A man may attain to all these ordinances, he may keep his path hidden in iniquity for a season, but the time will come when every evil doer will stand before the Lord in his own naked deformity, he will be stripped of his hypocrisy and subterfuge of lies. The gigantic superstructure of Satan, that has so long wielded influence on the earth, will be swept away, and in that day all who stand will do so by their own virtue and integrity.[26]

No ritual can, of itself, assure us of any blessing of heaven. It is not enough to observe the "letter" of temple marriage—the "spirit" must be present as well if the ordinance is to be endowed with life. Consequently all ordinances performed by the priesthood must be sealed or validated by the Holy Ghost (the Holy Spirit of promise) if they are to be in force after death.[27]

For example, the admonition to "receive the Holy Ghost" at the time of confirmation does not of itself assure one that gift. We are simply given the authorization to receive it; personal worthiness determines whether or not we actually do so. Elder Marion G. Romney observed:

Now, we have the Holy Ghost. Every one of us who are members of the Church has had hands laid upon our heads, and we have been given, as far as ordinance can give it, the gift of the Holy Ghost. But,

---

[25]See D&C 41:5; 58:31-33; 82:10; 130:21, 22; 132:5, 6.
[26]Daniel H. Wells, JD 16:128.
[27]For an excellent summary statement on this point see McConkie, *Mormon Doctrine*, pp. 331-332.

78   as I remember, when I was confirmed, the Holy Ghost was not directed to come to me; I was directed to "Receive the Holy Ghost."[28]

By the same token, a temple sealing must be ratified by the Holy Spirit before it is fully efficacious.[29] Man proposes, God disposes. Were this not the case, unworthy persons could obtain the choicest blessings of heaven by the simple expedient of going through a ritual.

When a man and a woman, in all sincerity, enter into a covenant of marriage for time and all eternity (and after they have "overcome by faith," and are "just and true"), *the Holy Ghost—who is the Spirit of Promise—bears record of or ratifies that sealing.* In other words, *he seals the promises appertaining to the marriage covenant upon them. . . .* If one or both of these covenanting persons break that covenant by which they were sealed by the Holy Spirit of Promise, then *the Spirit withdraws the seal* and the guilty party, or parties, stand as if there had been no sealing or promise given. *All covenants are sealed based upon faithfulness.*[30]

The Lord is the keeper of the gate of the straight and narrow way leading unto eternal life; he employs no servant there.[31]

Equally Yoked

It is impossible for the Holy Spirit of Promise to seal (ratify) a marriage in which one mate is faithful to the covenant while the other is not. There must be "a whole and complete and perfect union, and welding together" of all things in God.[32] Just as the Church—the bride of Christ—must become "holy and without blemish" before it can be permanently sealed to him, so must every husband and wife become sanctified via their mutual obedience to the commandments if their marriage is to endure.[33] In eternity all matrimony is

---

[28]CR, September 30, 1961, p. 60. See TJS, p. 148.
[29]See D&C 132:7.
[30]Smith, DS 2:98. Italics original.
[31]See 2 Nephi 9:41.
[32]See D&C 128:18.
[33]See Ephesians 5:27; Revelation 21:2.

holy matrimony between holy men and holy women.[34] A
marriage having one foot in heaven and the other on earth
is unacceptable to the Lord. It cannot continue forever because the parties to it are unequally yoked.

> Be ye not unequally yoked together with unbelievers: for what
> fellowship hath righteousness with unrighteousness? and what com-
> munion hath light with darkness?[35]

Paul's warning against marrying those not of the faith is
also applicable to those who are not valiant or who have
apostatized from the faith. Indeed, such persons may be
more spiritually blind than those who never entered into
covenant at all.[36]

Assuming that true repentance on an errant mate's part
is not forthcoming, what is to become of a faithful saint
under these circumstances? Paraphrasing the second Article
of Faith, we believe that a man or woman will be punished
for their own sins and not for a mate's transgressions. Individuals can do lasting harm only to themselves. Others
may hinder their progress and cause them much suffering,
but they cannot rob them of salvation. Consequently, an
unworthy husband or wife cannot prevent a faithful companion from obtaining exaltation. We are reminded of the
Savior's words to those who "shut up the kingdom of heaven
against men: for ye neither go in yourselves, neither suffer
ye them that are entering to go in."[37] Those who have been
sealed to partners who will not honor their covenants will,
in due time, be provided with the opportunity to select
another companion and go on to perfection.

To be equally yoked implies much more than a surface
commitment to the same religious system or to the same
professed interests, ideals, values and goals. It involves an
actual affinity of natures, of characters, of hearts and minds.

---

[34]See Moses 6:57; D&C 1:31; Alma 45:16.
[35]2 Corinthians 6:14, See JD 26:120.
[36]See Alma 12:10, 11.
[37]Matthew 23:13.

80   The problem of joining dissimilar natures is analogous to that encountered in transplanting tissue or an organ from one person to another. The recipient's own body is inclined to reject the foreign substance and attempts to slough it off. Only by introducing powerful chemicals which serve as anti-anti-bodies can this resistance be overcome. Even so, the transplant may not be successful. Likewise, the permanently successful yoking of a man to a woman can only be achieved if both come under the regenerating influence of the Holy Spirit. For, as George Q. Cannon noted, "It is the spirit of God that unites heart to heart, that unites man and woman with bonds that are stronger than death—death cannot break them."[38]

A true saint cannot be wholly bound in heart and mind to someone who does not share his or her commitment to God. Said Brigham Young:

> I do not believe it possible, since I have been baptized into this Church, for a woman to be presented to me that I could love, were she not in the Church of Jesus Christ and did not love the Gospel. That is my feeling to-day, and I expect it to remain from henceforth and for ever.[39]

The more one's spirit becomes united with the Spirit of God, the more difficult it becomes to give one's affections to an "infidel." Fidelity to the truth is the sword which sunders the children of light from the children of darkness. A God-oriented love is paradoxical. As it grows, one's desire to show mercy, compassion and concern for others increases while one's inclination to be bound in heart, mind and soul to those who do not share that love diminishes.[40] Jesus ministered to unrepentant publicans and sinners, but he did not call them "friends."[41]

Though blood may be thicker than water, spirit is

---

[38] JD 22:241.
[39] JD 8:209; See JD 5:92, 282, 283.
[40] See TJS, pp. 147, 241.
[41] See John 15:13-15; James 4:4; D&C 45:5; 93:45, 46.

thicker than blood. All lasting relationships spring from the spirit, not from the flesh. Informed that his earthly mother and brothers wished to speak with him, Jesus asked the rhetorical question, "Who is my mother? and who are my brethren?" Then, indicating his disciples, he answered, "Behold my mother and my brethren! For whosoever shall do the will of my father in heaven, the same is my brother, and sister, and mother"[42] And, we might add, wife and husband.[43]

This is in harmony with President Young's feelings:

> Fathers, mothers, brothers, and sisters are no more to me than are any other persons, unless they embrace this work. Here are my fathers, my mothers, my sisters, and my brethren in the kingdom, and I have none outside of it, neither in any part of the earth, nor in all the eternity of the Gods. In this kingdom are my acquaintances, relatives, and friends, —my soul, my affections, my all.
>
> I will carry this idea a little further, for the sake of those who are unmarried. Since I was baptized into this Church and kingdom, if all the female beauty had been simmered down into one woman not in this kingdom, she would not have appeared handsome to me; but if a person's heart is open to receive the truth, the excellency of love and beauty is there. How is it with you, sisters? Do you distinguish between a man of God and a man of the world? It is one of the strangest things that happens in my existence, to think that any man or woman can love a being that will not receive the truth of heaven. The love this Gospel produces is far above the love of women: It is the love of God—the love of eternity—of eternal lives.[44]

This love is the touchstone of all other loves, serving to protect the Lord's people against its many counterfeits. It also provides both the way and the means of loving one's neighbor—be he parent, mate, child, friend, enemy or stranger—as he *should* be loved. Putting God first precludes any human being, or anything, becoming either our master or our slave. Love of God is the spiritual gyroscope which creates an intelligent balance in all inter-personal relation-

---

[42]Matthew 12:48-50.
[43]Luke 14:26.
[44]JD 8:199, 200.

82

ships. Possessing it, we are able to love *every* one without hurting or demeaning *any* one. This is the essence of love's integrity and, therefore, of its authenticity.

The issue in marriage, then, is affinity. We are expected to love our neighbors—even our enemies—but we are not required to become one with them. Oneness is a product of alikeness: only as we become like Christ—Christ-like—do we become one with him. So too, oneness in marriage is achieved only as the two natures coalesce. This is the human sealing which, to an extent, must precede the divine sealing.

> For intelligence cleaveth unto intelligence; wisdom receiveth wisdom; truth embraceth truth; virtue loveth virtue; light cleaveth unto light; mercy hath compassion on mercy and claimeth her own; justice continueth its course and claimeth its own; . . .[45]

Such a claiming can be virtually instantaneous or it may take years. The rapidity with which it is accomplished is dependent upon the quality of the marriage. Doubt, fear, ignorance, sin and the dross in man's fallen nature are barriers which must be removed before a celestial marriage can come into being. This is why personal salvation via the sanctifying influence of the Holy Ghost is pre-requisite to the joint exaltation of husband and wife. We become free to love others only as we free ourselves of those negative factors which keep us alienated from God.

If feelings of bitterness, disappointment or frustration are present in a marriage, there can be no free flow of spirit between husband and wife. The union is unsealed. God cannot accept them because they have failed to accept one another. Under such conditions, the Holy Spirit would be imposing God's will on their wills were he to seal them up. The Lord comes to us only *after* we have come to him.[46] Indeed, effective communion with God depends upon right relationships with his other children.

---

[45]D&C 88:40.
[46]See D&C 88:63.

Therefore if thou bring thy gift to the altar, and there remember-
est that thy brother hath ought against thee, Leave there thy gift before
the altar and go thy way; *first be reconciled to thy brother,* and then
come and offer thy gift.[47]

David Whitmer tells of an incident in the lives of Joseph
and Emma Smith which bears out the Savior's words:

> One morning when he was getting ready to continue the transla-
> tion, something went wrong about the house and he was put out about
> it. Something that Emma, his wife, had done. Oliver and I went upstairs
> and Joseph came up soon after to continue the translation but he could
> not do anything. He could not translate a single syllable. He went
> downstairs, out into the orchard, and made supplication to the Lord;
> was gone about an hour—came back to the house, and asked Emma's
> forgiveness and then came upstairs where we were and then the transla-
> tion went on all right.[48]

God's acceptance of us and his forgiveness of our sins
depends upon our acceptance of others and our forgiveness
of their trespasses against us.[49] If God will not justify barriers
between brothers or neighbors, will he excuse them between
wives and husbands? The burden of proof that any marriage
should, in fact, be perpetuated into the eternities rests with
the covenanting couple, not with the Holy Spirit. Only after
they have demonstrated their mutual love for God and for
one another will the Lord justify the ordinance by uncondi-
tionally sealing them up unto Eternal Life.

Thus love is a sealing power. It seals God to man, man
to woman, parent to child, and saint to saint.[50] All relationships must be "rooted and grounded in love"—which is to
say, in Christ, if they are to endure.[51] No ceremony, no
ritual can seal a man to a woman unless they first seal them-

---

[47]Matthew 5:23, 24.

[48]B. H. Roberts, *Comprehensive History of the Church,* Deseret News Press, Salt
Lake City, Utah, 1930. Vol. 1, p. 131.

[49]See Matthew 6:12-15; 18:15-35; I John 4:20; D&C 64:8-12.

[50]Elder H. W. Naisbitt spoke of love as "the only element that will bind together
in its original purity the family circle". JD 26:119.

[51]See Ephesians 3:17.

84   selves to one another through mutual affection. And this "sealing power" must flow "without compulsory means," it cannot be demanded or coerced. We may work at it, but as long as it is *work,* it is a compromise at best. We should aspire to the labor *of* love, not to a labor *for* love. A true mother does not have to work at feeling affection for the infant in her arms. Nor should husband and wife have to labor at loving one another. Mutual affection should grow between them like a living thing. Faith and love are inseparably connected principles. As we develop one, we develop the other. But before we can perfect them, we must possess them.

A mighty oak can develop from a small acorn but there must be an acorn. Likewise, a successful marriage need not begin in meteoric showers of poetry, music and high romance, but faith and love must be present in some degree if it is ever to be immortalized.

> There is no evil in love; but there is much evil resulting from the want of love. No woman should be united in marriage with a man unless she have some love for him; and if she love him in a small degree, this is capable of being increased to perfection.[52]

The realization of this perfection need not rob the marriage of its individuality. Even in perfection there is variety. Were this not so, heaven would be nothing more than a hall of mirrors in which every reflection was one's own! Personality would be swallowed up in the anonymity of a shared divinity. However, the human personality is sacred to God. He will not sacrifice it in the process of sanctifying it. Every celestial marriage will partake of the individuality of its partners. Every love will have a quality all its own.

Spiritual Consummation

The temporal order exists only because it is infused with life by its spiritual counterpart. This principle is equally valid in the creation of eternal relationships. Adam and Eve were

---

[52]Pratt, *The Seer,* p. 154.

mated in spirit before they were ever mated in flesh. A spiritual consummation preceded the physical consummation of their union. Being of one mind and one heart before becoming one flesh, they virtually eliminated the threat of later incompatibility. Frequently, it is more a case of wives and husbands *being* incompatible rather than *becoming* so. However, initially, the condition is obscured by physical, material, and emotional attractions and considerations. The irony is that the very factors which deceived them into believing that they were well mated in the beginning are often the same factors which later convince them that they are incompatible! When the facade falls in decay, they are brought face to face with the inner reality of their relationship. Which is to say, they discover what they really were to each other all of the time. However, not realizing what has happened, they think, "We don't *love* each other *anymore.*" In truth, only a part of them was committed, and that part succumbed to the ravages of time. But when spirit and flesh are inseparably connected, the union of husband and wife is holy and, quite literally, *soul-*satisfying.

Obviously, then, the more unequal the spiritual commitment, the more unstable the union. Yet there are few marriages in which one partner is not more devoted than the other. The human condition being what it is, this is to be expected. Since an imperfect order can only produce imperfect men and imperfect social arrangements, the truly symmetrical personality or relationship is virtually non-existent in this world. "But when that which is perfect is come, then that which is in part shall be done away."[53] When wives and husbands are perfected in the resurrection, their love for one another will be total and, to that extent, equal. But for now we must be content with something less than the ideal! The fall has taken its toll; everything is skewed at least a little. Consequently, we should neither expect nor desire flawless symmetry in anything pertaining to mortality.

---

[53] 1 Corinthians 13:10. See JD 5:315.

86   Indeed, it is essential to the plan of salvation that we be
tried with the imperfect order of things. The perfect God
loved his imperfect brothers and sisters enough to lay down
his life for them. Those who would emulate him, cannot repudiate others for their limitations without indicting themselves. The pure love of Christ vitalizes, blesses, forgives,
sustains, and edifies. It lifts and bears the burdens of others.
It could do none of these things were it not for human
limitations and failings. Needs must exist before service can
be given. Love seizes the opportunities life affords it. Love
is non-competitive. Where it exists between husband and
wife, each will strengthen and support the other. It is significant that when Adam began "to eat his bread by the sweat
of his brow, as I the Lord had commanded him . . . Eve,
also, his wife *did labor with him.*"[54] His burden became her
burden. Such is the way of love. And if it has its way *all
the way*, it will, in time, perfect everyone and everything it
touches.

However, human love is, of itself, quite imperfect and
limited in scope. It is an admixture of faith and doubt,
knowledge and ignorance, wisdom and foolishness, strength
and weakness. The *sum* of what we are dictates the quality
of our love. God, being a perfected, holy man, can only
love with a perfect, holy love. It is holy because it is un-
alloyed with any negative trait or factor; hence, it is known
as "the *pure* love *of* Christ."[55] It is altogether intelligent
because it is in complete harmony with all that is light
(spirit) and truth.[56] But because men differ in spiritual development, its manifestations among them are quite varied.[57]
For example, while "the Spirit giveth light to every man that
cometh into the world,"[58] the gift of the Holy Ghost is
restricted to God's faithful sons and daughters.

---

[54]Moses 5:1.
[55]Moroni 7:47. It was this type of love to which Paul referred in 1 Corinthians 13.
See also 1 John, chapters 3 and 4.
[56]See D&C 93:36, 37.
[57]See JD 20:228.
[58]D&C 84:46.

Even Jesus had his "beloved" apostle. Nor did the Savior love the world at large as he loved his own disciples.[59] The world did not permit him to do so; it would not receive him. President Joseph F. Smith, a most kindly man, said that he loved his enemies and would do good to them:

> . . . but I do not love them with that affection with which I love my wife, my brother, my sister or my friend. There is a difference between the love we should bear towards our enemies and that we should bear towards our friends.[60]

One having a celestial disposition has more love to give than can be received by those of a lesser spirit. Our Heavenly Father loves us more than we are capacitated either to accept or understand. Perhaps this is one reason why his work and glory is centered in his endless posterity. He needs an infinite outlet for his infinite love.

While the saints are admonished to aspire to the pure love of Christ, it is not self-attainable; it is an endowment from on high.[61] When husband and wife possess it, they cannot fall out of love with one another unless one or both first falls *from* love. The lovers must change before the love can die. And this change must be *fundamental*. It must involve a fall from a celestial to a lesser spiritual state of being. Temporal circumstances alone cannot destroy a spiritually based union. Youth may pass, beauty fade, health be lost, worldly possessions slip away and life be taken, but the love will endure. Like the blue sky, it may be hidden for a time, yet it remains. Night passes, clouds roll on and we see again what was always there.

Even from a temporal standpoint alone, a marriage in which there is a true union of spirits—which is to say, of minds—can be one of life-long constancy and devotion.

---

[59]See John 17:9-11.
[60]JD 23:285.
[61]Moroni 7:48.

88

Let me not to the marriage of true minds
Admit impediments. Love is not love
Which alters when it alteration finds,
Or bends with the remover to remove:
O, no! it is an ever-fixed mark,
That looks on tempests and is never shaken;
It is the star to every wand'ring bark,
Whose worth's unknown, although his height be taken.
Love's not Time's fool, though rosy lips and cheeks
Within his bending sickle's compass come;
Love alters not with his brief hours and weeks,
But bears it out even to the edge of doom:—
    If this be error and upon me proved,
    I never writ, nor no man ever loved.[62]

Unfortunately, such constancy is lacking in most pre-marital and marital associations because they are wrongly conceived from the first. Not only are they inverted in design in that they begin with the flesh rather than the spirit, but they become fixed in that condition. There is no upward movement, no ascending. The relationship remains earthbound. It begins in dust; it ends in dust. Such affairs simply mirror the world at large which is inclined to assign first priority to those things which gratify the senses. In spite of Jesus' warning, the human race is prone to try to live by bread alone. Everything and everyone is a consumable commodity. Human beings are valued as things to be bought, sold, manipulated and otherwise *used*. In nothing is the inversion and stagnation of human relations more evident than in the area of sexual conduct.

It is not uncommon to hear of husbands beating and otherwise abusing their wives while still insisting upon their conjugal rights. Then there are those marriages which exist under a constant pall of quarrels, recriminations and general unhappiness, yet accompanied by habitual sexual activity. While it might be argued that such intimacies serve to keep these marriages going, it should be noted that they keep them going in circles—nowhere. Whether in or out of mar-

---

[62]William Shakespeare, "Sonnett CXVI."

riage, physical intimacy without spiritual compatibility partakes of the spirit of prostitution. The greater the alienation
of minds, the more predominant that spirit becomes. The
harlot and her companion differ more in degree than kind
from those who are also devoid of any genuine feeling for
or lasting commitment to the one with whom they become
physically involved. Flesh, alone, kills; it is the spirit which
gives life. When the marriage relationship has been spiritually
consummated, the foundation for a celestial union has been
laid.

Selecting A Mate

Few other decisions in life are so critical to spiritual success as the selection of a marriage partner. The right mate
can do more to assist one in keeping the commandments than
any other thing, save only the Holy Spirit. Therefore, once
a man or woman have determined to live with an eye
single to God, they should seek his guidance in finding a
companion who will help them realize their righteous
desires. God will counsel those who seek his counsel if their
lives are in harmony with his will.[63]

Now, I tell you that you can make every decision in your life
correctly if you can learn to follow the guidance of the Holy Spirit.
This you can do if you will discipline yourself to yield your own feelings
to the promptings of the Spirit. Study your problems and prayerfully
make a decision. Then take that decision and say to him, in a simple
honest supplication, "Father, I want to make the right decision. I want
to do the right thing. This is what I think I should do; let me know if
it is the right course." Doing this, you can get the burning in your bosom,
if your decision is right. If you do not get the burning, then change
your decision and submit a new one. When you learn to walk by the
Spirit, you never need to make a mistake. I know what it is to have
this burning witness. I know also that there are other manifestations of
guidance by the Spirit.[64]

---

[63]See Alma 34:17-29.
[64]Marion G. Romney, CR, Sept. 30, 1961, pp. 60, 61.

90

The heart should not be mindless. Intelligence is meant to dictate the who, the when and the how of "falling in love." It lies within the mind's power to control emotions *before* the heart is given free rein. Too many young people reach the affectional point of no return before they give any serious thought to their commitment. From then on, reason whispers while the heart shouts. It is a rare person who will surrender anything for logical reasons that was initially accepted for purely emotional ones.[65] Marriage should only take place in the presence of two witnesses: the mind and the heart.

If I were a lady I should be careful whom I married: I should want to be pretty sure that the man tried to live his religion as revealed to us. Young folks generally marry because they love, sometimes because they are pretty. It is said that beauty is "only skin deep," and I believe it is so, it will shortly fade away. We should be reasonable on this subject, as well as on others; but when a person is love struck, there is no reason in them. We should never be struck very bad. We should love so that we could throw him off at any time if he does not do right.[66]

This is wise counsel. The heart should not be given in a single burst of emotion, but line upon line, grace for grace as the loved one proves worthy of it.

Marriage is an act of faith that is only as valid as the evidences upon which that faith rests. The more our trust in others is predicated upon a discerning spirit in ourselves, the more justified that trust will be. Faith in the Lord should include faith in his providential care and in his willingness to assist his righteous daughters in both seeking and finding a fit companion.

Our daughters should seek, by all the faith that they can exercise before God, to obtain good husbands—husbands who will build them up instead of holding them down; who will strengthen their hands in the work of God, who will make them mothers of a righteous seed and

---

[65]This is one reason early childhood is the most important period of character development.

[66]John Taylor, JD 19:167. George Q. Cannon said: "Our daughters should be taught to control their feelings and affections, and not let them go out without any regard to these circumstances to which I have alluded." JD 25:368.

posterity, with whom they can rejoice in the eternal mansions of our Father and our God; and no woman who has the faith of the Gospel within her, will want to bear a child to a man of whom she will be ashamed, and who cannot lead her into the presence of the Lamb. She will rather exercise faith before the Lord that God will give unto her a husband in whom she can trust, in whom she can have confidence, whose word will be as the word of God to her. And in the midst of the troubles, afflictions and trials that belong to this mortal existence, she will feel comforted by the knowledge that her husband is indeed a man of God, a man who will be true and faithful to her under all circumstances. This is a constant cause of strength and comfort to every woman, to know that she has wedded a man whom she can trust, upon whom she can rely, who will never fail her, that is, as far as human nature will permit a man to be free from infallibility. This is the course we should all take.[67]

Those possessing deep spiritual inclinations sometimes err in selecting a mate and may, therefore, be burdened with unhappy marriages. Their misfortune stems from the disparity in religious commitment existing between themselves and their partners. Being more other-worldly than this-worldly in orientation, the spiritually-minded are very much in the minority; they are exceptional people. In identifying with the ancient prophets who sought for a day of righteousness and found it not, they, too consider themselves "strangers and pilgrims on the earth" rather than its eager denizens and property owners.[68] Whereas most mortals can readily find others to marry whose tastes and dispositions are similar to their own, the spiritually motivated are hardpressed to find suitable companions. Like rare pearls, they are too few in number, too widely scattered and too hidden to be properly matched up without the greatest difficulty. However, a primary purpose for the latter-day gathering of Israel out of the nations is to facilitate this very matching. Even so, those with an astute, discerning nature, embark upon marriage only after the most careful forethought. Others, however, not yet really knowing themselves, or lacking their spiritual

---

[67]George Q. Cannon, Ibid., p. 369.
[68]See D&C 45:11-14; Hebrews 11:13-16.

92 growth, naively marry with little consideration to the question of overall compatibility.

Paradoxically, the individual with a pronounced spiritual need may find more peace and contentment with someone who is indifferent to religious matters than with someone whose spiritual interests are only nominal and perfunctory. In other words, a spouse from "Babylon" may be less of a frustration and disappointment than one from "Laodicea." Why? Because the spiritual dichotomy in the former instance is more honest and clear-cut than would be true of the latter. Being so, false religious expectations will not exist nor will false hopes for a spiritual oneness arise. There will be no illusions, the relationship will be what it appears to be. Perhaps this is one reason the Lord berated the ancient saints of Laodicea for their spiritual indecisiveness.

> I know thy works, that thou art neither cold nor hot: I would thou wert cold or hot. So then because thou art lukewarm, and neither cold nor hot, I will spue thee out of my mouth. Because thou sayest, I am rich, and increased with goods, and have need of nothing; and knowest not that thou art wretched, and miserable, and poor, and blind, and naked: . . .[69]

We reiterate, like-minded people can be happy only with their own kind. The prospect of finding the right wife or husband is far greater when one conscientiously strives to reflect the character of the marriage partner he or she is seeking. Since like attracts like, one who would have a companion with the potential for exaltation, must also be such a person. Those who desire the best, must be the best. What we are, dictates what we may possess. Indeed, maintaining the highest standards of virtue and commitment to God, serves to repel the overtures of those prospective marriage partners whose ideals and conduct would, like some moral gravity, tend to pull us down. This does not mean that one should demand a perfect mate. Few have lived in this world.

---

[69]Revelation 3:15-17.

And even if one came along, we would have to be perfect ourselves to recognize so rare a wonder (since it takes one to know one) or to be accepted in marriage by such an individual. We can be too demanding where mortals are concerned. The object, therefore, should not be a perfect mate, but one who has the potential and the desire to achieve perfection in and through Christ. We marry, not because we are perfect, but to become so.[70]

93

Ordinarily, it is best not only to live, but to marry within one's means. Much unhappiness results from men and women reaching beyond their own *unalterable* limitations. Recall, the prince did not fall in love with Cinderella, the harassed scullery maid, but Cinderella the beautiful charmer who magically appeared at the royal ball. He chose a lovely girl who had been *disguised* in rags; he did not select one of her undeniably homely sisters with their undeniably big feet. It is one thing to rise to your potential and quite another to transcend it. So too, we should accept the facts concerning our own assets and liabilities and seek fulfillment in terms of those facts. The average person lacking such added endowments as money, talent or status, seldom attracts the handsome prince or the dazzling beauty. Most of those who dream of such a mate experience frustration, self-rejection, and heartbreak. Even those who do manage to marry above themselves pay a price for their "success." The old insecurities do not go away, indeed, they may become intensified. The plain woman with the handsome husband often experiences a gnawing fear of losing him to some attractive female predator. The untalented mate of an accomplished artist is seldom at ease among that mate's peers. And so it goes. Many young people subject themselves to needless pain and despair over their presumed inadequacies. Covetousness may be the life-blood of commerce, but it is the bane of the insecure personality. It is a creator of hells and of the devils who inhabit them. Satan himself is the

---

[70]See CR, October 5, 1947, p. 153.

94 product of a ruthless, unremitting envy which grants him no peace.[71] Happiness results from filling the measure of one's own creation, not from possessing the measure of another's.

Too many young people allow purely physical and material factors to determine their choice of a mate. This is a grave error. The rising tide of marital disharmony, emotional breakdown, delinquency and divorce witness to the fruits of the popular fallacies associated with mate selection. We are victimized by deceitful priorities: beauty; money, charm, status, etc. The very qualities which led men to reject the Savior of mankind who "hath no form nor comeliness; and when we shall see him, there is no beauty that we should desire him."[72]

Nor should we forget that we wed the soul—not just its "outward adorning." The core reality—the spirit—will remain after the flesh and the things thereof have faded away under the relentless battering of time. An eternal marriage must be based upon values which transcend mere temporal considerations. Samuel the prophet was greatly impressed with the physical appearance of Jesse's son, Eliab, but the Lord warned him:

> . . . Look not on his countenance, or on the height of his stature; because I have refused him: for the Lord seeth not as man seeth; for man looketh on the outward appearance, but the Lord looketh on the heart.[73]

Brigham Young put the matter a bit more bluntly:

> A great many women are more nice than wise. If they can get a man with a pretty face, they think it is all there is about it. Some men think if they can get a woman that has a handsome face, that is all there is of it. But it is that woman that has a head and sensibility,— I do not care if her head is three feet long,—it has nothing to do with the character that lives in the body. It is the character that is in the man's house, the spirit that is in the man; it is the spirit that in in the woman and in the house that makes the woman and that makes the man.[74]

---

[71]See Moses 1:12-22; 4:1-4.
[72]Isaiah 53:2.
[73]I Samuel 16:7.
[74]JD 5:92.

Then too, it is well to remember that all mortal imper- **95**
fections result from sin (the violation of law) and that when
sin is finally vanquished in the resurrection, beauty of face
and form will be the natural endowment of every celestial
man and woman.

I think it has been taught by some that as we lay our bodies down,
they will so rise again in the resurrection with all the impediments
and imperfections that they had here; and that if a wife does not love
her husband in this state she cannot love him in the next. This is not
so. Those who attain to the blessing of the first or celestial resurrection
will be pure and holy, and perfect in body. Every man and woman that
reaches to this unspeakable attainment will be as beautiful as the angels
that surround the throne of God. If you can, by faithfulness in this life,
obtain the right to come up in the morning of the resurrection, you
need entertain no fears that the wife will be dissatisfied with her husband, or the husband with the wife; for those of the first resurrection
will be free from sin and from the consequences and power of sin.[75]

While the Spirit is a guide for the faithful, it will not
usurp man's agency or guarantee that all of the heart's
desires will be granted in mortality. For many reasons, some
are not given the opportunity to marry the man or woman
of their choice. Social custom makes mate selection a particularly frustrating matter for most women since they are
obliged to play the part of flower rather than bee. While
this is no problem for those females possessing sought-after
attributes, it presents serious difficulties for some of their
less-favored sisters. Fear of lonely years of spinsterhood or of
failing to keep the commandments have prompted many
women to marry someone they did not love or who was
morally and/or spiritually their inferior. While this is a decision each must make for herself, no faithful saint need
feel obligated to marry in order to be assured of a companion in the life to come.

You good sisters, who are single and alone, do not fear, do not
feel that blessings are going to be withheld from you. You are not under

---

[75]Brigham Young, JD 10:24.

96 any obligation or necessity of accepting some proposal that comes to you which is distasteful for fear you will come under condemnation. If in your hearts you feel that the Gospel is true, and would under proper conditions receive these ordinances and sealing blessings in the temple of the Lord, and that is your faith and your hope and your desire, and that does not come to you now, the Lord will make it up, and you shall be blessed—for no blessing shall be withheld.[76]

While the celibate life is an unnatural one, when sustained in it by one's fellow saints and by the Spirit of the Lord, it can be far more rewarding than a loveless marriage to an alien spirit.

There is not a young man in our community who would not be willing to travel from here to England to be married right, if he understood things as they are; there is not a young woman in our community, who loves the gospel and wishes its blessings, that would be married in any other way; they would live unmarried until they could be married as they should be, if they lived until they were as old as Sarah before she had Isaac born to her. Many of our brethren have married off their children without taking this into consideration, and thinking it a matter of little of importance. I wish we all understood this in the light in which heaven understands it.[77]

A Wife In The Lord

Paul counseled the women of the Church to honor their husbands in their callings.

Wives, submit yourselves unto your own husbands, as unto the Lord. For the husband is the head of the wife, even as Christ is the head of the church: and he is the saviour of the body. Therefore as the church is subject unto Christ, so let the wives be to their own husbands in every thing.[78]

The true order of marriage, being founded upon the power and the authority of the Holy Priesthood, is patriar-

---

[76]Joseph Fielding Smith, "Elijah The Prophet And His Mission," p. 31, 32.
[77]Brigham Young, JD 11:118. See JD 12:97.
[78]Ephesians 5:22-24. Hugh B. Brown remarked: "This requirement of the wives to submit to their husbands presupposes righteousness on the part of the husbands." CR, October 1, 1954, p. 15.

chal in design. The husband leads because he is the living 97
embodiment of that priesthood which governs all things. A
celestially-oriented wife understands this and fully sustains
her worthy mate in his position.

> If our wives would remember and keep faithfully the covenant
> they have made, they would observe the laws of their husbands, and
> teach their children to honor every law of God, and to love, honor,
> and obey their earthly father. If I keep my covenants, I shall be saved
> in the presence of God; if I violate them, I shall be damned; and so it
> will be with my family; and what applies to me in this respect will
> apply to all.[79]

A covenant wife is a man's God-given helpmate; she is
circumscribed by him as he is circumscribed by Christ. The
family is like an eternal time piece made up of wheels within wheels—each moving at its ordained pace in its ordained
place. Thus, each serves and is served by the other. But just
as the movement of one wheel depends upon the movement
of another, so does a wife's fulfillment depend upon the fulfillment of her husband. He, in turn, can only advance with
the help of God, the great main spring of all progress. This
principle lay behind the Lord's instructions to Emma Smith,
the Prophet's wife:

> Continue in the spirit of meekness, and beware of pride. Let
> thy soul delight in thy husband, and the glory which shall come upon
> him. Keep my commandments continually, and a crown of righteous-
> ness thou shalt receive. And except thou do this, where I am you can-
> not come.[80]

The wise woman will do this, for it is a matter of enlightened self-interest. There is no more reason for a woman
in Israel to chafe under this commandment than it is for a
child to resist the guidance of loving parents. Pride is the
number one killer of spirituality. It afflicts men and women
alike at every level of society. May the Lord deliver us from
it! It is the antithesis of all he stands for. It prevents the of-

---

[79]Heber C. Kimball, JD 11:211.
[80]D&C 25:14, 15.

98 fering of a broken heart and a contrite spirit—which offering is the basic prerequisite to the blessings of the atonement.[81]

On the other hand, willingness to sustain a leader who is less gifted or less knowledgeable than one's self is a mark of genuine humility. It is not difficult to bow before the superior attributes of another, this is the way of the world. But to honestly respect and support those whose endowments are seemingly less than one's own savors of godliness. Brigham Young decried the attitude of those who disdained their lawful stewards:

> A feeling exists in the minds of many of this people that they would be glad to submit to their presiding Elder or Bishop, but they do not think that he was knowledge sufficient to lead them. Says a wife, "I would be glad to submit to my husband; but I wish I had a husband that I could look upon as my superior—that I could look up to and receive his words and counsel: that would be my highest delight. O that I had a husband capable of dictating me; but, alas! I have not." Go among some of the children, and they say, "I would be glad to mind my parents in all things, but I believe that I know more than they do."[82]

The priesthood is greater than any man and is not bestowed upon men because of any presumed intellectual superiority over women. Wrote John A. Widtsoe:

> In the Church no adjustment can be made. The Priesthood always presides and must, for the sake of order. The women of a congregation of auxiliary—many of them—may be wiser, far greater in mental powers, even greater in actual power of leadership than the men who preside over them. That signifies nothing. The priesthood is not bestowed on the basis of mental power but is given to good men and they exercise it by right of divine gift, called upon by the leaders of the Church. Woman has her gift of equal magnitude, and that is bestowed on the simple and weak as well as upon those who are great and strong.[83]

---

[81]See 2 Nephi 2:7.

[82]JD 6:44. John A. Widtsoe observed: "It is undeniable that there are weak men as well as weak women, and it is equally true that such men are often attracted to and marry strong, capable women; and vice versa." PCG, p. 90.

[83]*Ibid.*, See CR, April 8, 1967, pp. 89, 90.

A wife may be better educated, more gifted, and wiser than her husband. This is often a trial to her, but it is for her to manifest a spirit of meekness and to honor him in his station. In doing so, she leaves him without excuse should he then fail to magnify his calling.

. . . I have seen women who, I thought, actually knew more about the business of life than their husbands themselves did, and were really more capable of directing a farm, the building of a house, and the management of flocks and herds, etc., than the men were; but if men were to live up to their privileges this would not be the case; for it is their right to claim the light of truth and that intelligence and knowledge necessary to enable them to carry on every branch of their business successfully.[84]

On another occasion President Young said:

Some mothers try to make father believe that a child five years old knows as much as the father. Another great cause of dissatisfaction is that so many women are such noble women, and know so much more than their husbands. They say, "This man is not capable of leading me." That is a positive proof to me that that man does not know his ability and calling. I will acknowledge that many women are smarter than their husbands. But when people are married, instead of trying to get rid of each other, reflect that you have made your choice, and strive to honour and keep it.[85]

A man's wife should be his best and most trusted counselor. She is in a position to do more for his betterment than any one else on earth. It lies within her power to be his dearest friend or most devasting enemy.

Woman's influence is all powerful: a woman can influence a man to almost anything if she knows how to proceed. She can lead him to the lowest depths of degradation, or to the grandest heights of noble deeds. She can cause a man to forsake his principles and those things which he knows to be right and do what he knows to be wrong, and what he would do under no other circumstances; while on the other hand she can, by her influence and efforts, cause a man to rise step by

[84]Brigham Young, JD 11:135.
[85]JD 9:39, 40.

100　　step from the low places into which he has fallen, till he is capable of the noblest things.[86]

A marriage "in the Lord" requires that a wife follow her husband *only* "in the Lord," for obedience to God takes precedence over obedience to any man.

> We have got to learn to stand or fall for ourselves, male and female. It is true that we are taught in the principles of the Gospel that man is the head of the woman, and Christ is the head of the man; and according to the order that is established in the kingdom of God, it is the duty of the man to follow Christ, and it is the duty of the woman to follow the man in Christ, not out of him. But has not a woman the same volition that the man has? Can she not follow or disobey the man as he can follow or disobey Christ? Certainly she can, she is responsible for her acts, and must answer for them. She is endowed with intelligence and judgment, and will stand upon her own merits as much so as the man.[87]

President Young put the matter in even stronger terms:

> The woman that says, "I will follow my husband to hell," will have the privilege. The man that says, "I will follow a woman to hell, but what I will have her," will have the privilege of following her there. It is a disgrace to a Saint to love anything that he would drop or forsake for his religion. Love your religion better than anything else. Love your God. Life everlasting is all in all to us.[88]

The story of Thomas B. Marsh, the first president of the Council of the Twelve, is a case in point. His pride and jealousy coupled with his determination to support his errant wife regardless of the consequences led him to betray the Saints in Missouri in 1838. He was excommunicated. Bitter years followed. Then, in 1857, he returned to the Church a broken man and requested re-baptism. In the heat of the moment he had once said that he would sustain his wife's character even if he had to go to hell for it.[89] His remarks

---

[86]Celia A. Smith, "Woman's Influence," *Young Woman's Journal* IV (March, 1893), p. 281.
[87]Joseph F. Smith, JD 16:247.
[88]Brigham Young, JD 8:141. See 1:77.
[89]JD 3:283, 284.

upon returning to the Church prove that he had done just
that.[90] There is a point beyond which love for and loyalty to
one's mate ceases to be a virtue. That point is reached when
the first great commandment is denied in order to affirm
the second.

The Lord is the *only* one we are commanded to love
with *all* of our being. He, alone, is worthy of such complete
devotion. Everyone else, including one's self, should be sustained only to the extent that they partake of the divine nature. Speaking of one who has been sealed up unto eternal
life, President Young asked:

> Now suppose that he gains the affection of a lovely woman and
> marries her, how much shall that righteous man love that woman? Shall
> he say, "I love this woman to such a degree that I will go to hell
> rather than not have her, I will do even this rather than lose my wife?"
> No, for you ought to love a woman only so far as she adorns the doc-
> trine you profess; so far as she adorns that doctrine, just so far let your
> love extend to her. . . . When the wife secures to herself a glorious resur-
> rection, she is worthy of the full measure of the love of the faithful hus-
> band, but never before. And when a man has passed through the vail,
> and secured to himself an eternal exaltation, he is then worthy of the
> love of his wife and children, and not until then, unless he has received
> the promise of and is sealed up unto eternal lives. Then he may be an
> object fully worthy of their affections and love on the earth, and not
> before.[91]

While many will regard President Young's words as extreme, they are fully in accord with all that the Savior taught
on this point and have the clear ring of truth about them.

In Summation

Whatever the reality of our lives, we must never forget nor surrender the divine ideal. Without it, we are lost.
Without it we cannot know what we might be or what we
might attain—therefore, we cannot know, in truth, what we

[90]See JD 5:28, 29, 115, 206-213.
[91]Brigham Young, JD 3:360, 361. See also 9:140; 22:125; CR, October 4, 1930, p. 79.

102   are and what we have attained. If the ideal is painful to us, so much the better. The very discomfiture we feel witnesses to the truth of that ideal and to our own longing for it. Pain precedes all sincere repentance. Better a leper crying out in desperation to a passing Jesus than a leper huddled in hopelessness among other lost lepers. The Savior personified all that is divine and noble in mankind. How impoverished we should be without his testimony of the hidden potential in us all! The following is a brief summation of the writer's understanding of what is meant by a marriage in the Lord— a celestial marriage.

A marriage in the Lord is a God-ordained, God-sustained union between a man and a woman of like natures. It is as immortal as the spirits of the parties to it. Because of their mutual love for and commitment to Christ, they are prepared to sacrifice all that they possess for his sake, knowing that he has sacrificed all that he possessed for their sake. In doing so, they become joint-heirs with him in all that the Father possesses.

While mindful that obedience to the whole law of God entails the postponement of some of their personal desires and ambitions, they are happy to take up the cross of self-denial and walk by faith in an ultimate vindication. They made the choice that had to be made between one law and another, and one world and another. They do not look back. Because they seek that city whose builder and maker is God, they are able to rise above the temptations and cares of this world knowing that mortality is not the "be all and end all" of life. They realize that celestial marriage is an act of mutual consecration. In coming to it, each surrenders all and each strives to magnify the stewardship which they are individually given in return. Loving their companion as themselves, each endeavors to assist the other in successfully fulfilling his or her stewardship. They bear one another's burdens that they might be less burdensome.

Their happiness is joyful. It permeates their lives and the lives of their children. It touches all who come within their circle. They know that peace which passes all human understanding. Insofar as mortals can, they enter into the rest of the Lord. Death's separation only serves to further intensify their appreciation for and devotion to one another. Absence does make the heart grow fonder because their union *was* of the heart—the spirit—and not of the flesh alone. Their marriage will be a thing of beauty, joy, and holiness throughout eternal time.

V

The Robe of Modesty

*Your beauty should reside not in
outward adornment—the braiding of
hair, or jewelery, or dress—but
in the inmost centre of your being,
with its imperishable ornament,
a gentle, quiet spirit, which is of
high value in the sight of God.*[1]

Modesty is becoming to men and women alike. It is a sister of humility and should be her constant companion. Gentle women and gentle men—those of genuine breeding and refinement—practice modesty and restraint as a matter of course. This does not mean that they are rigidly precise in their decorum. To the contrary, modesty is no stranger to the blithe spirit. Freedom of happy expression is quite compatible with modest behavior. Indeed, without it, presumed modesty may be nothing more than prim conformity. Modesty requires a sense of humor if it is to be truly modest.

---

[1]New English Bible, 1 Peter 3:3,4.

106 The devil is the author of the common notion that high standards of conduct are anathema to the good life. The reverse is the case: the Lord's way is the only authentically happy way. Modesty is one of the bright flowers we find growing along that way.

In opposition to that flower is the pandemic weed of immodesty. This ugly plant is highly variegated. Characteristically, it is the antithesis of the temperate, the balanced and the beautiful. It caters instead to the extreme, the excessive and the unnatural. The gaudy, the over-done, the irresponsible —all are varieties of immodesty. This behavorial defect is commonly associated with one's dress, grooming, demeanor, and speech. However, the Lord also considers loud and excessive laughter inappropriate for his people.

Therefore, cease from all your light speeches, from all laughter, from all your lustful desires, from all your pride and light-mindedness, and from all your wicked doings.[2]

Joseph Smith was characteristically of a naturally cheerful disposition, yet he did not approve of the unbecoming conduct of the Saints.

How vain and trifling have been our spirits, our conferences, our councils, our meetings, our private as well as public conversations—too low, too mean, too vulgar, too condescending for the dignified characters of the called and chosen of God, according to the purposes of His will, from before the foundation of the world![3]

Happiness does not require levity anymore than freedom requires intemperance. Indeed, in view of the times and the awesome responsibilities devolving upon the Church, levity is about as appropriate for the Saints as a square dance at a funeral. Immodesty is not limited to the foregoing, it is also manifest in such things as the ostentation of one's home or in an overweening pride stemming from affluence in ma-

---

[2]D&C 88:121. See *Ibid.*, 59:15; 88:69.
[3]TJS, p. 137.

terial wealth, education, intellect, abilities, status, physical attractiveness, etc. Those who succumb to such conceit gild the lily of human dignity.

While pride and immodesty are often fellow travelers, feelings of inadequacy can also prompt the self-doubter to unseemly behavior. The aging woman may overdress, over-groom or otherwise turn herself into a caricature of lost youth in a desperate effort to deny the undeniable. The in-secure man may assume a loud and overbearing manner in an effort to bolster his flagging ego. Some young people, emotionally unprepared to meet the demands of normal adulthood and naively assuming that a repudiation of the accepted trappings of the culture somehow places them above and beyond the status quo, bury their heads in rather extreme, even bizarre, styles of dress and grooming. While such immature behavior is to be regretted (since it wastes their time and energy on the trivia of life and makes them more vulnerable to deviate moral behavior), of itself, it need not be taken too seriously. For many young people, it is a matter of clinging on to childhood—playing dressup with their peers. Not having fully oriented themselves to reality, they feel a need to don one costume after another in the process of finding and accepting the one best suited to their part in the drama of life. There are many reasons for the foolish ways of mortals—some very pathetic. We should not be too judgmental of one another's foibles until we learn the why of them—perhaps not even then. With this understand-ing, we will consider the single phase of modesty relating to dress and its moral implications.

Origin of Modesty

When God placed Adam and Eve in the garden "they were both naked, the man and his wife, and were not ashamed."[4] But, as was previously noted, their subsequent fall brought them mortality and with it an awareness of the

---

[4]Genesis 2:25.

WOMAN AND THE PRIESTHOOD

108   deeper implications of maleness and femaleness. They were
as little children no more. They quickly made aprons of fig
leaves (there being no cloth or like materials at the time)
to partially cover themselves.[5] Thus was modesty—a sense
of personal decorum—introduced among men. Thereafter,
the Lord instructed the man and his wife more perfectly
in this principle and clothed them with durable coats made
of animal skins.[6] This suggests that Heaven's standard of
propriety was both more constant and more comprehensive
than that symbolized by the apron of leaves. A divine pattern of modesty had been given to fallen man which established the proper bounds and limitations for all human
fashions. Those bounds and limitations have been violated
again and again to the detriment of us all.

Nakedness was not inappropriate so long as the couple
retained their child-like innocence in God's presence. But
this condition no longer held; they were now two knowledgeable mortals facing, not God, but an alien world where
spiritual predators waited to destroy them. Like the Word
of Wisdom, the coat of skins was designed to be a safeguard
against the evils and designs of conspiring men yet unborn.[7]
The Lord is far more concerned with protecting his people
against the wickedness of men than the elements of nature.

If he deemed it important for so pure a couple—one
living in total isolation—to practice modesty, how much more
imperative it must be today! The more corrupting the times,
the more essential it is that strong defenses be maintained
against them. Whether it is due to ignorance, slothfulness or
outright perfidy, many continue to play moth to the flame of
indecency. Sophisticates argue that it is only prudery and
evil-mindedness which prompts the call for modesty. The

---

[5]*Ibid.*, 3:7. See JD 9:168. The fact that Adam and Eve practiced modesty in one
another's presence while still alone on the earth suggests that this principle should be
observed in the privacy of the home as well as in public. Husbands and wives who
habitually go about uncovered before one another and, far worse, before their children,
violate this principle.

[6]*Ibid.*, 3:21. See JD 11:357.

[7]See D&C 89:4.

human body, they contend, is a beautiful creation of God which should be seen without shame or censure. These enlightened souls either do not know or do not believe that the race is fallen and corrupt. Indeed, there are few who are not relatively carnal, sensual and devilish.[8] Most men do not view the body as the temple of the spirit; they see it as an instrument of titillation and gratification.

Those who quote Paul's words, "unto the pure all things are pure. . ." in defense of "freedom of expression" neglect to complete the apostle's statement: "but unto them that are *defiled and unbelieving* is nothing pure; but even their mind and conscience is defiled."[9] Are not most humans *unbelieving* where the Gospel of Jesus Christ is concerned? It is precisely because our age is rife with uncleanness that women should cover their nakedness before men—and men before women. No, the body is not evil—but the world is. All things are not pure because all men are not pure. Heaven, not earth, is the only place where nakedness could be practiced without evil consequences.

The Flow of Moral Opinion

Satan is devilishly clever! He persuades men to believe that what does not embarrass them or disturb their consciences is thereby proven acceptable. Alexander Pope's couplet succinctly sums up the manner in which Satan leads the unwary "carefully down to hell."[10]

Vice is a monster of so frightful mien,
As, to be hated, needs but to be seen;
Yet seen too oft, familiar with her face,
We first endure, then pity, then embrace.[11]

---

[8]See Alma 34:9; 42:10.
[9]Titus 1:15
[10]See 2 Nephi 28:19-21; Alma 30:60.
[11]Alexander Pope, "Essay on Man," Epistle II, lines 217-220. The Library of Liberal Arts. Bobbs-Merrill Co., Inc. New York, 1965. p. 25.

110   In this way each generation justifies its conduct. Each delights in pointing out how earlier generations decried the changing fashions of their day only to finally accept and, indeed, often go beyond them.

The moralist is caricatured as a would-be-Jeremiah sounding the monotonous cry of "wolf" only to have the fearful creature eventually embraced for the innocent "lamb" it always was. The fact is, God's standards *have* been violated in different ways by each succeeding generation, cycles of fashion notwithstanding. But as fashions in dress or morals change, there is always a period of lag while *what is* passes and *what will be* assumes dominance. A rip-tide of opinion is created when the ebbing flow of the old order is met head-on by the surging force of the new. But it doesn't last. The old finally turns to join the flow of the new so that for a time the sea of human fashions presents a serene face to the moon of human folly. These tidal reversals are coming with ever-increasing rapidity; they are meeting with diminishing moral resistance and they are drawing mankind ever downward.

Immodest fashions have characterized many different cultures in human history. Nudity and near nudity have been practiced by savage and sophisticate alike with no thought of impropriety. But it is only since the first world war that women in so-called civilized nations have adopted the short skirt. Previously, the exposure of the ankle by women of refinement had been thought most daring; but to display the leg (or limb) was thought absolutely scandalous.[12] Today, the wearing of form revealing attire is common practice. The fact that such styles are widespread does not excuse them.[13] The argument of numbers is fallacious: forty million Frenchmen *can* be wrong. Morality is not a matter of majority opinion.

The very nature of our pluralistic society makes it im-

---

[12]See JD 12:299; 14:103; 15:39.

[13]Immodest—even vulgar—beach and street wear is not infrequently seen on the male of the species as well. Immodesty is not only a female problem. See JD 14:21.

possible to use abstractions with any degree of precision. Being of many different minds, our words are subject to various connotations or nuances which do not always allow for clear understanding. Consequently, telling someone to be modest, or virtuous or chaste may have little value—another abstraction. We know what snow, rain, and ice is—but what is modesty, virture, chastity? Clearly, these terms do not mean the same thing even to people in the same culture, not to mention those in a different culture. If there is to be consensus as to their meaning, abstractions must be specifically qualified—defined.

American democracy is hardly the same as Russian or Chinese democracy, yet all three nations claim to be democratic. Abstractions are always the victims of rationalization. We tailor them to our own purposes. If the saints are to be one where modesty is concerned, they must be provided with a model of modesty. In wearing the coat of skins the Lord tailored for them, Adam and Eve provided such a model for their children. A modern "coat of skins" is needed today. Lacking it, far too many of us have gone back to wearing fig leaves.

Isaiah employed strong language in prophesying the immodest behavior of the daughters of Zion in our generation.

> Moreover the Lord saith, Because the daughters of Zion are haughty, and walk with stretched forth necks and wanton eyes, walking and mincing as they go, and making a tinkling with their feet: Therefore the Lord will smite with a scab the crown of the head of the daughters of Zion, and the Lord will discover their secret parts. . . . And it shall come to pass, that instead of sweet smell there shall be stink; and instead of a girdle a rent; and instead of well set hair baldness; and instead of a stomacher a girding of sackcloth; and burning instead of beauty.[14]

Isaiah's words bring to mind Alma's denunciation of the hypocrisy of the Zoramites.

---

[14]Isaiah 3:16, 17, 24.

112

Behold, O my God, their costly apparel, and their ringlets, and their bracelets, and their ornaments of gold, and all their precious things which they are ornamented with; and behold, their hearts are set upon them, and yet they cry unto thee and say—We thank thee, O God, for we are a chosen people unto thee, while others shall perish.[15]

One of the chief responsibilities of the shepherds of Israel is to guide the Lord's sheep along the right path in all important matters pertaining to their generation. Even with such guidance the sheep are prone to wander, but without it, they are sure to drift into the false paths of a world in darkness.[16] Unhappily, too many of the flock assume that the very presence of alternative paths justifies them in selecting the one most to their own liking. They become their own shepherd. Such an attitude makes for a kind of moral and spiritual solipsism.

The word of the Lord has been described as a *"rod of iron."*[17] It is not made of rubber. It cannot be twisted to one's liking, it cannot be fashioned into something else. His word has also been compared to the Liahonah—the sacred compass—which led Lehi's party through the wilderness.

For behold, it is as easy to give heed to the word of Christ, which will point to you a straight course to eternal bliss, as it was for our fathers to give heed to this compass, which would point unto them a straight course to the promised land.[18]

Both of these metaphors emphasize the firm, unchanging nature of the law of Christ.[19] Obedience to it must become as total as immersion in the covenant waters of baptism, it should be applied to everything in life, for what aspects of life are irrelevant to the issue of perfection?[20] Although we may not wish to yield some facet of our behavior to the divine ideal, still, we cannot in all honesty deny that ideal. The

---

[15]Alma 31:28.
[16]See Isaiah 53:6.
[17]1 Nephi 15:23, 24.
[18]Alma 37:44
[19]See D&C 88:21.
[20]See CR, April 3, 1971, p. 47.

Gospel standard is as independent of worldly fashions in behavior as it is of theological fashions in religion.

For truth is an absolute monarch. If honored, it conquers the democracy of relativism where men's ideas are given equal deference. It topples error's proud castles. At the same time, error exists only because truth exists. False religion is invaribly preceeded by true religion. It is the same in matters of dress, entertainment, music, art, literature, politics, economics, etc.. For each of them there was a divine standard long before there was a human deviation. There is a true and false, a right and a wrong for everything in any given system subject to divine law.[21] Hence, it is God, not couturiers in Paris, artists in Rome, writers in London, or musicians in New York, to whom modern Israel should look for guidance in all things.

A divine ideal should dictate the basic design of the clothing we wear, the food we eat, the songs we sing, the dances we dance, the books we read, and—in fine—the lives we lead. For God approves the design of all things in the celestial world. His will is done there as it is to be done on earth during the millennial reign of Christ. If his design for temporal life is rejected, when shall the saints prepare themselves to accept his design for eternal life?

Thirty year's experience has taught me that every moment of my life must be holiness to the Lord, resulting from equity, justice, mercy, and uprightness in all my actions, which is the only course by which I can preserve the Spirit of the Almighty to myself. What is your experience? It is the same as my own.[22]

A Fashion Of Our Own

Mormon, in commenting on the dress of the Nephite women in Alma's day wrote: "they did not wear costly ap-

---

[21]See D&C 93:30, 88:36-39.
[22]Brigham Young, JD 9:220.

114

parel, yet they were neat and comely."[23] Modern Israel has been commanded: "thou shalt not be proud in thy heart; let all thy garments be plain, and their beauty the beauty of the work of thine own hands . . ."[24] This principle was stressed from the days of Joseph Smith.[25] Again and again, the modern prophets have counseled the Saints to become independent of the world and to establish "a fashion of our own."

> My discourse will have to be brief, and I am going to ask my sisters in particular to stop following these foolish fashions, and to introduce fashions of their own. This is the place, and this the time to make known the word of the Lord to the people. It is vain and foolish, it does not evince godliness, and is inconsistent with the spirit of a saint to follow after the fashions of the world. I wish to impress these remarks especially on the minds of my young sisters—the daughters of the Elders of Israel. Not but what our wives as well as daughters follow many fashions that are uncomely, foolish and vain. What do you say? "Shall we introduce a fashion of our own, and what shall it be?"[26]

A Latter-day Saint fashion would be a light to the world. Nor would it call for drab sameness since each could and should style that fashion in a manner most suitable to themselves. The preservation of one's individuality is vital to personal happiness. The Lord knows this and delights in the endless variety of His creations. President Young understood this principle and pointed out that clothes, houses, gardens, families, etc., should reflect the Saint's own personality and creativity.

> Thus a variety of talent would be brought forth and exhibited of which nothing would be known, if houses and dresses and other things were all alike. But let the people bring out their talents, and have the variety within them brought forth and made manifest so that we can behold it, like the variety in the works of nature. . . . Now let us

---

[23]Alma 1:27. It is interesting to note how often the prophets associated the wearing of costly clothing with apostasy. See Luke 16:19; Revelation 18:16; 1 Nephi 8:27; Jacob 2:13; Alma 1:6, 32; 4:6; 31:27, 28; 32:2; 4 Nephi 24; Mormon 8:36, 37.

[24]D&C 42:40. See JD 10:311.

[25]See JD 6:212.

[26]Brigham Young, JD 14:16, 17.

develop the variety within us, and show to the world that we have talent and taste, and prove to the heavens that our minds are set on beauty and true excellence, so that we can become worthy to enjoy the society of angels, and raise ourselves above the level of the wicked world and begin to increase in faith, and the power that God has given us, and so show to the world an example worthy of imitation.[27]

Such a course respects both God and man. For it would allow the Lord to exercise His agency in establishing the *fashion* most appropriate to His children while permitting them to exercise their agency in selecting their own *style* of that fashion!

However, many Saints are yet to catch the vision of President Young's counsel. Both he and his successors pled with the sisters in particular to assert their faith and their independence and become a light of fashion to the world.[28] In carrying out President George Albert Smith's instructions to "preach modesty," Elder Spencer W. Kimball told the students of Brigham Young University: "We do not have to do anything we do not want to do. We can create our own styles and costumes."[29] In spite of this, an undeniable decline in dress and other standards has taken place in obvious conformity with those of the world at large. The fact that so many Latter-day Saints are prepared to approximate the ever-changing styles of the general society is far more significant than *how* they do so. A lack of integrity toward any righteous principle is far more basic to morality than the diverse ways such a lack may be expressed.

From time to time, popular dress may actually conform to more acceptable standards of modesty, however, this is no credit to those whose accidental commitment to the principle was dictated by the style requirements of the moment. Modesty is an eternal principle, it should be constant, as valid in this world as it is in heaven itself.

---

[27]JD 11:305.
[28]See JD 12:220, 221; 14:16-19; 15:161, 162; 18:129.
[29]"A Style of Our Own," A Devotional Assembly address, February 13, 1951.

116   Suppose that a female angel were to come into your house and you had the privilege of seeing her, how would she be dressed? . . . She would be neat and nice, her countenance full of glory, brilliant, bright, and perfectly beautiful, and in every act her gracefulness would charm the heart of every beholder. There is nothing needless about her. None of my sisters believe that these useless, foolish fashions are followed in heaven. Well, then, pattern after good and heavenly things, and let the beauty of your garments be the workmanship of your own hands, that which adorns your bodies.[29]

The Lord's fashion would enable every female—from the little girl to the mature woman—to be attractively dressed without the excessive financial expense and sheer labor now required to maintain costly and elaborate wardrobes. Then too, the wearing of expensive and/or form revealing clothes may tempt the less richly endowed female to become envious and covetous. While immodesty may be the glory of the well disposed female, what of those who are less attractive? So-called sex appeal is deemed extremely important to the husband-seeking girl. Many a "plain Jane" has lowered her moral standards in order to compete with her more desirable sister. And what of the older woman—or the woman who may be suffering from some deformity such as varicose veins? Should she be required to choose between exposing her condition or being out of style with her sisters? If modesty were practiced today as it was by those in the past, everyone could present a neat and comely appearance before the world. Perhaps women would then be honored and cherished more for their true worth and beauty rather than those trappings which time eventually strips away.

Most men and women want to present as pleasing an appearance as possible. This is as it should be. We are children of God; we seek, consciously or otherwise, the divine ideal. However, there are some who feel that it is wrong to use cosmetics or other aids in an effort to improve one's appearance. They argue that God made men and women a certain way and they should not try to change it. Such is not

---

[29]Brigham Young, JD 16:21. See JD 19:6.

the case. God did not make the race the way it is; all imperfection has come about through the violation of natural and moral law. God did not give any one a large nose, flat feet, poor complexion or any other physical defect. We may blame these things on heredity, diet, lack of proper exercise or anything else—but not on God. In discussing the divine objectives for the Word of Wisdom, Hyrum Smith wrote:

> When God first made man upon the earth, he was a different being entirely to what he now is, his body was strong, athletic, robust, and healthy; his days were prolonged upon the earth; he lived nearly one thousand years, his mind was vigorous and active, and his intellectual faculties clear and comprehensive, but he has become degenerated; his life has dwindled to a span; Disease preys upon his system; his body is enervated and feeble; and his mental and intellectual faculties are impaired, and weakened; and man is not now that dignified, noble, majestic, honorable, and mighty being that he was when he first proceded from the hands of his maker . . . Everything has become degenerated from what it was in its primitive state; 'God made man pure, but he has found out many inventions;' his vices have become innumerable, and his diseases multiplied; his taste has become vitiated, and his judgment impaired; he has fallen—fallen—fallen, from that dignified state that he once occupied on the earth; and it needs a restorative that man has not in his possession—wisdom which is beyond the reach of human intellect;—and power which human philosophy, talent and ingenuity cannot control.[30]

None want to be sickly or unattractive anymore than they want to live in a shanty. "What fools these mortals be!" The aged patriarch glories in his white locks, while his less fortunate brother considers a toupee! According to the anonymous author of Second Kings, even the prophet Elisha was offended by the taunts of some youths who cried after him: "Go up, thou bald head; go up, thou bald head." Elisha then "cursed them in the name of the Lord"—with rather disastrous results.[31] The apostle Paul (described by one early writer as "an ugly little Jew"), contrasted "our vile bodies" with those of resurrected beings.[32] Poor mortals have

---

[30]"Times & Seasons," Vol. III, No. 5, p. 799. June 1, 1842.
[31]2 Kings 2:23, 24.
[32]Philippians 3:21.

118   a right to do what they can, within reason, to make themselves more attractive. Let them put on, take off, pull in, push out, cover over or hide under what they will—no one should take offense. It is altogether good for women to be neat and comely—and to teach their children how to be the same.

> Let the sisters take care of themselves, and make themselves beautiful, and if any of you are so superstitious and ignorant as to say that this is pride, I can say that you are not informed as to the pride which is sinful before the Lord, you are also ignorant as to the excellency of the heavens, and of the beauty which dwells in the society of the Gods. Were you to see an angel, you would see a beautiful and lovely creature. Make yourselves like angels in goodness and beauty. Let the mothers in Israel make their sons and daughters healthy and beautiful, by cleanliness and a proper diet. Whether you have much or little clothing for your children, it can be kept clean and healthy, and be made to fit their persons neatly. Make your children lovely and fair that you may delight in them.[33]

The foundation of modesty, as with all basic principles of life, should be laid in childhood. It is unrealistic to assume that modesty can be suddenly imposed on youth who have been accustomed to wearing abbreviated styles from the time they were little children. This fallacy is as much responsible for the difficulty encountered in teaching modesty to youth as any one single factor. If proper dress is worn from earliest childhood, it is less likely that modesty will ever become a serious issue thereafter. The early inculcation of a sense of decorum is to be highly prized; for there is something to be said for the gentle ways of the "Little Women" of bygone days. How far we have departed from them! But even then, the prophets were warning the very young against immodesty:

> Little girls, permit me to ask you, Won't you be so kind and so good as to take those pins or the india-rubber cords out of the back of the skirts of your dresses, so that you will look comely. They make you look uncomely, to see your dresses drawn around you, showing your

---

[33]Brigham Young, JD 12:201-202.

form. Mothers ought to be ashamed of teaching their children such things. Dress your children and yourselves in that comely, angelic manner that, were an angel to visit you, you would not feel ashamed.[34]

The seeds of every form of virtuous conduct are meant to be planted in the rich soil of innocence. Modesty is no exception.

Indeed, modesty may have far more to do with the attitudes of youth toward temple marriage and the subsequent wearing of the garment than many parents realize. More than one young woman has declined a temple marriage rather than deny herself the wearing of the popular styles of both under and outer clothing. Elder Harold B. Lee echoed the warning of other leaders of the Church when he said:

Careless mothers who permit even in childhood or babyhood nudity or semi-nudity in dress are but sowing the seeds of disregard for standards of modesty which if taught and adhered to in her growing up years will prepare a daughter for entrance into the holy and sacred ordinances of the Lord.[35]

Clearly, modesty should be thought of as a way rather than as a mere acquisition of life.

Paradoxically, the moral pluralism of our day makes a Latter-day Saint fashion quite feasible. We can employ the same freedom of expression in matters of taste and behavior that the world demands for itself. If the world claims the negative privilege of disobeying God and practicing every species of immorality, his "peculiar people" can claim with equal enthusiasm the positive privilege of serving him with all of their heart, might, mind and strength. Why must freedom always be thought of in terms of lawlessness? Liberty is a two-way street. The saints are as free to do what is right (letting the consequence follow) as the world is to do what is wrong! We are as free to practice outright modesty as we are to play the hypocritical game of semi-modesty.

---

[34]Brigham Young, JD 19:64, 65.
[35]CR, April 5, 1957, p. 24.

120 Those who are animated by a substantial degree of the Spirit of God use the liberty of the times to come as close as possible to the divine ideal. Those who employ that same liberty to get as far as they dare from that standard while still assuring themselves that they are not doing anything "wrong" are, at the very least, slothful servants. The Lord knows the thoughts and intents of our hearts; He cannot be deceived by feigned expressions of devotion.

Before the world coming of Christ occurs, the saints will build the New Jerusalem, a city of holiness uncontaminated by any form of immodesty.[36] The spirit of that city, of Zion, ought to be developed among the Lord's people here and now. Although practical considerations preclude a complete break with the present order of things, what the saints can do, they should do. Then, while their efforts may be short of the mark, the Lord can accept their offering and bless them for it. But, O, what contempt he has for the grudging gift.[37]

Because it harmonizes with all that is true and natural, genuine modesty is enhanced by its association with whatever is virtuous, lovely and praiseworthy. It increases in loveliness as it blends with the spiritually beautiful. The prophets understand this. Peter counseled the women of the Church:

> "Your beauty should reside, not in outward adornment—the braiding of the hair, or jewelery, or dress—but in the inmost centre of your being, with its imperishable ornament, a gentle, quiet spirit, which is of high value in the sight of God."[38]

Love and Modesty

Speaking of his Father, Jesus said, "I do always those things that *please him.*"[39] Perfect love produced perfect

---

[36]See D&C 45:28-33, 64-71; 84:2-5.
[37]See D&C 58:26-29; Moroni 7:5-11.
[38]New English Bible. 1 Peter 3:3, 4. See 1 Timothy 2:9, 10.
[39]John 8:29.

obedience. Jesus did not reason, argue, or debate the issues of life; he determined his course by one simple test: will it please the Father? We want to please those we truly love. Because their heavenly Father loved them, Jesus' disciples were comforted with the assurance: "Fear not, little flock; for it is your Father's good *pleasure* to give you the kingdom."[40] True disciples of Christ are anxious to please God, not themselves or the world.[41] When a choice must be made, love should dictate what it will be.

The faithful saint will not want to do anything which will lead another into temptation. The argument is frequently heard that one has the "right" to behave in a certain way, that he or she is not doing anything "wrong." Paul answered this rationalization nearly two thousand years ago when certain saints at Corinth felt that they had the "right" to eat the flesh of animals slaughtered in connection with the rituals of the pagans.[42] These saints saw nothing "wrong" with the meat even though some of their fellow members considered it spiritually unclean. In dealing with the issue, Paul expressed a principle which applies to every situation where exercising one's "rights" may jeopardize the well-being of another.

This principle is summed up in the following passages:

> But take heed lest by any means this liberty of yours become a stumbling block to them that are weak. . . . For though I be free from all men, yet have I made myself servant unto all, that I might gain the more. . . . To the weak became I as weak, that I might gain the weak: I am made all things to all men, that I might by all means save some. . . . Give none offense, neither to the Jews, nor to the Gentiles, nor to the church of God: Even as I please all men in all things, not seeking mine own profit, but the profit of many, that they may be saved.[43]

Clearly, no true follower of Christ will say or do anything which—though presumably not wrong—will needlessly

---

[40]Luke 12:32.
[41]See Romans 8:8; 15:3; 1 Thessalonians 4:1; Hebrews 11:5.
[42]See 1 Corinthians 8-10.
[43]1 Corinthians 8:9, 9:19, 22; 10:32, 33.

122 weaken the faith or endanger the virtue of another. Charity—the pure love of Christ—"doth not behave itself unseemly, *seeketh not her own.*"[44]

Further, we should heed the apostle's warning against over-confidence as to our own security. He reminds us that thousands of those ancient Israelites who had committed themselves to Christ (Jehovah) were subsequently destroyed for immorality. "Wherefore let him that thinketh he standeth take heed lest he fall."[45] Who is so secure in his or her own purity of soul as to be beyond all threat of sin? If there are any among us, they would be the last to sacrifice another on the altar of personal vanity.

When love rules, we avoid doing anything which will make it more difficult for others to keep the commandments. We do not knowingly subject them to temptation. For how can we pray "lead us not into temptation" when we are deliberately leading others into temptation? If need be, we lay down some aspect of our lives for our weaker "friends;" we do not exploit them. Men do not want their wives, daughters or other females to dress or behave immodestly. Women do not deliberately comport themselves in a manner to attract either envy or salacious attention. The spirit of competition is alien to the Spirit of Christ. Those who are true to that spirit have no desire to out-do or out-shine their fellows. Life is replete with inequities of every description. Insofar as we can, we should seek to minimize, not accentuate, them. We do not love our neighbor as ourselves if we rejoice in the fact that we are richer or healthier or younger or stronger or better educated or more talented or more influential or more attractive than someone else.

Whittier wrote a charming poem in which an aged man recalls the words of a childhood sweetheart who had excelled him in spelling:

---

[44]1 Corinthians 13:5.
[45]1 Corinthians 10:12.

"I'm sorry that I spelt the word:
    I hate to go above you,
Because, "—the brown eyes lower fell,
    "Because, you see, I love you!"

In his closing lines, the poet spoke a sad truth.

He lives to learn, in life's hard school,
    How few who pass above him
Lament their triumph and his loss,
    Like her, —because they love him.[46]

When we love, we become joined in spirit with the object of that love. That is why we cannot help but seek our neighbor's interest along with our own.[47]

The White Robe

Before man and woman left paradise and entered this fallen state, the Lord clothed them in sacred garments—the wearing of which symbolized, among other things, submission to his will. This "coat of skins" stands in opposition to the fashions of the world. For this reason, the saints have been admonished to "come forth out of the fire [the divine crucible], hating even the garments spotted with the flesh."[48] Those who do so are heirs of salvation: "He that overcometh, the same shall be clothed in white raiment; and I will not blot out his name out of the book of life, but I will confess his name before my Father, and before his angels."[49] The sum of those claimed by the Savior constitutes the assembly of the redeemed seen in vision by John the revelator.[50]

In that vision, one of the twenty-four elders was heard to ask, "What are these which are arrayed in white robes? And whence come they?" The answer was "These are they which came out of the great tribulation, and have washed

---

[46]John Greenleaf Whittier, "In School-Days," *The Pocket Book of Popular Verse,* ed. by Ted Malone (New York, 1945), pp, 273-274.
[47]See D&C 59:6; 82:14.
[48]D&C 36:6, See also Jude 23.
[49]Revelation 3:5.
[50]*Ibid.* 7:9.

124   their robes, and made them white in the blood of the Lamb."[51]
They, and they alone, possess the "wedding garment" of the
Lord.[52] Having rejected the world and its fashions and faithfully worn the "coat of skins" in time, they have the glorious
robe of righteousness and salvation placed upon them in
eternity.[53] Such is the ultimate blessing of modesty and
obedience in all things.

---

[51]*Ibid.* 7:13, 14.
[52]Matthew 22:2-14.
[53]See 2 Nephi 9:14; D&C 109:75, 76.

Chastity: God's Delight

For I, the Lord God, delight in the chastity of women. And whoredoms are an abomination before me; thus saith the Lord of Hosts.[1]

Woman is "one of the fairest gems of all God's creation."[2] She is the epitome of everything virtuous, lovely and praiseworthy. And chastity is her crowning glory, her most precious possession. Its loss is one of the saddest things that can befall her. Death itself is a lesser thing by comparison. Indeed, more than one prophet has considered the death of his children preferable to their loss of innocence.[3] Such an attitude is alien to these times; it reflects the spirit of a bygone era when chastity was a more closely guarded and highly prized endowment than it is now. These days call for more mercy than justice, more compassion than condemnation and more vigilance than unquestioning trust. It is an evil hour; virtue will not triumph by default.

[1]Jacob 2:28.
[2]See Proverbs 31:10-31.
[3]See JD 2:322; 24:186. CR, April 6, 1921, p. 169; April 5, 1954, p. 71.

126   **The Wounding of Delicate Minds**

One of the Lord's announced purposes in bringing Lehi's family to America was "that I might raise up unto me a righteous branch from the fruit of the loins of Joseph."[4] But soon after the death of Nephi a plague of immorality broke out among his people for the first time.[5] The Lord gave Jacob, Nephi's brother, the painful assignment of calling the erring men to repentence.[6] Noting the presence of women and children, Jacob said,

> And also it grieveth me that I must use so much boldness of speech concerning you, before your wives and your children, many of whose feelings are exceedingly tender and chaste and delicate before God, which thing it pleasing unto God;[7]

The sensitive, even apologetic, manner in which the prophet introduced his message provides a striking contrast to the unseemly candor currently found in many books, magazines, plays, motion pictures and, yes, even classrooms. This deluge of profanity, pornography and promiscuity would lead one to believe that some malevolent agency is determined to drag us into the very vortex of hell.[8] It has become a cliche to speak of the rapid deterioration of morals during the second half of the twentieth century. The assault on traditional Christian standards by a vocal and influential minority is no passing fad. The world *is* changing. For many reasons, it will never be the same again. Although these moral iconoclasts do not represent today's average person, they are in fact, the precursors of tomorrow's orthodoxy. Hopefully, most people will not accept the most extreme views of these sexual revolutionists, but if history can be

---

[4]Jacob 2:25.
[5]It is ironic that the problem did not originate with the "loathsome" Lamanites but with the "delightsome" Nephites. See Jacob 3:5-9.
[6]See Jacob 2:22-3:12.
[7]Jacob 2:7.
[8]See D&C 1:35, 36; 38:11, 12; Moses 7:24, 25.

trusted, there is no doubt but what society will be influenced by them. Indeed, it has been already.

We have witnessed the emergence of a seemingly amorphous but very real movement calculated to eliminate the sexual inhibitions of the rising generation. The moral disintegration of millions of young men and women is being accomplished before our eyes. This campaign is not only abetted by many artists, writers, publishers, producers and others associated with the various media, it is also supported by some scientists and educators as well. In the name of freedom, knowledge and education, consciences are being seared with the hot iron of brutal frankness and vulgar candor. In the name of scientific research every nuance of man's sexual nature is being probed down to the minutest detail—a profane examination of the temple of the human spirit. Nothing is sacred because nothing is divine; men are only animals with animal needs and drives; good mental hygiene calls for them to accept themselves as such.

Many classes in so-called sex education are nothing more than exercises in pornography. Being presented in a classroom setting, such instruction can be more damaging to the minds and morals of receptive children than anything they might learn in the streets. Some bonafide psychiatrists and psychologists—along with an army of non-professionals —have introduced programs aimed at ridding their clients of any moral or emotional blocks to a free and unrestrained expression of feelings and desires. The negative effects of these hedonistic programs are already apparent. Children are being robbed of their innocence before the due time, spiritual awareness is failing, emotions are becoming desensitized and our ability to be shocked—a first line of moral defense— is being destroyed.

Jeremiah's indictment of his generation comes to mind.

Were they ashamed when they had committed abomination? nay, they were not at all ashamed, neither could they blush: therefore they shall fall among them that fall: at the time that I visit them they shall be cast down, saith the Lord.[9]

---

[9]Jeremiah 6:15. See also D&C 112:23.

128   We are on holy ground when we discuss the human body and the means by which life is organized. Unfortunately, the blatant candor of our times has robbed the subject of the sensitive treatment it merits. The nomenclature of the physiologist is stark and dehumanizing when contrasted with that used by the Lord and his prophets. Scripture provides us with a spiritual nomenclature for those things pertaining to human reproduction which can add needed dimension to any purely scientific treatment of the subject. While the language of science may be more precise in describing the physical aspects of sex, the language of the Lord lifts us above the flesh and reveals its soul. Contrast the following:

Language of Science	Language of Scripture
1. To menstruate	1. The custom of women.
2. Sperm	2. Seed
3. To be unfertile or sterile	3. To be barren
4. The uterus	4. The womb
5. To have intercourse	5. To know one
6. To become pregnant	6. To conceive
7. Pregnancy	7. To be with child
8. A baby	8. The fruit of the womb

While some technical terms must, of necessity, be used when teaching the young the nature and functions of the body, such instruction would be far more effective if the spiritual implications of these terms were also considered. When human maturation is taught in the context of the physical alone, it is a half-truth at best. Only when the subject is placed in its proper spiritual setting can it be rightly understood and appreciated.

When schools are prevented from teaching anything of a spiritual nature, they are thereby disqualified from teaching sex at all, for

in its very nature, sex is spiritual and inseparably connected with the 129
creative work of God.[10]

In spite of all of the programs set up to teach the young about themselves, immorality and illegitimacy have never been more rampant. The truth may be that these programs have actually abetted this trend! Said J. Reuben Clark, Jr.:

Parents are grasping at straws in an effort to hold their children. The cry is raised that the Church needs a book on sex. But what should such a book tell? Already the schools have taught sex facts *ad nauseam.* All their teachings have but torn away the modesty that once clothed sex; their discussions tend to make, and sometimes seem to make, sex animals of our boys and girls. The teachings do little but arouse curiosity for experience. It is said these courses tell enough about the generation of human beings to enable the youth, largely, to escape parenthood. Books are written, courses are given about courtship and marriage. To what point? We have not too far to go to get to the heathenish abominations and practices in pre-Christian and early Christian times, against which the Lord again and again lashed out to ancient Israel and to early Christians.[11]

The dangers cited by President Clark prompted the First Presidency to speak out against the introduction of sex education into the curriculum of the public schools:

We believe that serious hazards are involved in entrusting to the schools the teaching of this vital and important subject to our children. This responsibility cannot wisely be left to society, nor the schools: nor can the responsibility be shifted to the Church. It is the responsibility of parents to see that they fully perform their duty in this respect.[12]

If the counsel of the First Presidency is not followed, the teaching of sex education will be left to the mercy and the morality of men and women of uncertain commitment to Christian ideals. In too many instances, this will mean the propogandizing of the innocent with the object in mind of making them sexual sophisticates. Already, familiarity with

---

[10]Mark E. Petersen, CR, April, 1969, p. 64.

[11]CR, Oct., 1949, p. 194. See Cr, April, 1969, p. 13.

[12]CR, April, 1969, p. 13.

130   the purely physical dimension of sex has bred contempt in millions of young people for the law of chastity. Instructing the young in sexual matters in a moral vacuum has too often proven to be education for death.[13] Such instruction is a part of the very ills it purports to cure. Its aim is to adjust the young to the world as it is, not to prepare them for the world as it should be.

It is primarily for parents—armed with correct knowledge and gifted with inspiration—to provide their children at the right time, in the right way, with the right amount of instruction in these matters. The very nature of the subject requires that it be custom-tailored to the individual child's nature and needs. Mass indoctrination can only do violence to the innocent. Such "education" is a bull in a china shop, a thoughtless rampage in the temple of the human spirit. Neither those who come to teach nor those who come to be taught can enter the house of the Lord without a recommend. Let those who have been called to instruct their own magnify that calling, not forgetting that there is no better way for the young to appreciate the sacredness of their own being than for those who instruct them in its mysteries to do so with wisdom and reverence.

The Price of Immorality

Only God knows what sexual immorality has cost the human race in spiritual well-being, social stability, family unity and personal happiness.[14] The price is beyond human calculation. Strife, life-long guilt, ravaging disease and bitter lives have been left in its wake from time immemorial. The sad participants are not the only ones to suffer; our sins are almost always visited on those around us one way or another. Innocent infants conceived by diseased parents often suffer the fruits of their misconduct in the form of blindness, crippling, malformation and mental retardation.

---

[13]See *Ibid.*, pp. 54-57, 63, 64.

[14]The widespread use of alcohol and drugs only adds to the incredible toll.

And even those who escape overt damage are often made to   131
suffer emotional hurt because they were illegitimate, unwanted, even resented. Not infrequently such parents un-
consciously impose their own guilt on the child by the strained
and spiritless atmosphere of the home in which it is obliged
to grow up. Accidental marriages resulting from accidental
conception are seldom characterized by happy parents
with happy children. Being built upon moral sand, the
stresses and storms indigenous to life eventually take their
toll and expose the misbegotten alliance for what it always
was—a sin against truth. Only the presence of genuine repentance, love and devotion between the parties involved can
mitigate the situation and sweeten what must otherwise be a
bitter and tenuous union.

Jacob's Family

As the Old Testament so abundantly testifies, immorality
has stalked Israel from its beginning. The blessings of Jacob
upon the heads of his sons provide evidence of the patriarch's
understanding of their individual characters; he knew them
for what they were. Unlike many parents, Jacob did not make
his children more than they were. Reuben, his firstborn, lost
the birth right because of an incestuous affair with Bilhah,
his father's concubine. Of him Jacob said:

> Unstable as water, thou shalt not excel; because thou wentest up
> to thy father's bed; then defiledst thou it: he went up to my couch.[15]

Further disgrace was heaped upon Jacob when his
daughter Dinah was seduced by a young Canaanite, Shechem.[16]
Word of the incident reached Jacob who "held his peace"
until his sons returned from their field labors. Dinah's full
brothers, Levi and Simeon, were incensed: Shechem had
wrought folly in Israel in committing fornication with Dinah
—"which thing ought not to be done." Although it was finally

---

[15]Genesis 49:4.
[16]See Genesis 34.

132   agreed that their sister could marry the Canaanite, her brothers plotted against Shechem and murdered him and every male in his village. When Jacob learned of the massacre, he told Levi and Simeon: "Ye have troubled me to make me to stink among the inhabitants of the land. . . ."[17] It was this incident which prompted Jacob's last words concerning them:

> Simeon and Levi are brethren; instruments of cruelty are in their habitations. O my soul, come not thou into their secret; unto their assembly, mine honor, be not thou united: for in their anger they slew a man, and in their selfwill they digged down a wall. Cursed be their anger, for it was fierce; and their wrath, for it was cruel: I will divide them in Jacob, and scatter them in Israel.[18]

Joseph and Potiphar's Wife

Adam and Eve were not only forbidden to eat of the tree of mortality (knowledge), they were told not to touch it. Sin is born in the touching stage; if we are to avoid the bitter harvest of wrong doing, we must nip the initial thought or suggestion in the bud so that it cannot bear fruit in desire or action.[19] Unfortunately many do not do this, they foolishly expose themselves to temptation when they are morally weak and vulnerable. The typical rationalization for doing so is that weaknesses can only be overcome by placing one's self in situations where temptation must be faced and resisted.[20] Just the opposite is true. The time to deliberately confront temptation is when it no longer *is* temptation. Never meet any enemy in weakness. An enemy must either be defeated, surrendered to, compromised with, or run from.[21] Discretion is the better part of valor where sin is concerned.

Joseph was a man of just such discretion. After entering the employ of the wealthy Egyptian, Potiphar, the handsome

---

[17]Genesis 34:30.

[18]Genesis 49:5-7.

[19]James 1:13-15.

[20]Those who use this rationalization are often guilty of self-deception; subconsciously they want to succumb to that which they pretend to resist.

[21]See Luke 14:31-32.

youth became an object of desire on the part of Potiphar's 133
wife.[22] With little or no hesitation, the idle woman commanded him to have relations with her. But Joseph refused,
pointing out that her husband trusted him implicitly. He
asked her, "How then can I do this great wickedness and
sin against God?"[23] But neither God nor her husband meant
anything to the promiscuous woman; day after day she
entreated the youth. His position was most untenable;
she must have made his life miserable. We can but wonder
at his own inner strugglings. Did he find her at all desirable?
Was he tempted to succumb to her wiles? Or was the whole
affair repugnant to him?

Finally, a day came when the two were alone in the
house. She would not be denied. "And she caught him by
his garment saying, Lie with me: and he left his garment
in her hand, and fled, and got him out."[24] *And he got him
out!* He did not *touch* the fruit of adultery. He did not play
with sin. Nor did he stay to speak to her of virtuous principles or to teach her the Gospel, or to ask her if she had
read any good books lately. He got him out! Hell having no
fury like a woman scorned, the frustrated seductress accused
Joseph of making improper advances, whereupon he was
imprisoned for two years. Once more the great Jehovah
overruled and Joseph thereafter became governor of all
Egypt, a prophet, seer and revelator,[25] and the father of the
ruling house of Israel throughout the eternities.[26] What
blessings would have been lost had Joseph failed his God in
that critical period of trial!

What devastation adultery produces when it occurs in a
marriage between fundamentally decent people. Its memory
hangs like a pall over the once happy home long after its

---

[22]See Genesis 39:1-20.

[23]Genesis 39:9.

[24]Genesis 39:12.

[25]See 2 Nephi 3.

[26]See Genesis 37:5-11. Joseph's dreams implied more than his rule over his family
during their Egyptian sojourn; they pertained to the everlasting primacy of Joseph's posterity.
See D&C 133:34; Jeremiah 31:9.

134 flames have died away. Was it a sadder but wiser Solomon who counseled the following?

> My son, keep thy father's commandment, and forsake not the law of thy mother: . . . Can a man take fire in his bosom, and his clothes not be burned? Can one go upon hot coals, and his feet not be burned? So he that goeth in to his neighbors wife; whosoever toucheth her shall not be innocent. Men do not despise a thief, if he steal to satisfy his soul when he is hungry; But if he be found, he shall restore sevenfold; he shall give all the substance of his house. But whoso committeth adultery with a woman lacketh understanding: he that doeth it destroyeth his own soul. A wound and dishonor shall he get; and his reproach shall not be wiped away. For jealousy is the rage of a man: therefore he will not spare in the day of vengeance. He will not regard any ransom; neither will he rest content, though thou givest many gifts.[27]

How can the wrong of unchastity be undone? How can "the rage of a man" whose wife has been defiled, be satisfied? What will make things right again? In honoring God, Joseph honored himself and his master, Potiphar—the man who had "made him overseer over his house, and all that he had he put into his hand."[28] There would be no adultery if every man were as pure of heart and clean of hand as Joseph. He kept his father's commandment and did not forsake the law of his mother.

David and Bathsheba

One who forgot that eternal vigilance is the price of virtue as well as of liberty was David, Israel's great poet-king. His life provides a classic example of how illicit love affairs destroy once virtuous men and women. Such human bondage has seen honor, position, fortune, loved ones—even salvation itself—sacrificed upon the altar of unchecked passion. How many basically fine persons caught in a moment of carelessness, fatigue, depression, or loneliness have permitted their unguarded emotions to sweep them along into regretted behavior?

[27]Proverbs 6:20, 27-35.
[28]Genesis 39:4.

There is no sadder example in all scripture than that of   135
David, the shepherd boy who became Israel's mightiest king.
Gifted with a poet's soul, blessed with the charisma of a
great leader, young David had been chosen by Jehovah himself to replace Saul as king of Israel. David was a man after
the Lord's own heart. Only glory lay before him until a
chance incident stepped in to alter his destiny forever. Walking upon his upper porch late one afternoon he saw a beautiful woman bathing herself. Upon learning her identity,
he summoned her to his apartment and committed adultery
with her.[29] She later informed David that she had conceived by him. Fearing public disgrace and the law's judgment,[30] David attempted to cover his guilt by making it
appear that she had conceived by her husband, Uriah, a
soldier in David's army. But Uriah's very fidelity to David
caused the king's plan to fail. Desperate, David then ar-
ranged the murder of his loyal soldier by having him
abandoned by his comrades on the battlefield. Sin begets sin;
adultery fathered murder. It wasn't meant to be that way,
but it had happened. The sweet singer of songs who penned
the sublime words, "The Lord is my Shepherd" had by
his conduct given the lie to those sentiments and lost his
exaltation.[31] And it was all for nothing! The crime was soon
known throughout Israel; it is written in detail in the holy
scriptures.

David married Bathsheba, but the son they conceived
in adultery died soon after birth.[32] From that time forth the
family of David was torn with immorality and violence. The
Lord's word through Nathan the prophet was fulfilled:

Now therefore the sword shall never depart from thine house; because thou hast despised me, and hast taken the wife of Uriah the Hittite
to be thy wife. Thus saith the Lord, Behold, I will raise up evil against

---

[29]See 2 Samuel 11.
[30]Adultery called for the death penalty. Leviticus 20:10.
[31]See D&C 132:39; TJS, 339.
Bathsheba later bore Solomon.
[32]2 Samuel 12:10-12.

136   thee out of thine own house, and I will take thy wives before thine eyes, and give them unto thy neighbor, and he shall lie with thy wives in the sight of the sun. For thou didst it secretly; but I will do this thing before all Israel, and before the sun.[38]

Can kings do wrong? Does great artistic talent, genius of mind or services rendered to God or man set anyone apart and allow them to be a law unto themselves? David's fate provides us with the answer.[34]

Amnon and Tamar

How often the love that is supposed to condone acts of immorality proves to be nothing more than the masked face of lust seeking to gratify its pernicious appetite. But at the time who is willing to admit this? It is only after consuming itself that the counterfeit nature of such emotions are exposed. Amnon and Tamar, two of David's children[35] vividly illustrate this point.[36] Young Amnon became obsessed with the desire to seduce his virginal half-sister, Tamar. By feigning illness he obtained his father's permission to have the unsuspecting girl wait upon him in his private apartments. With elaborate effort he finally managed to get Tamar alone in his room where he asked her to submit to fornication with him. Her wise response suggests that she actually favored Amnon as a husband but not as an illicit lover:

And she answered him, Nay, my brother, do not force me; for no such thing ought to be done in Israel; do not thou this folly. And I, whither shall I cause my shame to go? and as for thee, thou shalt be as one of the fools in Israel. Now therefore, I pray thee, speak unto the king; for he will not withhold me from thee.[37]

But Amnon did not love the *soul* of Tamar; he only wanted the use of her body. Employing brute strength, he

---

[34]There is no substitute for obedience. See D&C 52:14-20; Matthew 7:21.
[35]By Ahinoam and Abigail respectively. See 2 Samuel 3:2, 3 13:1.
[36]See 2 Samuel 13.
[37]Ibid., 13:12, 13.

proceeded to rape the young virgin. Immediately upon spend-
ing his passion (as so often is the case) he turned on the
shamed Tamar with angry spite.

> Then Amnon hated her exceedingly; so that the hatred wherewith
> he hated her was greater than the love wherewith he had loved.[38]

The violated girl, having lost her virginity for all mortal time, pled with Amnon to claim her as his wife.

> And she said unto him, There is no cause: this evil in sending me
> away is greater than the other that thou didst unto me. But he would
> not hearken unto her.[39]

But he would not! He wanted nothing more to do with
her. His great "love" was proven nothing more than raw
lust. Calling his servant, Amnon ordered, "Put now *this
woman* from me, and *bolt the door after her.*" Amnon's conduct brings to mind the words of Brigham Young:

> Every virtuous woman desires a husband to whom she can look for
> guidance and protection through this world. God has placed this desire
> in woman's nature. It should be respected by the stronger sex. Any
> man who takes advantage of this, and humbles a daughter of Eve to rob
> her of her virtue, and cast her off dishonored and defiled, is her destroyer,
> and is responsible to God for the deed. If the refined Christian society
> of the nineteenth century will tolerate such a crime, God will not; but
> he will call the perpetrator to an account. He will be damned; in hell
> he will lift up his eyes, being in torment, until he has paid the utter-
> most farthing, and made a full atonement for his sins.[40]

Absalom, Tamar's full brother, learned of the incident
and after waiting two years revenged his sister by successfully
plotting the murder of Amnon.

Although David loved Absalom dearly, he banished him
from his presence as a *persona non grata*. In time, the alienated
son—fearing that he would not be chosen as David's suc-
cessor—conspired to seize the throne. His rebellion eventuated

---

[38]Ibid., 13:15.
[39]Ibid. 13:16.
[40]JD, 11:268. See CR, April 6, 1947, pp. 119, 120.

138 in his death at the hands of Joab, the king's general. Upon learning of his son's fate, David cried out in an agony of grief:

> . . . O my son Absalom, my son, my son Absalom! would God I had died for thee, O Absalom, my son, my son![41]

What tragedy came to the house of David, the shepherd lad, the sweet singer of songs! When did it begin? With Amnon's violation of Tamar? With Absalom's revenge? With his conspiracy against his father? Or did it begin one pleasant afternoon when David, walking alone upon the porch of his palace, first beheld Bathsheba, the beautiful wife of Uriah, the Hittite?[42]

Homosexuality in Israel

The book of Judges tells of a certain Levite whose concubine returned to her father's house in Bethlehem.[43] The Levite followed her and persuaded her to come back to him. On their way home they spent a night in Gibeah, a village belonging to the tribe of Benjamin. Certain men of the village, learning of the presence of the stranger, demanded that he be turned over to them for homosexual purposes. The Levite's host offered them his own daughter and his guest's concubine rather than that they should do "so vile a thing." Finally, the Levite gave his concubine to the men who ravished her until morning when she fell at the door of the man's house and died. When the Levite awoke, he found the poor creature, "and her hands were upon the threshold." Not knowing she was dead and with astonishing insensitivity he said, "Up, and let us be going." Subsequently he took her corpse and cut it into twelve pieces and "sent her into all of the coasts of Israel." The men of Israel were incensed and demanded that those responsible for the crime be delivered

---

[41]2 Samuel 18:33.
[42]Psalm 51 is David's poignant plea for mercy.
[43]See Judges 19-21; Genesis 19:1-11.

to them for death. But the Benjamites refused. A fratricidal war ensued in which the tribe of Benjamin was virtually decimated; only 600 men survived.

Then the tribes, not wanting Benjamin to die out, plotted to provide wives for the surviving 600. Having sworn an oath that their own daughters would not be given to any man of Benjamin, they attacked and destroyed the village of Jabesh-Gilead because it had not joined the tribes against Benjamin. The only survivors were 400 virgins who were then given to the men of Benjamin for wives. Israel then had the men who still lacked wives abduct a sufficient number of young women from the village of Shiloh during the annual grape festival when the girls came together to dance. The anonymous chronicler ends the account with the revealing words: "In those days there was no king in Israel: every man did that which was right in his own eyes."[44]

If the story of the Levite and his concubine seems a terrible one, it should be remembered that it was also terrible to the people of ancient Israel. All that heard it said, "There was no such deed done nor seen from the day that the children of Israel came up out of the land of Egypt unto this day. . . ."[45] Israel was far from being that "peculiar people" the Lord wanted them to become, but it is to be wondered if they were not more sensitive to vileness and lewdness than is the case with many in our enlightened age. Crimes of equal debauchery are so commonplace in our society as to be hardly worthy of notice. We live in a day when homosexuality is not only practiced by an increasingly large number of men and women, but when it is defiantly justified by its practitioners and defended by certain social scientists and members of the clergy. That the writer of Judges should deal with one incident in such detail says something in favor of that much maligned people.

---

[44]Judges 21:25.

[45]Judges 19:30. The conduct of the Benjamites was more typical of the Cannanites who were given to acts of gross immorality and perversion in conjunction with their religious worship.

140   We can hardly overestimate the evil which results from the satanic doctrine that sexual gratification is an end in itself to be sought heterosexually or homosexually—within or without the bonds of marriage—at the rightful discretion of the individual. Male and female homosexuality is reaching epidemic proportions. What was once whispered of in secret is brazenly broadcast before the world. Not only are many of its practitioners not ashamed of their perversion, they express pride in it and demand its social and legal acceptance. The unspeakable vileness of the devils in hell (from whence all things profane and obscene originate) is paraded before us as a legitimate and morally acceptable mode of sexual conduct. Supposedly responsible religious and political leaders defend the practice even to the point of advocating the legalization of homosexual marriages.

Whereas sexual intimacy was long regarded (if not honored) as a concomitant of the marriage state alone, the number of men and women who are prepared to pay even lip service to that viewpoint is declining. It is being supplanted with the notion that since men are just animals, and since all animals have a natural sex drive, it may be appeased in any manner the animal desires. Those who defend either normal or abnormal immorality are undermining the very idea of male and female together with all that those terms were meant to connote.

We again emphasize that the primary external cause of mankind's follies is either its ignorance of or rejection of the true God. The apostle Paul, after showing that the practice of idolatry followed in the wake of the ancient world's apostasy from that God, wrote:

Wherefore God also gave them up to uncleanness through the lusts of their own hearts, to dishonour their own bodies between themselves: Who changed the truth of God into a lie, and worshipped and served the creature more than the Creator, who is blessed for ever. Amen. For this cause God gave them up unto vile affections: for even their women did change the natural use into that which is against nature: And likewise also the men, leaving the natural use of the woman, burned in their lust one toward another; men with men working that which is unseemly, and receiving in themselves that recompence of their error which was meet. And even as they did not like to retain God in their knowledge, God gave them over to a reprobate mind, to do those things which are not convenient; . . .[46]

Who can doubt that a correct understanding of the character of God is the keystone of personal and societal morality?

The homosexual is most pitiable. Especially those who are trapped in a psychological nightmare from which they would awaken if only they could find the strength of will to do so. It is far easier to judge such a person than it is to understand them. But they need mercy—as do we all—and should be given all possible support. They are, in fact, deviating from a true principle. For it is intended that men should love men, and women, women. Indeed, a special bond of brotherhood has characterized the relationships of some great men.[47] It is tragic when this righteous principle is defiled and perverted by Satan in his assaults against the integrity of the male and female natures of those who, for one reason or another, have misplaced their true identities.

WHY CHASTITY

A Father's Delight

Mormon described chastity and virtue as "that which was most dear and precious above all things."[48] This is in harmony with the Lord's clear and uncompromising statement to the prophet Jacob:

---

[46]Romans 1:24-28.
[47]Said David of Jonathan: "thy love to me was wonderful, passing the love of women." 2 Samuel 1:26. Speaking of Joseph and Hyrum Smith, John Taylor wrote: "In life they were not divided, and in death they were not separated." D&C 135:3. A special bond of affection seems to have existed between Jesus and John, the traditional apostle "whom Jesus loved." John 13:23. See also JD 4:277.
[48]Moroni 9:9.

142

For I, the Lord God, delight in the chastity of women. And whoredoms are an abomination before me; thus saith the Lord of Hosts.[49]

Why does the Lord *delight* in their chastity? Does he comprehend a principle that we blind mortals fail to see? Undoubtedly so; still we may perceive some of the reasons for his high regard for female virtue.

For one thing, all women are literally his spirit daughters. They were conceived in the bonds of celestial marriage and brought forth by a holy wife and mother. The Father naturally rejoices in the purity of his children; for purity implies wholeness, unity and perfection. The Most High cannot accept or condone any degree of imperfection (sin) in himself or in any of those who would be one with him.[50] He desires oneness with his family and delights in those principles which make it possible.

Also, it is the Father's work, glory and good pleasure to organize the primal intelligences of men so that they too can know the joy that is his.[51] Woman is uniquely blessed in being privileged to assist—both spiritually and temporally—in this greatest of all enterprises. Celestial mothers provide spirit tabernacles for those "organized" intelligences; their mortal co-creators complete the labor by providing those spirits with physical bodies. Thus men are "added upon" by their mothers! Woman alone conceives the tiny germ of life. It is in her womb that the incredible miracle of organization occurs. Only she can bestow the grand key to a fulness of joy upon the waiting offspring of God.[52] For the temporal body is all-essential; it is what universal birth and death are all about. Only those endowed with flesh and bone can hope to attain to the excellence of the Gods. To be denied a physical body is to suffer the punishment of Satan himself![53]

---

[49]Jacob 2:28. The chastity of his sons is also of paramount importance to God.
[50]See D&C 1:31; Alma 45:16.
[51]See Moses 1:39.
[52]See D&C 93:33, 34.
[53]See TJS, pp. 181, 297.

To deny our waiting brothers and sisters this immortal blessing is to threaten them with his fate.

Then too, the Father is anxious that the pre-mortal purity of his daughters be perpetuated and added upon in their temporal estate so that they can emulate their heavenly mother in bringing forth righteous offspring of their own. It is a universal law that like begets like. Virtuous and wise mothers are best qualified to "train up" noble children. The example of virtue is far more potent than the precept of virtue. The spirit of a mother's own purity can distill itself like the dews of heaven upon the souls of susceptible children. They will drink of her unspoken goodness. This alone is cause enough for the young women of modern Israel to jealously guard their chastity. In doing so, they are expanding their hearts beyond the borders of mortal time and expressing love and concern for their unborn posterity.

Further, every blessing of God requires obedience to the law upon which it is predicated.[54] Eternal life is the greatest of them all,[55] but in order to qualify for it one must enter into the new and everlasting covenant of marriage.[56] And in order for such a union to be eternally valid, it must be sealed by the Holy Spirit of Promise.[57] The *Holy* Spirit will not seal up *unholy* men and women—the law of chastity *must* be obeyed if the blessing of eternal marriage is to be realized.[58]

Finally, God delights in the chastity of his daughters because He would spare them that special suffering and heartbreak that is the lot of womankind. Unchastity perpetrates a unique crime against the female nature that the male—being generally less committed in body, mind and heart—tends to escape. Sexual intimacy for those women who are not hardened in such things is an act of the *soul*. It is the giving of her whole being. The virtuous girl or woman who allows

---

[54]See D&C 130:20, 21.

[55]See D&C 6:13.

[56]See D&C 131:1-4.

[57]See D&C 132:7, 19.

[58]Those who have violated the law of chastity *may*, upon sincere repentance still obtain this vital sealing.

144 herself to be drawn into an immoral relationship—one that offends the Spirit of God—cannot escape without deep hurt.[59] She will either be left with a bleeding, open wound and in agony of guilt and remorse, or else she will become emotionally scarred, unfeeling and bitter. In either case—or any variation thereof—something precious but intangible will have been lost. The relationship that was designed to unite and fulfill man and woman in the Lord has the opposite effect when entered into unlawfully: it becomes a crippler of lives, a destroyer of peace, a divider. The Father knows this. He knows that his way is the only way of lasting happiness.[60] He delights in the chastity of his daughters because he wants them to walk in his way and find that happiness.

The Third Sin

Since chastity is so highly esteemed, it follows that its loss is a grave matter. And so it is; Alma told his errant son, Corianton,

> Know ye not, my son, that these things are an abomination in the sight of the Lord; yea, most abominable above all sins save it be the shedding of innocent blood or denying the Holy Ghost.[61]

The three sins cited by Alma share a common element: they violate the principle of life. The first repudiates God's infinite sacrifice.[62] It is perpetrated by those who know by the power of the Holy Ghost that Jesus is the Chirst yet disclaim that truth.[63] Such spiritual liars have "crucified him unto themselves and put him to an open shame."[64]

The second is the destruction of life. A living soul is "put asunder" by forcing the spirit to abandon its lawful

---

[59]A loveless marital relationship can also do great damage to a woman's emotional and spiritual well-being.

[60]See Alma 41:10, 11.

[61]Alma 39:5.

[62]John 14:6.

[63]See John 8:31, 32.

[64]See D&C 76:35, 132:27.

home.[65] In bringing anyone's mortal estate to an end we assume a prerogative belonging only to God and to those whom he authorizes to exercise it in his behalf.[66]

The third offense tampers with life. It strikes at the very nature and glory of God: the sacred power of procreation. It is this power which most clearly distinguishes those endowed with the gift of "eternal lives" from those angels who "cannot be enlarged, but remain separately and singly, without exaltation, in their saved condition, to all eternity. . . ."[67] Mortals are granted this power on a temporary basis so that they might provide bodies of flesh and bone for God's spirit offspring. This is a "talent"—a stewardship—for which there must be an accounting. If the talent is misused or repudiated, it may be taken from the offender forever. Unchastity is the third most serious sin because it is the third most damaging assault on the spirit of man. It is the soul against itself; the flesh and the spirit unite in a venture of self-destruction. The apostle Paul understood this and admonished the saints to:

Flee fornication. Every sin that a man doeth is without the body; but he that committeth fornication sinneth against his own body.[68]

Yet we are not our own; we are bought with a price.[69] The body belongs to God, not to the spirit which is presently occupying it. Indeed, we own nothing of self or the earth until it is sealed upon us in the resurrection.

Let us esteem all that we are permitted to possess as given to us of the Lord; whether it be gold, silver, goods, houses, lands, or wives and children, they are all the Lord's. These blessings are only lent to us. When we have passed this earthly ordeal and have proven to the heavens that we are worthy to be crowned with crowns of glory, immortality and eternal lives, then the Lord will say these are yours, but until then we own nothing.[70]

---

[65]D&C 88:15.
[66]See Genesis 9:6; D&C 42:19, 79; 134:1, 8.
[67]D&C 132:17.
[68]1 Corinthians 6:18.
[69]1 Corinthians 6:20.
[70]Brigham Young, JD 9:136.

146   Therefore, we have no right to misuse the body for it is not our property.

Unchastity is the illegal, unauthorized or perverse use of the physical body for sexual purposes. In most instances such acts are ends in themselves; the objective is pleasure for its own sake. Marriage alone endows men and women with the key of authority for entering into sexual relationships. When rightly done, the words of Hebrews applies:

> Marriage is honorable in all, and the bed undefiled: but whoremongers and adulterers God will judge.[71]

If we assume the intimate prerogatives of marriage without assuming its obligations, we are thieves and robbers. We are stowaways on the ship of matrimony, seeking the pleasures of the voyage, but unprepared or unwilling to pay the passage. Such irresponsible cruises are often taken at the expense of both the living and the unborn.

> Every soul is entitled to the right to come into this world in a legitimate way—in the way the Father has willed that souls should come. Whosoever takes a course contrary to this is guilty of an almost irreparable crime. Is there any wonder, then, that the Lord places the violation of this covenant of marriage and the loss of virtue as second only to the shedding of innocent blood? Is there not, then, sufficient reason for the severity of the punishment which has been promised those who violate this eternal law? The demand for personal purity is made by the Church upon both men and women equally. There is no double standard of judgment. "If purity of life is neglected," President Joseph F. Smith said once, "all other dangers set in upon us like the rivers of waters when the flood gates are opened."[72]

The fountainhead of life should be pure. Only *holy* men and women will retain procreative power in the resurrection. Their offspring will partake of their divine natures, being begotten without any physical or moral imperfection. Like will beget like. Orson Pratt wrote:

---

[71]Hebrews 13:4.
[72]Joseph Fielding Smith, CR, October, 1965, p. 28. See also Joseph F. Smith, *Gospel Doctrine*, 1961 ed., p. 313.

Could wicked and malicious beings, who have irradicated every feeling of love from their bosoms, be permitted to propogate their species, the offspring would partake of all the evil, wicked, and malicious nature of their parents. . . . It is for this reason that God will not permit the fallen angels to multiply: it is for this reason that God has ordained marriages for the righteous only: it is for this reason that God will put a final stop to the multiplication of the wicked after this life: it is for this reason that none but those who have kept the celestial law will be permitted to multiply after the resurrection: . . . for they alone are prepared to beget and bring forth offspring whose bodies and spirits, partaking of the nature of the parents, are pure and lovely, and will manifest, as they increase in years, those heaven-born excellencies so necessary to lead them to happiness and eternal life.[73]

Fornication and adultery defile the fountainhead of life and rob both the living and the unborn of the richest blessings of chastity.

When a man takes to himself a woman that properly belongs to another, and defiles her, it interferes with the fountain of life, and corrupts the very source of existence. There is an offspring comes forth as the fruit of that union, and that offspring is an eternal being—how can it be looked upon? To reflect upon it, wounds the finest feelings of human nature in time, and will in eternity. For who can gaze upon the degradation of their wife, and the corruption of their seed, without peculiar sensations?[74]

Such betrayals of the marriage covenant cannot help but taint the legitimate expressions of love within that covenant. The marital relationship is adulterated; confusion results. For this reason Paul admonished the ancient saints (who, in partaking of the sacrament, became spiritually "one flesh" with Christ) not to also partake of the meat of pagan rituals.

Know ye not that your bodies are the members of Christ? shall I then take the members of Christ, and make them the members of a harlot? God forbid. What? know ye not that he which is joined to an harlot is one body? for two, saith he shall be one flesh. But he that is joined unto the Lord is one spirit.[75]

---

[73]Orson Pratt. *The Seer*, pp. 156, 157. See JD 13:186.
[74]John Taylor, JD 1:232.
[75]1 Corinthians 6:15-17; See also *Ibid.*, 10:16-21.

148   Unchastity is an act of spiritual murder against those almost indefinable feelings which lend a righteous union its wonder, joy, and strength.[76] It destroys that confidence which is the life-blood of all viable relationships and, as Moses Thatcher observed, "where confidence dies, there you may dig the grave of love."[77]

For since we are, at any given moment, the sum of the past—it follows that in marriage we become the unique sum of two lives. If either of those lives have been marred by immorality, that marring becomes an unavoidable constituent of the marriage itself. It is, therefore, in the marital relationship that the fruits of unchastity are the most bitter. No other human association involves so complete and intimate an amalgam of hearts and minds or is subjected to so many stresses. The moral purity of husband and wife is a significant factor in meeting them successfully. President David O. McKay observed:

A chaste, not a profligate, life is the source of virile manhood. The test of true womanhood comes when the woman stands innocent at the court of chastity. All qualities are crowned by this most precious virtue of beautiful womanhood. It is the most vital part of the foundation of a happy married life and is the source of strength and perpetuity of the race.[78]

The loss of virtue is most keenly felt when the need for virtue is the most compelling. One reason so many people see nothing wrong in many things the Lord brands sin is that the "wrong" becomes apparent only with the passage of time. It is in the reaping, not the sowing, that we determine the ultimate nature of all things. Nor can we expect to reap a harvest we did not sow.[79] Past performance dictates present possibilities. We cannot change the past; we can only react to it.

---

[76]See Jacob 2:9; Alma 36:14. President David O. McKay referred to unchastity as "the prostitution of love." CR, October 5, 1951, p. 8.

[77]JD 26:315.

[78]CR, April, 1967, p. 8.

[79]See Alma 41.

The moving Finger writes; and, having writ,
Moves on: nor all your Piety nor Wit
Shall lure it back to cancel half a line,
Nor all your Tears wash out a word of it.[80]

There are three occasions in the life of a spiritually sensitive young woman when past mistakes are most likely to cause her pangs of regret. The first occurs when she finds true love with the one who would claim her as his wife, only to realize that she cannot bestow upon him a woman's greatest gift: her untarnished virtue.[81] Once virginity is given, it is given for all mortal time; no power on earth or in heaven can restore it. The second occurs when she kneels at the altar of the Lord. The shadow of things past may sweep across the moment to becloud what otherwise would have been a clear day of happiness. President David O. McKay beautifully described how that occasion should be.

The bridegroom kneeling at the altar has in his heart the dearest possession that a husband can cherish—the assurance that she who places her hand in his, in confidence, in marriage, is as pure as a sunbeam—as spotless as the snow newly fallen from the sky. He has the assurance that in her purity and sweetness she typifies divine motherhood. Now, young man, is not that complete faith and confidence worth everything else in the world? And equally sublime is the assurance the young girl has that the man she loves, to whom she gives herself in marriage, comes to her with that same purity and strength of character which she brings to him. Such a union will indeed be a marriage ordained of God for the glory of his creation.[82]

But perhaps the most bitter-sweet moment of all occurs when she finally cradles her firstborn in her arms and realizes that she is a mother. She then sees the ultimate reason for chastity—it sleeps upon her breast.

---

[80]Edward Fitzgerald, Rubiyat of Omar Khayyam, LXXI. This is true from a human point of view; only the blood of Christ can remit any part of the past.

[81]President J. Reuben Clark said, "Chastity is the costliest jewel a girl can bring her husband." Deseret News, Church Section, May 7, 1952.

[82]Improvement Era, April, 1953, p. 222. President McKay noted: "Marriage is a failure when manhood is a failure." CR, April 6, 1958, p. 8.

150   Even though the ideal has not been realized, a truly repentant couple may still look forward to a happy and rewarding life together. Their very mistakes may draw them even closer, deepening their affections and reinforcing their determination to rise above the past. Such courageous marriages are sometimes more vital and productive of good than others which—although not tainted with unchastity—are devoid of those affinities which are the soul of any enduring union. Love can work wonders. It is God's balm of Gilead. It can heal broken hearts and bring peace to anxious minds. It can overwhelm yesterday's follies and free the repentant from the tyranny of the past. We must never forget that men are greater than their sins and that as deplorable as unchastity is, the power of love can transcend it. Men and women can triumph over their mistakes *if only they love enough.* But it must be remembered that God is the source of all true devotion. There can be no permanent mending of lives without him. Unchastity takes its awesome toll not only because it is a leprosy of the spirit, but also because so few of its victims will sincerely cry out to the one Physician who could heal them, "Unclean, unclean, Jesus, have mercy on us!" Christ can bless an insecure marriage. But if he is not invited into such a union, its inherent weakness will—like a stone cast into still waters—send out ripples of disharmony to mar its peace and threaten its existence.

A Breach of Promise

Every Latter-day Saint should feel committed to their future mate from childhood. They should regard any unchastity on their part as an act of infidelity against the one they will someday marry. The common practice of engaging in varying degrees of pre-marital intimacy is to be deplored. It is tantamount to love-play with another man's wife or another woman's husband. Young people consider this statement extreme until they are reminded that while they are engaged in such conduct, the likelihood is that their own future mate

is doing the same! Both are spoilers. Each is failing to save
the tender expressions of love for the coming of love. Each
is living out of due time, out of step with virtue and happiness.

> . . . I urge *loyalty to your future companion*. When harmony,
> mutual consideration, and trust pass out of the home, hell enters in. A
> memory of a simple indulgence in youth sometimes opens hell's door.
> Girls, choose a husband who has respect for womanhood! Young man,
> choose a girl who, in her teens, has virtue and strength enough to keep
> herself true to her future husband! Down the road of indulgence are too
> many good young girls, seeking vainly for happiness in the by-ways
> where people grovel but do not aspire. As a result their search for
> happiness is in vain. They grasp at what seems substance to find only
> ashes.[83]

And each is forgetting that, as immortal spirits, they are
as much in eternity now as they ever will be. It is myopic to
assume that the law of chastity is only meant to safeguard
mortal alliances. While there is no official doctrine on this
point, it is conceivable that some troths were plighted in
man's first estate. Some marriages may, indeed, have been
"made in heaven." Observing the celestial union of their
parents must have stirred deep longings in God's worthiest
sons and daughters for a like relationship. They could hardly
live in the presence of perfect love and not aspire to it. It
is not unreasonable to suppose that hearts claimed hearts
and pledges were given in anticipation of a later reunion.
Many had their "great expectations." Unchastity is a breach
of promises made before time began. For irrespective of any
possible pledges of fidelity men and women may have made
to one another, there is no doubt but that all promised to do
the Father's will on earth as they had done it in heaven.
Chastity is God's will for his children, whether in time or
eternity.

Spirit of Chastity

Although usually associated with the body, unchastity is

---

[83]David O. McKay, CR, April 6, 1956, p. 8. (Italics original). See CR, April 6, 1967,
p. 8.

152   essentially a spiritual problem. For the body is amoral; it is the spirit which must *will* to be virtuous, it cannot look to its house of clay for any moral support. Thus sin is not an inevitable consequence of being mortal. Jesus demonstrated this.[84] The spirit sins out of weakness, ignorance, fear, insecurity, loneliness, etc.——but not out of innate necessity. The "soul of man" comes into being when the spirit enters its fleshy tabernacle.[85] Each is meant to bless the other. In the resurrection they will be "inseparably connected," becoming an integrated spiritual being.[86] But in mortality the physical body is of the earth, earthy. It is the unperfected vehicle of expression employed by the spirit during its temporal sojourn. The relationship is that of master to servant. Salvation depends upon the spirit's ability—with God's grace—to rule that servant in righteousness.[87] However, should their roles be reversed, the spirit—in yielding to the flesh—will lose its original purity and the *soul* then becomes "carnal, sensual and devilish."[88]

Being welded to the flesh in the resurrection, an unrepentant spirit cannot return to God, for no unclean thing can dwell in the presence of the Man of Holiness.[89] The blessing becomes a curse; wings become chains. The physical body which was designed to lift man to the glory of the Father becomes instead a prison house of death.[90] Spirit and flesh will rise or fall together.

We have to fight continually, as it were, sword in hand to make the spirit master of the tabernacle, or the flesh subject to the law of the spirit . . . Did their spirits have their choice there is not a son or daughter of Adam and Eve on the earth but what would be obedient to the Gospel of salvation, and redeem their bodies to exaltation and glory. But there

---

[84]Fifth "Lecture On Faith," paragraph two.

[85]See D&C 88:15. The uncreated essence of man is composed of highly refined spirit matter rather than the gross element comprising the temporal body. See D&C 93:33; TJS, pp. 352-355.

[86]See D&C 93:33; Alma 11:45.

[87]See D&C 88:26, 27.

[88]See Moses 5:13; Mosiah 3:19; Alma 42:9, 10.

[89]See Moses 6:67.

[90]See D&C 93:35; 132:25; Matthew 7:13, 14.

is a constant warfare between them, still they must remain together, be saved and exalted together, or neither of them will be saved and exalted with the salvation and the exaltation which the Gospel offers.[91]

If chastity is to be taught as a positive ideal rather than as a proscription against human desire, it is helpful to explain this duality of the soul. Sexual desire is not evil, but it does need to be sanctified through the permeating influence of the spirit in man in union with the Spirit of God. Thus sanctified, it becomes one of those exalting principles of intelligence which will rise with the righteous in the resurrection.[92]

There is no reason to suppose that conjugal relationships are limited to mortality. To the contrary, those associations which are most sacred and compelling in time are to be glorified and perpetuated in eternity. Parenthood cannot be divorced from the act which makes it possible. The sexual relationship is sacred precisely because it is an essential part of eternal marriage. Speaking of how God begot his children, Brigham Young declared:

> He created man, as we create our children; for there is no other process of creation in heaven, on the earth, in the earth, or under the earth, or in all the eternities, that is, that were, or that ever will be.[93]

Orson Pratt was explicit in maintaining that "sexual love" will not only continue but be magnified for those who are exalted in the resurrection:

> When the sons and daughters of the Most High God come forth in the morning of the resurrection, this principle of love will exist in their bosoms just as it exists here, only intensified according to the increased knowledge and understanding which they possess; hence they will be capacitated to enjoy the relationships of husband and wife, of parents and children, in a hundred fold degree greater than they could in mortality. We are not capable, while surrounded with the weaknesses

---

[91]Brigham Young, JD 9:287, 288.

[92]See D&C 130:18, 19.

[93]JD 11:122. See also, TJS, p. 373. The literal paternity of God is an established doctrine of the Church.

154 of our flesh, to enjoy these eternal principles in the same degree that will then exist. Shall these principles of conjugal and parental love and affection be thwarted in the eternal worlds? Shall they be rooted out and overcome? No, most decidedly not. According to the religious notions of the world these principles will not exist after the resurrection; but our religion teaches the fallacy of such notions.[94]

Life is feeling and response. A fulness of joy is not possible without a fulness of life. No one is so alive as God. He wants to share this aliveness with his children. Therefore, his creations are designed not only to sustain life but to enrich it:

Yea, all things which come of the earth, in the season thereof, are made for the benefit and the use of man, both to please the eye and to gladden the heart; Yea, for food and for raiment, for taste and for smell, to strengthen the body and to enliven the soul.[95]

The virtuous life is truly the good life, the happy life, the abundant life—both now and in the world to come. There is no price too high, no sacrifice too great for its possession.

PROTECTING VIRTUE

Eve in a Fallen World

Children need to be educated in the principle of virtue much as they need to be taught good nutrition. Neither moral nor physical health should be left to chance. While Eve remained in the garden she could—with but one exception—freely eat the fruit of every tree; it was all good for food. Her well-being was assured almost automatically. Today, that happy state does not exist for the Father's little Eves. Having left their celestial garden, their's is a fallen and corrupt world filled with many, many forbidden fruits. Nor can they return to the tree of life, it has been taken away; thorns, thistles and

---

[94]JD 13:187; See 1:293; 4:143.
[95]D&C 59:18, 19.

noxious weeds cover the ground where it once stood. What,
then, are these little Eves to eat? They must have something.
Unfortunately, few of them will just naturally ferret out virtue
and goodness.

For this reason we must "train up a child in the way
he should go" unless we want a wild flower.[96] Temporally
speaking, righteousness is an acquired taste. The natural disposition of mortals is to yield to fleshy impulses and drives.[97]
Man is topsy-turvy; when he fell, he landed upside down.
The forbidden fruit was the least desirable of all things in
man's realm when he first walked with God. But having
fallen from the Lord's presence, man seldom eats anything
else! The sad irony of it all is that so many have come to
prefer the fruits of spiritual death to those of the tree of life.[98]
This is why children must not only be guided to the most
nourishing moral food available, but also taught a liking for
it. Lacking such direction, most will—like Eve—succumb to
the beguiling temptations of a world where forbidden fruits
are "pleasant to the eyes" and sweet to the taste.

Awakening the Giant

The sexual nature of man is God-given and psycho-physi-
cally intrinsic to his whole being. God *made* us "male and
female"; he is the author of sexuality in all of its dimensions.
The so-called sex drive is only one of those dimensions. Being
the most obvious and, for many, the most compelling, it
tends to overshadow all others. Even divine law places particular emphasis on this drive. Sooner or later, one way or
another, we must deal with it. Since it is a natural biological
phenomenon, it cannot be purged out of one's system anymore than the need for food and rest can be overcome. It is
all part of being mortal; we must accept it as an appetite to
be reckoned with all of our lives. Nor should we want to be

---

[96]See Proverbs 22:6; 2 Nephi 4:5; D&C 68:25-28.
[97]See Moses 6:55; Mosiah 3:19; 16:3, 4; 27:25, 26; Ether 3:2.
[98]See 1 Nephi 8:4-28; Alma 36:41, 42; Revelation 22:2.

156 bereft of this drive. Life is not only made possible for others through its gratification, it is made richer and more complete for the honorable parents of that life as well. Both the begettors and the begotten are blessed. As with most things, the sex drive is a potential force for good or evil, but this is hardly a reason for repudiating it. Better to sanctify it to the glory of God and the happiness of man than to destroy it, thereby robbing life of both its purpose and future continuance.

Sexual fulfillment is a sleeping giant in the very young, but once awakened many years will pass before it begins to grow drowsy again. And, as in natural rest, some hapless souls have a harder time getting back to sleep than do others. They will toss and turn while struggling to control its urges. Regimens calling for proper associations, moral direction, rest, exercise, diet, activity, etc., meet with varying degrees of success. But, again, they do not eliminate the drive, they can only serve to control it. Those who are forced by circumstance to more or less permanently dam their sexual desires are especially burdened and merit especial help and consideration. The celibate life is an unnatural one; most adults are, of themselves, incapable of living it without being adversely affected in some way.[99]

... God has implanted, for a wise purpose, certain feelings in the breasts of females as well as males, the gratification of which is necessary to health and happiness, and which can only be accomplished legitimately in the married state, myriads of those who have been deprived of the privilege of entering that state, rather than be deprived of the gratification of those feelings altogether, have, in despair, given way to wickedness and licentiousness; hence the whoredoms and prostitution among the nations of the earth, where the "Mother of Harlots" has her seat.[100]

Our lovely daughters should be gently awakened from their sexual slumber by their virtuous and considerate hus-

---

[99]Jesus counseled against it. Matthew 19:12. And Paul acknowledged that not all men had the self-control he possessed. 1 Cor. 7:5-9.
[100]George Q. Cannon, JD 13:195.

bands, not roused into wakefulness by the lust of an uncaring and uncommitted despoiler. It is for a devoted husband to come to his bride as the noble prince came to Sleeping Beauty. His kiss, not another's, should bring her to life and awareness. Ideally, all expressions and dimensions of intimate affection should begin with marriage, the divine setting for sexual love. When a young couple enter this phase of life together, they are equally yoked in the experience. Neither is ahead of or behind the other. They learn the nuances of married love *together*. One is not a naive novice while the other is a sophisticate in sex. They are not insecure with one another, wondering if their mate's pre-marital affairs with others were more exciting or more fulfilling. They begin together as they grow together in all of those dimensions of married love which serve to make the two as one.

Parents should act (not overreact) with intelligence and understanding in protecting their children from sexual stimulation and experimentation via questionable companions, improper sex education, music, books, magazines, television, movies, etc. However, the world being what it is, we cannot hope to isolate children from all of its diseases. Indeed, to attempt such a course could weaken their natural powers of resistance and render them even more vulnerable to the very illnesses parental oversolicitation sought to prevent! Neurotic fears on the part of parents may induce a prurient interest in sex on the part of children. A wise principle to follow in guiding children is to help them face and evaluate what cannot be avoided. Help them to see the world for what it really is by exposing the face behind the mask of what it appears to be. A proper "shot" of the offending organism can effectually innoculate a healthy spirit against the disease itself.

This done, parents should work and pray to keep their children from becoming involved in overt sexual activity. For once they are consciously introduced to it, they will find the shadow of that giant falling across their path forever after. Consequently, the conduct desired of the sixteen year-old

158   should be taught the eight year old. It is the young child who should learn that early dating and car ownership will not be allowed.[101] The time to discuss such issues is when they are not issues. Let the child grow up with an understanding of what will be expected of him or her in later years. Give them time to assimilate the future before it becomes the present.

Wings of the Priesthood

The Father never willed that his daughters should ever be alone or unguarded. The wings of the priesthood were meant to always cover them. However, the Lord has observed, "men do not always do my will."[102] Untold millions of females of all ages have suffered greatly because of this.[103] Still the ideal will yet be realized.

Initially, a girl has the right to look to her father for love, sustenance, guidance and protection. If he magnifies his fatherhood, he can play a vital role in her emotional preparation for adult life. A special bond of affection, understanding and respect will be forged between them which will have a stabilizing influence on her in the critical years of adolescence. For, ordinarily, fathers provide little girls with their first significant experiences with and understanding of the male temperament. Deep and lasting impressions for good or ill often result from those experiences. A woman's unconscious attitudes toward and reactions to men frequently stem from those childhood associations—or lack of them—with her father or some male surrogate. More often than not, her

---

[101]It is generally unwise for girls to date until at least sixteen, even then the boy should be less than two years her senior. The rate of male versus female physical and social maturation is variable; being so, the danger of unchastity tends to increase with the age differential between a boy and a girl.

[102]See D&C 103:31.

[103]It is unwise for most young women to leave home for any length of time before marriage unless they are provided with very responsible supervision. Many girls from the "best" of homes make serious mistakes when finding themselves "on their own." Lacking experience, emotional maturity and genuine inner commitment to moral principles, they are unprepared for that much freedom.

parent becomes the unrealized standard by which she measures other men. A positive father-daughter relationship can do much to insure a positive husband-wife relationship.

She will have been "trained up" to expect and demand courteous and honorable treatment from men. She will feel secure within herself as a person of worth. She will know that she is loved. She will be under no necessity of lowering her ideals or succumbing to tawdry affairs. A serene daughter makes for a virtuous girl and a happy wife. Brothers can reinforce a father's influence on his daughter. The kindness, consideration and respect shown their sister will further establish her good self image and aid in the development of a desirable feminine personality. Not only that, the righteous conduct of a girl's brothers becomes a standard to measure other young men by. Being accustomed to associating with males at their best, she will be less inclined to err in assessing the worth of friends and potential marriage partners. Having known the finest of men at home, she will be disinclined to associate with any but the finest of men away from home.

The presence of dissension between brothers and sisters should not be accepted as simply "normal" behavior. Normal behavior is for *normal* people; better things are expected of those who have committed themselves to Christ and claim to be led by his Spirit.

> And ye will not have a mind to injure one another, but to live peaceably, and to render to every man according to that which is his due. And ye will not suffer your children that they go hungry, or naked; neither will ye suffer that they transgress the laws of God, and fight and quarrel one with another, and serve the devil, who is the master of sin, or who is the evil spirit which hath been spoken of by our fathers, he being an enemy to all righteousness. But ye will teach them to walk in the ways of truth and soberness; ye will teach them to love one another, and to serve one another.[104]

Treating sisters or daughters with neglect, ridicule or abuse can engender attitudes of rejection, alienation and

---

[104]Mosiah 4:13-15.

anxiety: the seed bed for much immoral behavior.[105] No two girls react in just the same way to such mistreatment. There are those who in seeking to punish and humiliate their families deliberately involve themselves in illicit affairs. Others, hungry for affection and identity, also fall—only to be condemned for their misconduct by unloving loved ones.[106] The family of one so betrayed is unjustified in putting the full burden of guilt on her. There is a beam in their own eye as well. For like it or not, the absence of love at home leads most young people to seek it elsewhere—legitimately and otherwise. Then there are those wounded souls who, in an effort to protect themselves from further hurt, turn inward—damming up their longings. But love is like a river; it was meant to flow. When it does not, emotional stagnation sets in to poison the human spirit. Personality maladjustments—some mild, some serious—are the result.

Psychologists maintain that emotional problems are sometimes the cause and sometimes the effect of sexual problems. Of course, there are very few men and women who are not emotionally flawed in some way. Under normal conditions, such psychological defects are no excuse for immoral behavior. Some men and women simply possess a wanton spirit and a disdain for moral law. However, serious emotional disturbances stemming from fear, loneliness, insecurity, etc. may lead to widespread and/or intensive acts of sexual impropriety. Feelings of rejection, of being unloved, and of personal worthlessness accounts for much immoral behavior. While such feelings do not justify wrong conduct, beating the offender down with the commandments is not the answer. Humans have needs which, when met, enhance their ability to keep the commandments. Ignoring these needs while berating them for their sins bespeaks the attitude of the pharisees, not of the Savior.

---

[105]Jesus pointed out that we can kill someone's spirit by degrading or belittling them. Such treatment opens them up to despair and makes them vulnerable to sin. See Matthew 5:21-24.

[106]Orson Pratt wisely observed, "There is no evil in love; but there is much evil resulting from the want of love." *The Seer*, p. 154.

Complacent parents assume that all will be well with their children once their physical and material wants have been supplied and they have been "taught the gospel." Then, when one strays, they are at a loss to understand why. "Where did we fail; wasn't everything done for her?" In many instances the answer is no. Critical elements in the parent-child relationship may have been missing. The body can be provided with every essential nutrient except vitamin C and still develop scurvy. Although Jesus said that man does not live by bread alone, yet he fed the hungry multitude loaves and fishes. However, if after being properly nourished, a son or daughter still rebel against their parents, the sin will be upon their own heads.[107] God himself could not save Lucifer and those who joined him in his unwarranted rebellion. The Lamans and Lemuels along with the prodigal sons of this world are left without excuse; their blood does not stain the garments of their faithful fathers and mothers.

The same basic problems besetting the general society are relatively present among the saints. Among the most compelling is that of the lone—and lonely—woman. Separation, divorce and death have left thousands of women without husbands. Many of these sisters are also mothers with young children. Many are of very limited financial means. Their needs are great. In counseling some of these women through the years, the writer has heard the same basic story again and again from young widows and divorcees: they are lonely, they do not always feel comfortable around those who do not share their plight, married women distrust them, there are virtually no worthy men their age available in the Church, and they are considered fair game by men who have but one object in mind. Indeed, no point is stressed more often than that of men—usually middle-aged bachelors and widowers—attempting to take advantage of their condition. The attitude of these women ranges from amused contempt through despair to outright indignation.

While the program of the Church meets the general

---

[107]See D&C 68:25.

162   spiritual and temporal needs of its members, it cannot correct all of the social inequities to which they may be subject. However, it does lie within the power of the saints as individuals to mitigate some of these inequities. They can, spiritually and emotionally speaking, feed the hungry, give a cup of cold water to the thirsty, clothe the naked, visit the sick and the imprisoned and welcome the stranger—the dissimilar—into their homes.[108] In other words, they can do *something* "of their own free will" to alleviate the plight of those they call brothers and sisters whose circumstances impose an extra burden on their efforts to keep the commandments.

> Verily I say, men should be anxiously engaged in a good cause, and do many things of their own free will, and bring to pass much righteousness; For the power is in them, wherein they are agents unto themselves. And inasmuch as men do good they shall in nowise lose their reward. But he that doeth not anything until he is commanded, and receiveth a commandment with doubtful heart, and keepeth it with slothfulness, the same is damned.[109]

Most importantly, the men of the priesthood can rise to their calling as "Eve's" guardian and watch over her when she is left alone in this fallen world. She needs this consideration. She deserves it. And God will hold his sons accountable if she is denied it. There is abundant evidence that man's failure to love his neighbor as himself does not prompt God to intervene in behalf of the needy. If we do not feed the hungry and clothe the naked, they will go unfed and unclothed. "For ye have the poor always with you. . . ."[110] It is for us to comfort them until their Deliverer comes.[111]

The disparity between the lives of those who are safe, happy and secure and those who are not accounts for much human indifference. Genuine compassion is a rarity among individuals who have not experienced the trials of others.

---

[108]See Matthew 25:32-47.
[109]D&C 58:27-29.
[110]Matthew 26:11.
[111]See D&C 56:18, 19.

One reason Jesus entered the mortal state was that he might   163
know how to be responsive to the plight of his fellow man.

> Wherefore in all things it behoved him to be made like unto his brethren, that he might be a merciful and faithful high priest in things pertaining to God, to make reconciliation for the sins of the people. For in that he himself hath suffered being tempted, he is able to succor them that are tempted.[112]

Lacking Jesus' understanding and concern, many of his would-be disciples leave the needy to heaven, thereby practicing faith without works:

> If a brother or sister be naked, and destitute of daily food, And one of you say unto them, Depart in peace, be ye warmed and filled; notwithstanding ye give them not those thing which are needful to the body; what doth it profit?[113]

As for religion being a safeguard against unchastity, we must admit that it sometimes leaves something to be desired. *Being* religious and learning *about* religion are two different things. Effective gospel teaching has four essential, prerequuisites: a) the doctrine must be true, b) it must be relevant to the present, c) it must be taught with divine inspiration,[114] and d) there must be a readiness to receive it. The human spirit is like a field in early spring: it has to be tilled and otherwise prepared before a crop can be planted in it. The gospel seed cannot flourish in hard, shallow, impoverished or unbalanced soil. We are far more likely to respond affirmatively to religious training when it rests upon a home life characterized by mutual affection, esteem and consideration. Nor is all religious training good. Negative learning can occur both in the home and in the church. Church attendance does not guarantee spiritual development anymore than going to college assures true education.

---

[112]Hebrews 2:17, 18. See also Alma 7:11, 12.
[113]James 2:15, 16. See also Alma 34:28, 29.
[114]See D&C 50:17-22.

164   Too many Sunday school classes are little more than centers of irrelevance, boredom and levity where irreverence is inadvertantly taught with great effectiveness. Likewise, efforts at religious indoctrination through forced and spiritless home hours—being a contradiction of the real, day-to-day character of family life—only serve to expose the hypocrisy of such moralizing. More than one avowed atheist *learned* his disbelief at home from an obnoxious and over-zealous father.

Whether at home or at church, the letter of religion can be spoken but the Gospel itself must be lived. If it isn't a living thing, it cannot be *experienced*. And if it is not experienced—directly or vicariously—it cannot be known. It is in knowing the truth that we become free—not knowing *about* it. Jesus made it abundantly clear that there would be those who would profess his name and be associated with his Church who would never come to actually know Him.[115] The church, like the home, must look to its own conscience before it denounces its wayward sons and daughters. "Feed my sheep. Feed my lambs." Such was the Savior's commandment to those who are called as guardians of his fold. If the sheep stray into forbidden ways, the shepherds should first determine if they have failed to lead them to green pastures before sending the dogs after them. We cannot eat food we do not have—much less *digest* it. Nor will the reading of delicious recipes satisfy hunger. Is a cookbook an acceptable substitute for bread and milk? Love at home and in the church—our home away from home—coupled with intelligent moral example and direction, will do more to preserve the virtue and well-being of our youth than all the sermons on the evils of immorality ever given.

The right to lead implies the obligation to protect. It was previously noted that fathers, husbands and brothers should guard the moral and physical well-being of all woman kind. To fail to do so is reprehensible, but to actually abet the

---

[115]Joseph Smith's Inspired Version, Matthew 7:33, 25:11, hereafter abbreviated I.V., followed by the appropriate book, chapter and verse.

seduction and defilement of any female is a sin of the deepest **165**
dye. Said Brigham Young:

> Shall I say that the women are short-sighted? I will say they are
> weak; I will say that it is in their nature to confide in and look to the
> sterner sex for guidance, and thus they are the more liable to be led
> astray and ruined. It is the decree of the Almighty upon them to lean
> upon man as their superior, and he has abused his privilege as their
> natural protector and covered them with abuse and dishonor . . . there
> are many who will continue to ruin every virtuous woman they can,
> buying the virtue of woman with money and deception, and thus, the
> lords of creation proceed from one conquest to another, boasting of their
> victories, leaving ruin, tears and death in their pathway; and what have
> they conquered? A poor, weak, confiding, loving woman. And what have
> they broken and crushed and destroyed? One of the fairest gems of all
> God's creation.[116]

Nothing short of murder itself can be a greater offense
against a man's priesthood. Being, by ordination, an agent
and representative of Jesus Christ, the priesthood holder is
under covenant to emulate him in every way. "Therefore,
what manner of men ought ye to be? Verily I say unto you,
even as I am."[117] Jesus was a Savior and a sanctifier of women,
not a destroyer and a defiler. The times call for priesthood
vigilance over the chastity of every girl and woman. Irrespective of conditions in the world at large, every female
should feel secure in her virtue "in our country."

> I want to see it in our country that our young ladies in the com-
> pany of our young men, in any place and under any circumstances, in
> the darkest hours and in the most unprotected situations, will feel as
> safe as if they were in their mother's bed chambers so far as anything
> wrong from the opposite sex is concerned. I would rather see men
> punished with death—which we believe is a law that should be put in
> force against any man who ruins woman—than that there ever should be
> a time in our country when corruption and wrongs of this character
> should run riot and be unchecked. Virtue lies at the foundation of in-
> dividual and national greatness. No man can amount to much who is
> not a virtuous man, who is not strong in his virtue, I do not care who he

[116]JD 12:194, 195.
[117]3 Nephi 27:27.

166 is. He may be as talented as Lucifer; but if he is not a virtuous man his greatness will not amount to much. Virtue lies at the foundation of greatness. We mean to promote it and encourage it in the rising generation.[118]

A giant step forward in the fight against immorality could be taken if the Saints were to unite in breaking free of the deadly social patterns and attitudes of the world around them. The dating habits of many youth impose unrealistic burdens of self-control on those who are weak and uncommitted. Speaking of the moral excellence of our youth, Spencer W. Kimball said:

> But the devil knows how to destroy them. He knows, young fellows, that he cannot tempt you to murder or to commit adultery immediately, but he knows, too, that if he can get you to sit in your car late enough after the dance, or if he can get you to park long enough at the end of the lane, (because he has had thousands of years of experience) he knows that the best boy and the best girl will finally succumb, and will fall. He knows that they do have a limit to their resistance.[119]

Too much freedom of action has been granted to many young people. They are shouldered with obligations of sexual restraint at the very time the drive is gaining in intensity. Not only this, they are inundated with sexual stimuli of every description and from almost every quarter. Early dating, late hours, immodest dress, unrestricted liberty of choice as to amusements and a generally permissive attitude on the part of parents has and is taking its toll. These things need to be renounced, not simply modified. For those who try to avoid a direct confrontation with sin invariably compromise with it. Many a youthful offender is a victim of unwise and unnecessary parental compromise of principles. "Here I stand."

Many parents and children belonging to small religious bodies have refused to compromise their standards. Their commitments are clear and unmistakable. Unfortunately,

[118]George Q. Cannon, JD 24:224, 225.
[119]"A Style of Our Own," Devotional Assembly, (BYU, Provo, Utah), Feb. 13, 1951. See CR, October 6, 1951, p. 59.

the same cannot be said for all Latter-day Saints. The trumpet some hear gives an uncertain sound so that their response to correct principles is equally indecisive. We cannot play the devil's game and win a victory for the Lord. If the Saints are to be even as he is, they must be willing to do even as he did. We must be willing to pay the price of virtue if we are to possess virtue. Double-mindedness, halting between two opinions, indecision, an unwillingness to be in the world without being of the world—these are at the heart of the problem of immorality in the Church today. With chastity, as with all else, partial commitment can only produce partial success.

Holiness to the Lord

The immortal spirit of every man is of God godly. Its very presence animates and hallows the temporal body. But for those who "put off the natural man"[120] by coming unto Christ and being born again[121] through the Holy Ghost, the body becomes a living temple, a house of the Lord. Paul reminded the Corinthian saints of this fact:

What? know ye not that your body is the temple of the Holy Ghost which is in you, which ye have of God, and ye are not your own? For ye are bought with a price: therefore glorify God in your body, and in your spirit, which are God's.[122]

Immorality in mind or body, thought or deed, defiles that temple and drives God out of our lives. The following was given in connection with the building of the Kirtland temple but it is equally valid for all those who aspire to the gift of the Holy Ghost.

And inasmuch as my people build a house unto me in the name of the Lord, and do not suffer any unclean thing to come into it, that it be

---

[120]See Mosiah 3:19.
[121]See John 3:1-8; Mosiah 5:7; Alma 5:14.
[122]1 Corinthians 6:19, 20; See also John 2:19.

168   not defiled, my glory shall rest upon it; Yea, and my presence shall be there, for I will come into it, and all the pure in heart that shall come into it shall see God. But if it be defiled I will not come into it, and my glory shall not be there; for I will not come into unholy temples.[124]

To live without the gift of the Holy Ghost is to live without a bright hope of salvation.[125] It is to be without that directing, sustaining and sanctifying influence that is the unique endowment of the saints of the Most High. It is to be without that special guide appointed to lead the saints through this fallen world and back into the presence of the Father.[126] Without this gift we cannot go home again; it is *impossible* to qualify for celestial glory without it. It is the "unspeakable gift"[127]—the key that unlocks the treasury of heaven and makes all other gifts attainable.

No temple of wood or stone is so precious as that which houses the human spirit. The former, if rendered unclean, can be resanctified with little difficulty; but it is not so simple a matter to cleanse and reconsecrate the latter when it has been defiled by unchastity. Across the temple of the spirit of every child of God should be emblazoned the words, HOLINESS TO THE LORD.

A time is coming when unchastity with its attendant train of evils will be largely a thing of the past. Faithful and wise parents will raise their children "as calves of the stall" who "shall grow up without sin unto salvation."[128] There will be a return to Eden. The many forbidden fruits of this world will be destroyed in the glory of Christ's coming. For he will usher in the Lord's day, the day of righteousness, the millennial day. In the meantime, the saints are obliged to raise their families under wartime conditions—"for the enemy is combined."[129] There have been and will yet be many casualties. Mistakes are made, errors in judgment do occur. No one

---

[123]See Alma 41:11.
[124]D&C 97:15-17; See also *Ibid.*, 94:8, 9.
[125]See 2 Nephi 31:17-21.
[126]See D&C 45:57.
[127]See D&C 121:26.
[128]Malachi 4:2; D&C 45:58.
[129]See D&C 1:35, 36; 38:11, 12.

is safe. Even our little children are targets for destruction. While Satan cannot tempt them until they become accountable before the law,[130] still, he is able to attack them through those individuals who have allowed themselves to come under the Adversary's power. Young people are confronted with the trials and temptations indigenous to the hour. They need all of the example, affection, confidence, guidance and protection their parents and leaders can provide. They need to understand why the Lord delights in the chastity of his sons and daughters. But more than understanding, they need to share that delight with him.

---

[130]See D&C 29:47.

VII

Give Me Children Or I Die!

He maketh the barren woman to keep house, and to be a joyful mother of children. Praise ye the Lord.[1]

The desire for motherhood is a hallmark of the whole woman.[2] No other accomplishment, nor all other successes combined can effectively assuage her hunger for children. Compensate as she will, substitute as she may, the denial of the maternal imperative leaves her heart in quiet pain. A womb never filled is like a house never lived in. It is frustration and futility.

There are three things that are *never satisfied*, yea, four things say not, It is enough; The grave; and *the barren womb*; the earth that is not filled with water; and the fire that saith not, It is enough.[3]

---

[1] Psalms 113:9.

[2] The whole woman is herein defined as the woman who possesses all of the essential characteristics of a celestial wife and mother.

[3] Proverbs 30:15, 16.

172   **Barrenness A Reproach**

One of the blessings Jehovah promised Israel if it would live in obedience to the commandments was fertility in man and beast.

> And he will love thee, and bless thee, and multiply thee: he will also bless the fruit of thy womb, and the fruit of thy land, thy corn, and thy wine, and thine oil, the increase of thy kine, and the flocks of thy sheep, in the land which he sware unto thy fathers to give thee.[4]

On the other hand, Israel's disobedience would result in an awful cursing in this regard.[5]

The Israelitish woman considered barrenness a reproach from God.[6] It was a repudiation of her very nature, a denial of her right to fulfillment. Her life was centered in her husband and her children; she had no other temporal interests. To be a wife and a mother was her ultimate aspiration. Failing that, there was little she could do to survive—perhaps become a field laborer, a household menial or, at worst, a harlot. Life offered her few alternatives. And so a woman in Israel looked to her husband for security and affection and to God for the blessings of the womb. "He maketh the barren woman to keep house, and to be a joyful mother of children."[7] We can learn much from the women of Israel. For whether they were great or small, wise or foolish, they all sought fulfillment in motherhood.

Eve, The Mother Of All Living

Eve's maternal drive is revealed in the first recorded words she spoke after learning the "good news" of salvation through Christ, "Were it not for our transgression we never should have had seed . . ."[8] Even though she had been told that motherhood would mean pain and sorrow, she could

---

[4]Deuteronomy 7:13, 14; See also *Ibid.*, 28:4, 11; Exodus 23:26.
[5]See Deuteronomy 28:18; Job 24:19, 20.
[6]See Genesis 16:2; 30:23; Isaiah 3:16-4:1; Luke 1:25. JD 11:270; 13:41; 17:221.
[7]Psalm 113:9.
[8]Moses 5:11.

not deny her own nature. She had to bring forth no matter what the cost. And the cost was fearful! Her oldest sons and daughters "loved Satan more than God" and introduced carnality, sensuality, and devilishness into the world.[9] Earth's first family was not characterized by unity and love. But Eve, hopefully bore Cain saying, "I have gotten a man *from the Lord;* wherefore he may not reject his words."[10] What irony!

She had produced the temporal embodiment of Satan himself! No man in human history has surpassed the evil of Cain. Every mortal son of perdition bears the spiritual mark of this most infamous of men. And gentle, virtuous Eve had given him life! Seemingly, she had asked God for bread and received a stone. Up to this time not one son or daughter of record had brought Adam and Eve anything but sorrow. But then, still trusting in the goodness of heaven, she brought forth Abel, the first righteous mortal to be born on this earth. What happiness this son must have brought to his parents. And what grief! Who can comprehend the awful shock that must have been theirs when they learned that he had been murdered by his own brother. The horror of Cain's act escapes us because we have become hardened to man's inhumanity to man by millennia of crime and brutality. But such a thing was unheard of in that day. Not even Cain could conceive it. It remained for Satan to inspire him with the thought.[11] The murder of Abel looms even more terrible if, as is not unlikely, it was also the first death on earth of any human being.

If so, Abel's parents not only endured the shock of human death for the first time, but in a most heinous form, fratricide. If ever a woman would have been excusable in refusing to bring more pain and sorrow upon herself, it was Mother Eve. But she set the example for all of her daughters down through time. She continued to bear children.

---

[9]*Ibid.,* 5:2, 3, 12, 13.
[10]*Ibid.,* 5:16.
[11]*Ibid.,* 5:29-31.

174   After her many trials, came the blessing—Eve was rewarded with Seth, "a perfect man, and his likeness was the express likeness of his father, insomuch that he seemed to be like unto his father in all things, and could be distinguished from him only by his age."[12] The striking spiritual and physical resemblance between Adam and Seth must have been a source of especial delight to Eve. Seth was appointed heir to his father's throne. He was the covenant son through whom the blessings of the priesthood were to come to the righteous posterity of Father Adam and Mother Eve. The great matriarch did not cease to bear, for Adam "begat many sons and daughters."[13] It is conjectured by some that Adam had other wives unknown to us. But whether he did or not, the fact remains that it was Eve who bore Seth, the son through whom the entire human race traces its lineage to Adam.

Sarah, the Matriarch of Israel

Almost two thousand years of scriptural history pass before we come to another notable woman of record: Sarah, the wife of Abraham. But before considering her life, let it be noted that it is to the credit of the writers of the Old Testament that they did not expurgate the human element from their accounts of the lives of the men and women found therein. Who is completely free of those weaknesses and imperfections which are the despair of every man and woman who has ever aspired to holiness? The conflict between Sarah and Hagar is the story of real people living real lives; variations on its central theme were repeated many times in early Mormon history; the end is not yet.

With Sarah, we note the beginning of a common motif among the great matriarchs: barrenness. Although she was a woman of exquisite beauty (even Jehovah acknowledged it[14])

---

[12]D&C 107:43.
[13]Moses 6:11.
[14]Abraham 2:22; see also Genesis 12:11.

yet she was childless for ninety years—well past the period for child-bearing even in that day. Abraham suffered with her in this matter, for he longed for a son through whom the covenant might be fulfilled. He feared that he might have to appoint Eliezer, his housekeeper, as his heir, but the Lord assured him that he would have a son of his own body.[15]

In partial fulfillment of this promise, Abraham was instructed to take a second wife.[16] Sarah's trial was thereby compounded. But she loved the Lord and she loved her husband; she gave him[17] her Egyptian handmaid, Hagar.[18] Although it is not incorrect to refer to Hagar as Abraham's wife, it is more accurate to say that she was his concubine.[19] This did not make Sarah's lot any easier.

Her own frustration was compounded by the open derision she received from the younger woman who soon found herself with child.[20] *Jasher* provides the following interesting, albeit nonscriptural, account of the incident.

And when Hagar saw that she had conceived she rejoiced greatly, and her mistress was despised in her eyes, and she said within herself, this can only be that I am better before God than Sarai my mistress, for all the days that my mistress has been with my lord, she did not conceive, but me the Lord has caused in so short a time to conceive by him. And when Sarai saw that Hagar had conceived by Abram, Sarai was jealous of her handmaid, and Sarai said within herself, this is surely nothing else but that she must be better than I am.[21]

---

[15]*Ibid.*, 15:1-6.

[16]D&C 132:34.

[17]This is known as "the law of Sarah," it is associated with the plural form of celestial marriage. See *Ibid.*, 132:34; Genesis 16:1, 2.

[18]*The Book of Jasher* asserts that Hagar (the name means 'run-away') was a daughter of Egypt's Pharaoh by one of his concubines and that she was given to Sarah to be her handmaid. Sarah seemingly treated the girl like a daughter. "For Hagar learned all the ways of Sarai as Sarai taught her, she was not in any way deficient in following her good ways." The Book of Jasher, The Bible Corporation of America (Philadelphia, 1954), pp. 43, 46. Hereafter this source will be cited as *Jasher*, followed by the appropriate page number.

[19]A concubine was a slave wife—usually a foreigner—whose status was below that of a full wife. Her children did not enjoy rights of inheritance with those of free wives. Her offspring were considered as belonging to her mistress.

[20]Genesis 16:4.

[21]*Jasher*, p. 46.

176

The concubine exalted herself above the true wife of the great patriarch! The wine of status was too much for the Egyptian bond-woman just as it has proven to be too much for many another lesser spirit come too soon to high station. Hagar did not love Sarah; the younger woman exulted in her own new-found position without seeming gratitude to her aged mistress who had made it all possible. It was for Sarah to vicariously bear children through Hagar; it was for Hagar to do her part without arrogance. Although Abraham loved Sarah as he never loved Hagar, Sarah's lifelong failure in the light of the bondwoman's quick success caused the older woman to doubt her worth. She became both insecure with Abraham and jealous of the one who had so quickly transformed herself from an obedient handmaid into a disdainful rival.

Jasher suggests that Abraham was apparently unaware of the storm raging around him; he was blissfully enjoying the eye of a hurricane. Sarah was deeply hurt, not only over her own felt lack, but also because of her husband's seeming indifference to her pains and to the contemptuous manner in which she was being treated by Hagar.

And Sarai said unto Abram, my wrong be upon thee, for at the time when thou didst pray before the Lord for children why didst thou not pray on my account, that the Lord should give me seed from thee? And when I speak to Hagar in thy presence, she despiseth my words, because, she has conceived, and thou wilt say nothing to her; may the Lord judge between me and thee for what thou hast done to me.[22]

That Sarah did complain to Abraham about Hagar is confirmed in the following passage from Genesis.

---

[22]*Jasher,* p. 46. This statement should be tempered with Joseph Smith's tribute to Abraham:

"Abraham was guided in all his family affairs by the Lord; was conversed with by angels, and by the Lord; was told where to go, and when to stop; and prospered exceedingly in all that he put his hand unto; it was because he and his family obeyed the counsel of the Lord." TJS, pp. 251-252. See also I.V., Genesis 18:18.

And Sarai said unto Abram, My wrong be upon thee; I have given my maid into thy bosom; and when she saw that she had conceived, I was despised in her eyes: the Lord judge between me and thee.

But Abram said unto Sarai, Behold, thy maid is in thy hand; do to her as it pleaseth thee. And when Sarai dealt hardly with her, she fled from her face.[23]

An angel appeared to the aggrieved concubine and admonished her to return to Sarah and submit to her will. He comforted Hagar with the promise of a numerous posterity through her unborn son who was to be named Ishmael. Like his alien mother, he too, would know what it was to be at odds with men.[24]

Hagar was obedient. Thereafter, she bore her eighty-six year old husband his first child.[25] The rivalry between the two women never abated. Many years later, on the day Isaac was weaned, an incident took place which was to divide Abraham's posterity for many millennia:

And the child grew, and was weaned; and Abraham made a great feast the same day that Isaac was weaned. And Sarah saw the son of Hagar the Egyptian, which she had born unto Abraham, mocking. Wherefore she said unto Abraham, Cast out this bondwoman and her son: for the son of the bondwoman shall not be heir with my son, even with Isaac.[26] And the thing was very grievous in Abraham's sight because of his son. And God said unto Abraham, Let it not be grievous in thy sight because of the lad, and because of thy bondwoman; in all that Sarah hath said unto thee, hearken unto her voice; for in Isaac shall thy seed be called. And also of the son of the bondwoman will I make a nation, because he is thy seed.[27]

---

[23]Genesis 16:5, 6.

[24]*Ibid.*, 16:7-14.

[25]*Ibid.*, 16:6. Sarah was seventy-six years old.

[26]*Jasher* states that when Isaac was five years old, Ishmael who was then about 19, attempted to take the child's life. Sarah seeing the incident, asked Abraham to send Hagar and her son away. See *Jasher*, p. 58. Paul implies the persecution of Isaac by Ishmael in Galatians 4:29.

[27]Gen. 21:8-13. It was intended that Abraham should have several wives drawn from among different peoples for only in that way could he realize the divine promise that he would become "a father of many *nations.*" Indeed, because he was to become such, Jehovah changed his name from Abram (exalted father) to Abraham (father of multitudes). Likewise, Sarai (my princes) was renamed Sarah (my princess—ie., a queen of heaven). See Genesis 17:4-6, 15, 16.

178   Jehovah saw the end from the beginning; it was right that the posterities of the two sons should be separated.[28] Through Isaac and Isaac alone were the chosen people, the royal priesthood, to come to earth.[29] The house of Israel was to have the responsibility of taking the message of salvation to all men.[30] Mixing the seed of Isaac with that of other peoples could only lead to confusion, division and apostasy. Indeed, that very thing happened—first in Egypt and later in Canaan. Viewed in this light, Hagar's expulsion was best for all concerned. The bondwoman had been honored far beyond the possibilities of her original station in society.[31] Her son has become a patriarch in his own right to more than 100 million Arabs—most of whom are adherents of the faith of Islam. Her treatment was more than just.[32]

The trials of Sarah—barrenness, polygyny and female rivalry—finally ended in triumph. Fourteen years after Ishmael's birth, Sarah brought forth her one and only child, Isaac. She was ninety years old![33] Her sacrifice had finally brought her the blessing of Heaven!

Of her great integrity, President John Taylor said:

This Sarai, one of the noblest of women, received the promise of her son Isaac while in old age, a promise made to her by the angel of God, and this because of her barrenness and because too of the integrity of her heart towards her husband and her willingness to sacrifice her womanly feeling in giving to her husband other wives. And after she had given to Abraham Hagar, that she might bear him children, mark the Scripture: It was for the purpose that he might not be childless because she was childless. It was after she had thus sacrificed her womanly feeling, thereby manifesting her love and integrity to her husband, that the Lord had compassion upon her and granted the desire of her heart,

---

[28]Galatians 4:22-31.

[29]See Deuteronomy 32:8, 9; Ephesians 1:3-5; 1 Peter 2:9.

[30]See Abraham 2:8-11; Genesis 17:18-21.

[31]The same can be said for Keturah, whom Abraham married after Sarah's death, and for Bilhah and Zilpah—Jacob's two concubines from whom four of the twelve tribes of Israel are descended.

[32]Not infrequently our actions—right or wrong—serve the Lord's purposes. Part of the genius of God lies in his ability to utilize human attitudes and actions in fulfilling his own designs.

[33]Genesis 21:1-7; See *Ibid.*, 17:15-22; 18:9-15. She lived 127 years. *Ibid.*, 23:1.

promising her that she should in course of time bring forth a son, and telling her that his name should be Isaac, in whom and in whose seed all the nations of the earth were to be blessed.[34]

It was with good reason that Isaiah admonished modern Israel to "Look unto Abraham your father and unto Sarah that bare you. . . ."[35]

Rebekeh

Abraham and Sarah were both of semitic origin being descended from Shem the second son of Noah.[36] In order to insure the purity of the lineage of the chosen people at its fountainhead, the principle of endogamy was invoked by Abraham.[37] The Canaanites, among whom he was living at the time, were descendants of Ham through his son Canaan.[38] Therefore, to secure a wife for Isaac from among his own people, Abraham sent his servant back to Haran in Mesopotamia. The servant was successful; Rebekeh, the grandniece of the aging patriarch, agreed to return to Canaan and become the wife of the forty year old Isaac. The marriage was unfruitful for some nineteen years.

And Isaac entreated the Lord for his wife, because she was barren; and the Lord was entreated of him, and Rebekah his wife conceived. And the children struggled together within her; and she said, If it be so, why am I thus? And she went to enquire of the Lord. And the Lord said unto her, Two nations are in thy womb, and two manner of people shall be separated from thy bowels; and the one people shall be stronger than the other people; and the elder shall serve the younger.[39]

---

[34] JD 23:228.
[35] Isaiah 51:2.
[36] See Moses 8:12, Gen. 11:10-29, Abraham 2:2.
[37] It was Jehovah's will that Isaac's descendants refrain from contracting marriages with other nations. The violation of this principle was a major factor in ancient Israel's apostasy and consequent expulsion from the promised land. See Deuteronomy 7:1-6; JD 12:105; 16:76.
[38] Genesis 10:6, 15-19.
[39] Ibid., 25:21-23. See JD 25:363, 364.

180   Once more Jehovah willed that a division should be made within the family of Abraham so that the lineage of the chosen family might be distinct from all others. Rebekeh was honored in being the mother of the one to whom God gave the title, Israel.[40] It was she who secured the blessing of the first born for her younger son, for it was made known to her before his birth that Jacob was to receive the birthright.[41]

The passing years vindicated Jehovah's selection. Esau, "a cunning hunter, a man of the field," valued his birthright[42] so little that he surrendered it to his younger brother with little hesitancy.[43] He further dishonored himself and his parents by violating the principle of endogamy in marrying two Canaanite women of the Hittite clan. This was "a grief of mind unto Isaac and to Rebekeh."

Jehovah's earlier revelation to Rebekeh together with Esau's improper marriages go far to explain her conspiracy with Jacob whereby he obtained Isaac's favored blessing. God's will would have been frustrated had Esau been made its recipient.[44] Refusing to admit his own unworthiness, Esau blamed Jacob for his losses and vowed to murder him when Isaac passed away: (a further evidence of his character.) Learning of Esau's intent, Rebekeh determined to send Jacob to her brother's home in Haran. Apparently not wanting to trouble Isaac (who was then at least one hundred years old), his wife gave him another—equally valid—reason for suggesting that Jacob leave Canaan.

And Rebekah said to Isaac, I am weary of my life because of the daughters of Heth: if Jacob take a wife of the daughters of Heth, such as

---

[40]Genesis 32:28. Israel means "he who reigns with God."

[41]See Romans 9:10-13.

[42]The birthright entitled the eldest son to a double portion of his father's property as well as both temporal and spiritual leadership over the family. See Deuteronomy 21:16, 17. In surrendering the birthright, Esau lost the privilege of being the one through whom the chosen people were to descend.

[43]See Genesis 25-28.

[44]See Ibid., 25:23; 27:29. Clearly Isaac's favored blessing had to go to the one who attained the birthright; the one grew out of the other.

these which are of the daughters of the land, what good shall my life do me?[45]

Isaac concurred; he sent Jacob away after pronouncing the blessings of Abraham upon him and admonishing him not to marry a Canaanite but to choose a wife from among the daughters of Laban, Jacob's uncle.

Rachel, the Beloved Wife

Rachel, Laban's younger daughter, was probably in her early teens when the forty-odd year old Jacob arrived in Haran. She was "beautiful and well-favored" and quickly won her cousin's heart.[46] Jacob, not having any wealth of his own, could not pay the customary marriage price,[47] he therefore agreed to serve Laban for seven years and then claim Rachel as the reward of his labors.

And Jacob served seven years for Rachel; and they seemed unto him but a few days, for the love he had to her.[48]

But upon claiming his veiled bride, Jacob discovered that Laban had tricked him into marrying the willing, but unwanted, Leah—Rachel's dull-eyed older sister. Laban cleverly prevailed upon the unwitting bridegroom to accept the deception by assuring him that he could still marry Rachel if he would but claim Leah and labor yet another seven years.[48]

We can only wonder at Rachel's emotional state upon learning that Leah was to replace her as Jacob's bride. How was she restrained from warning Jacob? Disappointment, resentment and heartbreak must have commingled in her breast. Jacob too, probably reacted to the deception with similar feelings. The passing years saw the unfortunate beginning of his marriage to the two sisters compounded by

---

[45]*Ibid.*, 27:46.
[46]See *Ibid.*, 29, 30.
[47]Regarded as just compensation for the loss of a daughter's household services.
[48]*Ibid.*, 29:20; See *Ibid.*, verse 30.

182   their growing rivalry and antagonism toward one another.[49]

Leah, keenly sensitive to the fact that Jacob loved her less than he did Rachel, well understood the status enjoyed by a child-producing wife.[51] Upon bearing Reuben her first born, she exclaimed, "Surely the Lord hath looked upon my affliction; now therefore my husband will love me."[52] Three more sons quickly followed. Her hope of gaining Jacob's love is further reflected in her words upon bearing Simeon ("I was hated") Levi ("Now this time will my husband be joined unto me because I have borne him three sons!") and Judah ("Now will I praise the Lord"). It was after the birth of Leah's fourth son that Rachel, beset with envy and despair, cried out to Jacob, "Give me children, or else I die." With seeming want of compassion, Jacob remonstrated, "Am I in God's stead, who hath withheld from thee the fruit of the womb?"

Too many husbands finding themselves in a similar situation fail their unhappy wives at their moment of greatest need. The barren woman who longs for children should be comforted with reassurances of her husband's love and understanding. Certainly where an eternal union has been covenanted both must look to the time when all physical defects and limitations will be overwhelmed and when the "exaltation and continuation of the lives" will be an everlasting reality. No faithful wife should be made to feel rejected and unloved because of circumstances beyond her control. Like the poor widow, she gives her "two mites"—

---

[49]Jacob married Rachel soon after the traditional week of marriage festivities in honor of Leah were concluded. He was about forty-eight years old; Rachel was about twenty.

[50]Problems stemming from such marriages help to account for the Levirate law prohibiting the marriage of living sisters to one man. See Leviticus 18:18.

[51]Genesis 29:31 states that Jehovah blessed her womb because she was "hated." The word "hated" simply means to be held in lesser esteem.

[52]Speaking of those women who were tormented with the fear that their husbands did not love them, Brigham Young said: "I would not care whether they loved a particle or not; but I would cry out, like one of old, in the joy of my heart, "I have got a man from the Lord!" "Hallelujah! I am a mother!—I have borne an image of God!" JD 9:37.

all that she has. And like that poor widow, such a woman is beloved of the Lord and will be rewarded for the desires of her heart far beyond her fondest dreams. Love is tried in the crucible of sacrifice and adversity—of hopes unrealized, of needs unmet, of prayers ungranted. To love the gift more than the giver is idolatry and selfishness in the extreme. And to love only in the presence of gifts and blessings is not to love at all.

What husband could withhold his support from a wife whose need for fulfillment as a mother was more central to her nature than his need that she do so? Would such a man not pity himself if he were denied masculinity through no fault of his own? Would he not expect compassion if forces beyond his control prevented him from providing for his family? It is the same with the wife in her role.

Rachel could not be complete with her husband's love alone—vital though it was. She had to fulfill her creative need somehow. Like Sarah before her, she hoped to do vicariously what she could not do of herself: she asked Jacob to accept her maid, Bilhah, as a concubine saying, "she shall bear upon my knees, that I may also have children by her."[53] Thereafter Bilhah bore two sons.

And Bilhah conceived, and bare Jacob a son. And Rachel said, God hath judged me, and hath also heard my voice, and hath given me a son; therefore called she his name Dan. And Bilhah Rachel's maid conceived again, and bare Jacob a second son. And Rachel said, *With great wrestlings have I wrestled with my sister,* and I have prevailed: and she called his name Naphtali.[54]

And Leah, who had not conceived for some years, then gave Jacob her maid Zilpah to be his second concubine. She, too, produced two sons.

---

[53]Laban had given Zilpah and Bilhah to Leah and Rachel respectively as wedding gifts. See Genesis 29:24, 29. Although the text refers to Zilpah and Bilhah as wives, they were considered concubines. See Genesis 32:22; JD 13:188.

[54]Genesis 30:5-8.

184   And Leah said, A troop cometh: and she called his name Gad.
And Zilpah Leah's maid bare Jacob a second son. And Leah said, Happy
am I, for the daughters will call me blessed: and she called his name
Asher.[55]

Desperate for a child, Rachel asked Leah for some mandrakes Reuben had found in the fields.[56] Leah's response
makes clear the deep division between the two sisters. It
further suggests that Jacob still did not favor Leah with his
love or companionship: "Is it a small matter that thou hast
taken my husband? and wouldest thou take away my son's
mandrakes also?"[57] It is interesting to note that Leah, like
Esau, blamed someone else for her troubles. She had conspired to marry Jacob and yet accused Rachel of taking him
from her! But Rachel did not argue the point; she wanted
the mandrakes and agreed to send Jacob to her sister in exchange for them. The irony of the incident is that it was
Leah, not Rachel, who thereafter twice conceived, bearing
her last sons, Issachar and Zebulun. Leah felt that God had
blessed her because she had given Jacob her handmaid Zilpah to be his concubine. With the birth of Zebulun, Leah
expressed the hope, "God hath endued me with a good dow-
ry; *now will my husband dwell with me* because I have born
him six sons."[58]

It was after the birth of Leah's last child that "God
remembered Rachel," and she bore Joseph.[59] Rachel was vindicated; the last to bear produced the son who was to claim
the blessings of the first born.[60] Quality outshone quantity;
eventually the house of Joseph gained ascendancy over all
Israel both in time and eternity. For, one-by-one, those who
had preeminence by birth forfeited their right to rule the

---

[55]Genesis 30:11-13.

[56]Mandrake (or 'love apple') is a small pulpy tomato-like fruit. The ancients regarded it as an aphrodisiac capable of aiding in conception.

[57]Genesis 30:15.

[58]*Ibid.*, 30:20. She also bore a daughter, Dinah. Jacob's preference for Rachel was
constant; she was his favored wife unto death. See Genesis 33:1-2.

[59]Rachel's age at Joseph's birth cannot be stated with accuracy. If Jacob's sojourn
in Haran was only twenty years, she was probably less than thirty years of age.

[60]See I Chronicles 5:1, 2; JD 13:188.

chosen people. The scepter departed from the sons of Leah and was placed forever in the hands of Ephraim, Joseph's son of the right-hand blessing.[61]

Rachel's poignant plea, "give me children or else I die" proved prophetic. In bearing her second child, she suffered a hard and fatal labor. With her dying breath she called her new-born infant Ben-oni, son of my sorrow. But Israel[62] in an affirmation of his love for Rachel and of the Abrahamic covenant, named him Benjamin—son of the right hand. In laying down her life for a "friend" and brother from another world, Rachel expressed the "greater love" of which Jesus so eloquently spoke but hours before his own terrible ordeal. Rachel willingly accepted the ultimate implications of the law of sacrifice as it pertains to woman-kind: the giving of life for life. In doing this, she set an example for all the mothers in Israel—in all of their times and circumstances— who were to follow.

Israel's three great matriarchs—wives of Abraham, Isaac and Jacob—were women of superior merit. The counsel of Sarah and Rebekeh concerning the selection and protection of their covenant sons was most discerning. All three were tried with barrenness for a number of years, but in meeting that trial with faith and fidelity toward Jehovah, their husbands, and themselves, they were blessed far above other women even as their husbands were blessed far above other men. As it was with them, so will it be with their faithful daughters in every generation.

Hannah, A Prophet's Mother

Hannah had much in common with Rachel. Like her ancestress, she was barren; but she too was beloved of her husband, even though Peninnah, Elkanah's second wife had—Leah-like—given him many sons and daughters.[63]

---

[61]See *Ibid.*, 48:13-28; 49:10; D&C 133:34.

[62]Jehovah endowed Jacob with the title, Israel during the patriarch's return journey to Canaan and shortly before his reconciliation with Esau. See Genesis 32:24-29.

[63]1 Samuel 1.

186   Hannah's plight was compounded in that "her adversary provoked her sore, for to make her fret because the Lord had shut up her womb."

The annual trips to the house of the Lord at Shiloh were joyless occasions for Hannah who spent them in fasting and tears while the rest of the family enjoyed their portion of the sacrificial offering. But her husband, true to the male ego and confident of his own worth, sought with clumsy, albeit sincere effort, to comfort her. "Hannah, why weepest thou? and why eatest thou not? and why is thy heart grieved? am I not better to thee than ten sons?" Men have a marvelous faculty for missing the obvious and for being able to eat under the most trying circumstances. Elkanah was true to his gender. Hannah was somewhat comforted by her husband's words, but still "she was in bitterness of soul, and prayed unto the Lord, and wept sore." She vowed if Jehovah would "look on the affliction of thine handmaid" and grant her a male child, she would dedicate him to the Lord's service "all the days of his life."[64]

Better to experience the joys of motherhood and to pour love, like oil, upon a child for a season than never to know such happiness at all. Hannah's prayer was granted and she bore Samuel, the first of the prophets to be raised up after the time of Joshua. Thereafter, Hannah was further blessed with three more sons and two daughters because she had given her first born to minister in the house of the Lord at Shiloh.

Ancient Population Control

The Old Testament records what is perhaps the most ancient instance of any government establishing population control as an official policy. It was enforced with the death penalty. The Israelites flourished in Egypt, so much

---

[64]She was committing her son to a nazarite vow wherein he would be consecrated to Jehovah's service—in this case for his lifetime. A nazarite could not partake of any grape product, cut his hair, or touch any dead body.

so that they threatened to outnumber the native Egyptians. The Pharaoh,[65] fearing that these prolific foreigners might ally themselves with Egypt's enemies in time of war in order to escape from the land, placed them in hard servitude. Still they flourished. He then ordered the Israelitish midwives to kill all male infants at birth.[66] "But the midwives feared God" and not man. They could not destroy life even to save themselves, indeed, they would have lost eternal life had they valued temporal life too highly. It was a case of treasures on earth versus treasures in heaven. They chose wisely and Jehovah blessed them for it. Frustrated, Pharoah then ordered his own people to destroy the newborn male Israelites. The women of Israel continued to bear; not even the risk of seeing their sons drowned in the Nile deterred them. They left their tomorrows in God's hands. It was for them to bear children; it was for the Lord to preserve them or not as he saw fit.

It was under these perilous conditions that Moses was born.[67] Had his mother, Jochebed, obeyed the law of the land rather than God, she would have lost the high privilege of begetting one of the greatest prophets of all time. Since it was the appointed hour for Moses to come upon the scene, some other woman whose faith was stronger would have been appointed in Jochobed's place.[68] How many blessings have been lost through fear of men, fear of the unknown, or the want of selfless devotion?

God *does* move in a mysterious way his wonders to perform. The very conditions which seemed so formidable an obstacle to Israel's future existence produced the situation which brought little Moses into the family of Pharaoh and helped prepare him for his later mission as Israel's deliverer. Further, those oppressive years served to bring a measure of unity to Israel itself thereby making that stubborn people

---

[65]Probably Rameses II.

[66]See Exodus 1, 2; JD 26:14.

[67]The name, Moses (child or son), is Egyptian, not Hebrew. It was given him by the Egyptian princess—Thermutis or Merris (?) who adopted him.

[68]See Hebrews 11:23.

188   more amenable to Jehovah's will. In this respect, modern Israel has much in common with ancient Israel.

Lot's Daughters

The longing for children has led many a woman to unwise, even immoral actions. The maternal drive is virtually compulsive in some females; it is their magnificent obsession. Right or wrong, neither fear of pain, death or dishonor will deter them. Society's wrath and heaven's censure are forgotten in their single-minded quest for fulfillment. Indeed, this very thirsting after children has made such women peculiarly vulnerable to the male predator who turns this weakness to his own advantage. The woman seeks vindication as a woman; the man seeks sexual (and ego) gratification for its own sake.

> How is it among the nations of the earth? Why, women, in their yearning after the other sex and in their desire for maternity, will do anything to gratify that instinct of their nature and yield to anything and be dishonored even rather than not gratify it. . . .[69]

The story of Lot's two daughters is a case in point. Lot, Abraham's nephew, had chosen what he supposed to be the better part of the promised land only to be eventually forced to flee his home in Sodom and seek refuge in a cave. In these straitened circumstances his now motherless daughters, seeing no future for themselves or their father, conspired to conceive by him while he was in an intoxicated state. This they did that "we may preserve seed of our father."[70]

Although they "dealt wickedly"[71] in this incestuous affair, yet their sin seems to have been mitigated somewhat by their apparent anxiety over their father's threatened pos-

---

[69]George Q. Cannon, JD 13:207, See also JD 20:198.

[70]Genesis 19:30-36.

[71]I. V., Genesis 19:37. These girls were childless-widows; their husbands died in the destruction of Sodom. See Genesis 19:14.

terity. It is noteworthy that Lot's son by his elder daughter
was named Moab; from him descended Ruth, the Moabitess
—the great grandmother of David and a noble ancestress of
Jesus of Nazareth.[72] The younger daughter also bore a son,
Ben-ammi, father of the children of Ammon. So came into
being the Moabites and the Ammonites—Israel's antagonists,
both in ancient and modern times.

Tamar, Matriarch of Judah

A second example of the extremes to which some women
have gone to bear offspring is that of Tamar.[73] Shortly after
selling his brother Joseph into slavery, Judah became involved
with a Canaanite woman by whom he had three sons, Er,
Onan, and Shelah. Er married a woman named Tamar; he
was a wicked man "and the Lord slew him." Judah there-
upon ordered Onan to marry Tamar and "raise up seed unto
thy brother." But Onan refused to consummate the marriage
because he "knew that the seed should not be his." This
"displeased the Lord; wherefore he slew him also."

Judah then promised the childless Tamar that she could
claim his youngest son, Shelah, as a husband when he became grown. But the years passed and Judah did not honor
his word. Finally, Tamar put aside her widow's garb and
dressed herself in the manner of a harlot. Judah, not recognizing his daughter-in-law, gave her his signet, bracelets,
and staff as a guarantee of payment for her favors. Tamar
conceived and immediately returned to her former dress
and life. Some three months later it was reported to Judah
that his daughter-in-law had "played the harlot" and was
with child by whoredom. Judah ordered her burned to death,
but Tamar told him, "By the man whose these are, am I with
child." She then showed Judah his own properties, which he
acknowledged, confessing, "She hath been more righteous

---

[72]See *Ibid.*, 19:37; Ruth 4:17, 21; Matthew 1:5, 6; Luke 3:31, 32.
[73]See Genesis 38.

190   than I; because I gave her not to Shelah my son."[74] Judah's failing begot Tamar's sin.

The double standard of morality illustrated by this incident has always been abominable in God's sight. The manner in which men have glutted their passions on women only to abandon them to the merciless judgment of a hypocritical society is beneath contempt. It is of just such men that Jesus spoke when he said, "He that is without sin among you, let him first cast a stone at her."[75] God does not judge men by their actions alone (as we are prone to do), but by the thoughts and intents of their hearts. For this reason Jesus could tell the self-righteous Pharisees who rejected him, "Verily I say unto you, that the publicans and harlots go into the kingdom of God before you."[76] This was not mere prophetic hyperbole.

Brigham Young declared:

> When the books are opened, out of which the human family are to be judged, how disappointed the professedly sanctified, long-faced hypocrites and smooth-tongued pharisees will be, when the publicans and harlots enter into the kingdom of heaven before them; people that appeared to be full of evil, but the Lord says they never designed to do wrong; the Devil had power over them, and they suffered in their mortal state a thousand times more than you poor, miserable, canting, cheating, snivelling, hypocritical pharisees; you were dressed in purple and fine linen, and bound burdens upon your weaker brethren that you would not so much as help to lift with your little fingers. . . .
>
> You have fared sumptuously all your days and you condemned to an everlasting hell these poor harlots and publicans who never designed an evil. Are you not guilty of committing an evil with that poor harlot? Yes, and you will be damned while she will be saved.[77]

Tamar bore Judah twin boys, Pharez and Zarah.[78] Such is the origin of the tribe of Judah. Regardless of how one

---

[74]*Ibid.*, 38:26. The contrast between the conduct of Judah and that of Joseph when he was confronted with the opportunity to commit adultery is marked. (See Genesis 39: 7-13).

[75]See John 8:7.

[76]Matthew 21:31.

[77]JD 10:176.

[78]See Genesis 38:29, 30; Matthew 1:3; Luke 3:33. David descended from Pharez.

judges the conduct of Judah and Tamar, it seems providential that the posterity of Judah are descended from Tamar's sons rather than those of Shuah the Canaanite woman.

And so by the unsavory acts of two desperate women was that lineage established through which came the purest of "chosen vessels"—Mary, the mother of Jesus Christ! Truly, the great Jehovah "descended below all things" in taking upon himself mortality and the sins of the world. How gracious he is toward the weaknesses and foibles of the human family!

A Promise

Child-hunger is not limited to the great or the notorious women of scripture. It is a characteristic of certain classes of females in all times and circumstances. How many wives have sought conception in spite of the negative decrees of doctors and husbands? Others, though unmarried, have deliberately sought pregnancy by friends, lovers and strangers in virtual disregard of divine law or the stigma associated with such affairs—a stigma which was far more painful and ruinous in times past than it is today. Not only this, medical history is replete with cases of false pregnancy psychologically induced by intense yearning for maternity.

The widespread practice of adoption bears witness of the parental drive on the part of many married couples. (Even unmarried women are now adopting children.) A more extreme and less extensive phenomenon of the times is that of artificial insemination either employing the seed of the husband or that of an anonymous donor. In the latter instance, it would appear to be morally and psychologically very questionable; however, such measures demonstrate the lengths to which some are prepared to go in overcoming the problem.

Many childless women seek compensation by securing employment in homes, nurseries, schools and hospitals where they can be in daily contact with children. Enormous good

192 is done by such women; they shower warmth and affection on those children whose own parents starve them with indifference.

The untold millions of little children who die in Christ are all heirs of the celestial kingdom. They will come forth in the resurrection with glorious bodies of the same stature and at the same stage of physiological development they possessed at death. Many will need mothers to claim them and to raise them to the full maturity of their spirits. This will allow every faithful, but childless, woman to know all of the joys—intensified beyond human understanding—of motherhood.

There are born into the world countless thousands of children who die in their infancy whose mothers unfortunately shall not be worthy to go where these children shall be when, as little infants, they come up in the resurrection from the dead in their infant state to be, of necessity, under the care and direction of a loving mother until they grow to maturity; and no doubt worthy women who have not been granted the privilege of motherhood, shall have their hearts satisfied in the adoption and in the eternal right and possession of these motherless children.[79]

It is not the number of children that exalts a woman in God's eyes. Sarah had but one, Rachel but two. Those women who are denied motherhood through no fault of their own are fully acceptable to the Lord. Like the impoverished man who is forced to deny the beggar's plea, they can say in all honesty: "I give not because I have not, but if I had I would give."[80] Brigham Young comforted the childless women of the Church with this assurance:

Let me here say a word to console the feelings and hearts of all who belong to this Church. Many of the sisters grieve because they are not blessed with offspring. You will see the time when you will have millions of children around you. If you are faithful to your covenants, you will be mothers of nations. You will become Eves to earths like this; and when you have assisted in peopling one earth, there are millions of earths still in the course of creation. And when they have endured

[79]Melvin J. Ballard, Hinckley, op. cit., p. 207.
[80]Mosiah 4:24.

a thousand million times longer than this earth, it is only as it were the beginning of your creations. Be faithful, and if you are not blest with children in this time, you will be hereafter.[81]

The worthy, but barren or unmarried, woman need not envy her more fortunate sisters. Neither her need nor her sacrifice goes unnoticed.

Sing, O barren, thou that didst not bear; break forth into singing, and cry aloud, thou that didst not travail with child: for more are the children of the desolate than the children of the married wife, saith the Lord.[82]

---

[81]JD 8:208. See also 14:230.
[82]Isaiah 54:1.

VIII

Let There Be Life!

. . . Be fruitful, and multiply, and replenish the earth, and subdue it: and have dominion over the fish of the sea, and over the fowl of the air, and over every living thing that moveth upon the earth.
Genesis 1:28.

Our generation has seen this mandate challenged as never before. The clamor of voices calling for the denial of life and even the premeditated ending of life is heard everywhere. Motivated by selfishness, ignorance and fear, men and women the world over are decrying the so-called population explosion. "There are too many people! There isn't enough food or shelter or work or space for those now living, not to mention the vast increases predicted for the near future by our scientists. Something must be done, and now!" So goes the argument.

These are not the isolated views of a few unorganized

196 alarmists; an increasing number of political leaders and national governments are committing themselves to programs designed to curtail the birth rate of the world. This idea is not new. Said Brigham Young:

> To check the increase of our race has its advocates among the influential and powerful circles of society in our nation and in other nations. The same practice existed forty-five years ago, and various devices were used by married persons to prevent the expenses and responsibilities of a family of children, which they must have incurred had they suffered nature's laws to rule pre-eminent. That which was practiced then in fear and against a reproving conscience, is now boldly trumpeted abroad as one of the best means of ameliorating the miseries and sorrows of humanity.[1]

"In God We Trust" expressed the basic faith of America's founders; it does not reflect the honest convictions of many political leaders today. Naturally, their liberal views are receiving enthusiastic support from those who are disinclined toward large families since these views implicitly justify their own attitudes and conduct. It is not unusual for political morality to abet and vindicate personal morality. Caesar becomes god! Other elements in society are lending their active support to the political proponents of birth control because it serves their misguided purposes to do so. Chief among these are members of the clergy whose faith in God is over-shadowed by their faith in man. Lacking vision, they are nevertheless volunteering their services as blind leaders of the blind. They constitute the religious camp-followers of an unholy army of men and women who are without God in the world and who, consequently, look to the arm of flesh for their salvation.

They are fellow travelers with those "silly women laden with sins, led away with divers lusts, ever learning, and never able to come to the knowledge of the truth" who have distorted the cause of women's rights.[2] These caricatures of womanhood are determinedly leading their naive sisters into

---

[1] JD 12:120, 121, Cr, April 6, 1947, p. 120.
[2] 2 Timothy 3:6.

a bondage more degrading and more enslaving than any women have known before. What they once endured in innocence, they now embrace in guilt. For in renouncing marriage, motherhood and chastity and in aping the moral practices of their male counterparts, they are not only implicitly condoning the misconduct of men, they are also stripping themselves of that special dispensation which God granted them as the "weaker vessel" whose salvation lies in motherhood with all that that calling entails.[3]

Probability of over-crowding, famine, pollution, ecological imbalance and social upheaval are the major points currently cited by proponents of population control. Generally, however, more personal reasons are given for small families: inadequate finances, the desire to guarantee one's children a good education, the better things in life, or more personal attention than would be possible with a large family. Some frankly admit that they simply want to be unencumbered by parental responsibilities. Others, though not opposed to large families, have urged that the spacing of children is justifiable, even desirable. Again, such rationalizations as completing an education, getting situated in one's career, waiting for adequate finances or for a proper home, etc. figure prominently in their reasoning. The advent of more effective and usable methods of contraception, together with recent research into the presumed sexual nature and needs of women, has seen another defense advanced: the right of the female to be as sexually free and fulfilled as the male without the Damoclean sword of unwanted pregnancy hanging over her head. Thus freed, the argument goes, the marriage relationship will attain new heights of enjoyment, significance and stability. Needless to say, this hypothesis is yet to be demonstrated.

Justification for Birth Control

Morally speaking, the justification for birth control rests upon the particular theological and/or ethical frame

---

[3]*Ibid.* 2:15. See JD 13:207.

198   of reference employed by its advocates. In rejecting the literal fatherhood of God, Christians reject the notion that humans had any conscious, individual identity before their mortal conception (Catholic) or birth (Protestant). Consequently, immortality can only pertain to a future state, not to some previous life. Therefore, professing Christians, atheists, and agnostics agree that birth control only denies existence to the non-existent.

At face value, this position has the force of logic behind it. Under present circumstances, there are many serious problems facing mankind. Limiting population is one of the things that might be done to help solve some of them. The commandment to multiply and replenish the earth is, of itself, admittedly vague.[4] How much are we to multiply and how shall we know when the earth is sufficiently filled to be full?[5] Then too, traditional Christian theology stands all but mute before the question of why we exist at all, and is scarcely less vague when dealing with the nature and purpose of any future life. Birth and death remain a mystery to the most learned divines. Not knowing the beginning, they do not know the end. Is it any wonder that Christians support population control? Their error in this regard is only a part of a much larger pattern of deception foisted upon a benighted world by Satan and his mortal minions.[6]

Still, the traditional attitude of Christians has been to oppose the twin practices of conception prevention (contraception) and non-therapeutic abortion. The doctrine that conception marks the beginning of life for the soul is the basis for the Catholic practice of "baptising" the unborn embryo or fetus should the mother abort or the infant be stillborn. Not even therapeutic abortion is condoned in Catholic dogma; the right of the fetus to life supersedes the right of the mother to survive. Historically, the Protestant

---

[4]The term "replenish" is misleading. A more accurate rendering of the original Hebrew is "to fill" or "to make full."

[5]Modern revelation resolves this point. See page 201.

[6]See D&C 33:4, 123:12; Moses 7:26.

viewpoint, while less rigid, has reflected that of the Catholic church. The twentieth century has seen a decided shift of theological opinion on the entire matter. A majority of Protestant and a growing number of Catholic theologians no longer condemn contraception. In fact several leading Protestant denominations have officially endorsed the practice. What was once a shameful thing is now regarded as an act of social responsibility.

The changed attitudes of the clergy mirror those of the laity. The first world war was something of a watershed for Western civilization. An attitude of permissiveness and *laissez-faire* morality came into being in the 1920's which, except for brief pauses, has swept through all classes of society. What was once a small stream has burst its banks and become a raging flood. Abetted by such factors as the emergence of science as a new religion, the promulgation of the theory of organic evolution, the rise of atheistic communism, the defection of many Christian leaders from the basic faith of their fathers, the deterioration of the home's influence and a generally pervasive spirit of secularism and materialism— men and women in all strata of society are turning from the standards of the past. Old fences are being broken down with no apparent thought of replacing them.

Yes, the frame of reference is changing for many Christians and non-Christians alike. All things are, indeed, "in commotion." No individual, no family, no church, no society appears to be safe from the "gross darkness" that— like some living thing—is reaching out to engulf us.[7] However, the Gospel of Jesus Christ—the frame of reference of the Latter-day Saints—is still the same. The Lord's people possess a far greater understanding of the truth of "things as they are, as they were, and as they are to come" than does mankind at large.[8] Therefore, they cannot, in good faith, support the population control programs being currently advocated. They cannot justify a course of action which

---

[7]See Moses 6:15; D&C 38:11, 12; 88:49.
[8]See D&C 93:24.

200 would run counter to *their* faith by appealing to arguments premised upon an alien and contradictory faith. Try as we may, we still can't serve two masters. Apostle George Albert Smith wrote:

> Children are an heritage from the Lord, and those who refuse the responsibility of bringing them into the world and caring for them are usually prompted by selfish motives, and the result is that they suffer the penalty of selfishness throughout eternity. There is no excuse for members of our Church adopting the custom of the world to either limit the size of the family or have none at all. *We have been better taught than they.*[9]

The Capacity of Mother Earth

Moral considerations notwithstanding, is it not a fact that the burgeoning world population is a growing threat to the well-being, if not the very survival, of the human race? Has not mother earth's capacity to provide for her offspring been reached, if not exceeded? No one can deny that famine and pestilence take an awful toll of life on this planet. Great masses of hopeless people are trapped in an endless cycle of birth, poverty, hunger, and early death. The vast majority of those in the backward—"have not"—nations eke out the most meager existence while other peoples are blessed with an abundance of the necessities—even luxuries—of life. While millions suffer malnutrition and starvation, others glut themselves on the bounties of the earth. The problem is not one of production but of distribution. The Lord God, for whom the past, the present, and the future are "one eternal now"— organized this earth in such a way that it could amply supply the needs of his family during the intended seven-thousand years of its temporal existence.[10]

It is man, not God, who is responsible for the deplorable state of human affairs. The inequities of this world, with all of their attendant problems stem from broken law. It was

---

[9]Relief Society Magazine, Vol 4, No. 2, Feb. 1917 p. 72. Hereafter this source will be designated RSM, followed by the appropriate volume, page number and date.

[10]See D&C 77:6; 104:17.

never the Lord's will "that one man should possess that which
is above another." Because this condition exists, "the world
lieth in sin."[11] Were this imbalance due to God's faulty planning or to his arbitrary blessings and cursings, we might
justifiably accuse him of laying the foundation for human suffering. But such is not the case. His foreknowledge enabled
him to prepare every needful thing for those of his children
who were to sojourn on the earth during its temporal existence. All of these unembodied spirits were begotten by our
heavenly parents long before the physical earth was organized.[12] A major purpose of the marriage relationship is "that
the earth might answer the end of its creation;[13] and that it
might be filled with the measure of man, *according to his
creation before the world was made.*"[14]

Plainly, there is a fixed number of spirits destined for
embodiment on this planet prior to its death. Apostle Melvin
J. Ballard stated:

> About the throne of our Father are his children whose numbers are
> fixed and have not been changed or altered from the beginning, so far
> as those who were to come to this earth are concerned; for they were
> seen, even from the days of Adam, the host of the unborn. They have
> cried around the throne of the Father night and day for the privilege of
> coming into earth life, and they seek that opportunity today.[15]

Since only the spirit can endow its fleshly tabernacle with
life, the combined offspring of all mortal parents cannot
exceed that number. We cannot overpopulate the earth.
Viewed in this light, the two-pronged commandment to
multiply *and* fill the earth will not be kept until the last
spirit entitled to a mortal body has claimed it. Then, and only

---

[11]D&C 49:20.

[12]See Moses 3:4, 5.

[13]See 1 Nephi 17:36, Abraham 3:24.

[14]D&C 49:16, 17. Orson Pratt, in commenting on this verse, said that the human
family will continue to multiply "until the earth has filled the measure of its creation,
according to the number of souls that existed before the world was organized, in the family
of the two thirds who kept their first estate." JD 21:290. See *Ibid.* 16:178.

[15]Hinckley, *op. cit.*, p. 207.

202   then, will the earth be *full*. Thus, a more comprehensive statement of the commandment appears to be: Multiply and fill the earth *with the measure of man's spiritual creation*.

While all other divine decrees can be kept by individuals or groups, this one is unique in that it requires the cooperation of the entire race as such. A couple can multiply, but they cannot fill the earth. The imperative nature of this commandment is doubtless one reason for the universality of the sex drive. Lacking it, men would not obey the instruction to multiply with any more diligence than they do any other. President J. Reuben Clark told the priesthood of the Church:

> There is some belief, too much I fear, that sex desire is planted in us solely for the pleasures of full gratification; that the begetting of children is only an unfortunate incident. The direct opposite is the fact. Sex desire was planted in us in order to be sure that bodies would be begotten to house the spirits; the pleasures of gratification of the desire is an incident, not the primary purpose of the desire.[16]

Satan's varied efforts to blunt or pervert this drive are aimed at frustrating the plan of salvation. But he will not succeed. The unborn will live—for we can no more become perfect without those who are awaiting passage into mortality than we can become perfect without those who have taken passage out of it.

Cause of Present Conditions

The Father, knowing precisely how many spirits would be tabernacled in the flesh, prepared an earth adequate to their needs: it was pronounced "very good." Adam and Eve pioneered this *good* earth, becoming the parents of the mortal human race. The government of that race was to be literally a family affair under the patriarchal order of the priesthood. The constitution of that order—being modeled

---

[16]J. Reuben Clark, Jr., CR, Oct. 1, 1949, p. 194. See JD 23:225, 226; 26:217.

upon the theocracy of heaven—guaranteed every individual those unalienable rights so essential to human freedom and achievement. The religion of heaven was to be duplicated on earth so that there might be a heaven on earth. And the earth itself was to be shared by mankind *as a family:* belonging to all, serving all, and blessing all. She was capable, in spite of her fallen state, of yielding bounteously, for she would be responsive to the efforts of her righteous sons and daughters.[17] Thus the Lord God was prepared to do everything possible to make the mortal probation of his children both happy and productive.

But this was not to be. Satan—the spoiler, the kill-joy— entered the scene. He influenced Adam's children against their own father and inspired men in the ways of carnality and devilishness, thereby establishing his rule in opposition to the kingdom of God.[18] The rest is history: false and abominable cults and priesthoods practicing dehumanizing rituals soon developed. The "family quarrel" magnified into open warfare. Murder for territorial control and exclusiveness, murder for power, glory, possessions, and self-vindication became a way of life.[19] The political concept of separate, autonomous nations developed from the evil principle of survival of the fittest. Jungle law became man's law. Might made right. It was for the strong to rule, it was for the weak to submit.

Divine judgments followed one upon another down through the centuries culminating in the great deluge which swept virtually all life from the earth. The Lord, through Noah, then made another attempt at setting up the kingdom of God only to have Satan repeat his successes of the antedeluvian period.

In the beginning, after this earth was prepared for man, the Lord commenced his work upon what is now called the American continent, where the Garden of Eden was made. In the days of Noah, in the days

---

[17]See Moses 7:48. Isaiah 4:2; D&C 59:16-19.

[18]See Moses 5:13; 7:32, 33.

[19]See Moses 6:15.

204 of the floating of the ark, he took the people to another part of the earth: the earth was divided, and there he set up his kingdom. Did they receive his kingdom? No; they rejected it.[20]

Ours is the harvest generation of the second world order. The poor earth has been plundered and polluted, her body has been defiled by the blood of countless millions and carved up into scores of separate political entities. What began as one vast open vista has become a panorama of walled fields. God in his omniscience knew that man would wreak this folly. However, divine foreknowledge does not excuse human error. As Jesus warned:

> Woe unto the world because of offences! for it must needs be that offences come; but woe to that man by whom the offence cometh![21]

The natural results of man's offenses are everywhere apparent. He now proposes to solve his problems by compounding the very sins which produced them in the first place! He will *control* the population of this divided planet. He will not love his neighbor *as himself*. He will not live in harmony with nature. He will not abandon those practices which defile the environment and threaten the very existence of other forms of life.

He will not practice his science within the bounds of morality and humility. He will not deny himself needless luxuries and creature comforts. He will not sacrifice anything but one thing—life! And that, never his own. His appetites will be his undoing. But, for now, expediency—not repentance—dominates his thinking. Having brought this debacle upon himself by violating some of God's laws, he hopes to remedy his plight by lending official sanction and support to programs which run counter to still others. It is ironic that the same science which produced the present imbalance between birth and death now presumes to prevent birth while

---

[20]Brigham Young, JD 8:195.
[21]Matthew 18:7.

going to obscene lengths to delay death. A clear contradiction. Likewise, a society which refuses to execute guilty murderers does not hesitate to take the life of the innocent unborn! A monstrous hypocrisy—for God has explicitly commanded the former and forbidden the latter![22] Such duplicity can only bring added judgments upon mankind. Two wrongs don't make a right. We were wrong in the first instance; we will be wrong in the second as well.

If mankind—the transported family of a heavenly Father —would repent of its selfishness and turn to that Father in honest confession and contrition, pleading for divine forgiveness and support, he would respond. Every problem could be resolved. We could become a true family again. Sadly, this will not happen. Mankind's sickness is terminal in nature; it is only a matter of time before we witness the death of this, the second world order. Man's disobedience will bring about "a full end of all nations."[23] Then, and only then, will mankind become one nation under God. Then, and only then, will the will of the Father be done on earth as it is done in heaven. The kingdom of God, in all of its majesty and power, will stand for a thousand years.[24] Its king and lawgiver will be the Holy One of Israel—the Lord Jesus Christ.[25] He will bring justice, equity, and peace to a despairing humanity. So we will have the poor with us always until he reigns whose right it is to reign.[26] Only then will they be delivered from their burdens and finally rejoice.[27]

Meanwhile, it is for the saints and good men everywhere to do all that they can to ameliorate the suffering of their brothers and sisters—to feed the hungry, clothe the naked, and visit the sick and the imprisoned. It is for Israel to become, in very deed, a peculiar people. If the world insists upon programs which are at variance with that goal,

---

[22]See Genesis 9:6, 7; Exodus 20:13; Alma 34:11, 12; D&C 42:19.
[23]D&C 87:6.
[24]See Daniel 2:44, 7:13, 14, 27; D&C 65; 109:72-74.
[25]See D&C 38:21, 22.
[26]See Matthew 26:1.
[27]See D&C 56:18-20.

206   the saints must respectfully decline to support them. The Lord has said:

> For the earth is full, and *there is enough and to spare;* yea, I prepared all things, and have given unto the children of men to be agents unto themselves. Therefore, if any man shall take of the abundance which I have made, and impart not his portion, according to the law of my gospel, unto the poor and the needy, he shall, with the wicked, lift up his eyes in hell, being in torment.[28]

Those possessing faith will take him at his word. He is fully capable of providing for the lillies of the field, the lark that arches across the inner dome of heaven, and for his own spirit flesh and blood. It is for us to trust in him who "doeth all things well." God *will* provide if we are not of little faith. Now let us consider the commandment itself.

The First Commandment

The foreordained fall of Adam from an immortal to a mortal state was the *modus operandi* by which the spirit creations of God were to be provided with physical embodiment. Since man was made the lord of all creation, its destiny was placed in his hands.[29] Thus, when Adam fell all creation fell with him. In this way the gods made it possible for all forms of life to "be fruitful and multiply." The commandment was binding on both man and beast.[30]

The fall was a paradox. Should right come of wrong? Should life come of death? And yet it was so ordained from the beginning. Christ's great atoning sacrifice is heaven's own alchemy; it triumphs over broken law and transforms sin's base metal into the pure gold of righteousness. It wrests victory from defeat and makes the impossible possible.[31] The Savior of the world found life in death for himself and

---

[28]D&C 104:17, 18.
[29]Genesis 1:26.
[30]See *Ibid.,* 1:20-22; Moses 2:22, 28; Abraham 4:22, 28.
[31]See 1 Corinthians 15:55-57; Matthew 19:26.

for all mankind.[32] Therefore, upon hearing the "good news"
of divine pardon, Adam exclaimed:

> . . . Blessed be the name of God, for because of my transgression
> my eyes are opened, and in this life I shall have joy, and again in
> the flesh I shall see God.[33]

And Eve, having received the message of salvation from
her husband, responded:

> Were it not for our transgression we never should have had seed,
> and never should have known good and evil, and the joy of our redemp-
> tion, and the eternal life which God giveth unto all the obedient.[34]

The use of weakness and sin in bringing about lasting
benefits is a recurring theme in the story of God's dealings
with his family. As we have seen, more than one child was
begotten as a consequence of human imperfection only to
have eventual good come of it. It started with Eve; her
more erring daughters have access to the same grace she
found.

At first, Eve labored by Adam's side in the fields helping
him carry the burden God had placed upon him, but then
she had to assume her own responsibilities.

> And Adam knew his wife, and she bare unto him sons and daughters,
> and they began to multiply and to replenish the earth. And from that
> time forth, the sons and daughters of Adam began to divide two and
> two in the land, and to till the land, and to tend flocks, and they also
> begat sons and daughters.[35]

And so the family of Adam quickly spread across the
earth. In the days of Seth "the children of men were numerous upon all the face of the land."[36]

However, the *Book of Jasher* indicates that the practice

---

[32]See Matthew 10:39.
[33]Moses 5:10.
[34]Moses 5:11.
[35]Moses 5:2, 3.
[36]Moses 6:15.

208 of birth prevention began to be indulged in by certain of the ancients for very modern reasons:

> For in those days the sons of men began to trespass against God, and to transgress the Commandments which he had commanded to Adam, to be fruitful and multiply in the earth. And some of the sons of men caused their wives to drink a draught that would render them barren, in order that they might retain their figures and whereby their beautiful appearance might not fade. And when the sons of men caused some of their wives to drink, Zillah drank with them. And the child-bearing women appeared abominable in the sight of their husbands, as widows, *whilst their husbands lived*, for to the barren ones only they were attached.[37]

This and other sins eventually led to the flooding of the entire earth approximately 1656 years after the fall of Adam.[38] The deluge brought man's first world to an end. Of the many millions descending from Adam and Eve, only eight persons remained.[39] They constituted the tenuous thread which bound the Father's family together. Upon leaving the ark, Noah was instructed:

> Bring forth with thee every living thing that is with thee, of all flesh, both of fowl, and of cattle, and of every creeping thing that creepeth upon the earth; that they may breed abundantly in the earth, and be fruitful, and multiply upon the earth.[40]

And so the second world order began with the same divine injunction which prefaced the first.

The Great Promise

Abraham, having met his supreme test in being willing to sacrifice his son Isaac, had sealed upon him the greatest of all blessings: the gift of eternal life with its assurance of an endless posterity.[41]

---

[37]*Jasher*, Op. cit. p. 5. Italics original. Quoted in RSM. 4:71 Feb, 1917.

[38]Based on chronologies found in Inspired Version of Genesis, the Book of Moses, and the *Doctrine and Covenants*.

[39]See Genesis 6:18; 1 Peter 3:20.

[40]See Genesis 8:17; See also *Ibid.*, 9:17.

[41]That Jehovah did seal with a sure seal the blessing upon Abraham is attested by the writer of Hebrews. See Hebrews 6:11-17; D&C 131:5.

And the angel of the Lord called unto Abraham out of heaven the second time, And said, By myself have I sworn, saith the Lord, for because thou hast done this thing, and hast not withheld thy son, thine only son: That in blessing I will bless thee, and in multiplying I will multiply thy seed as the stars of the heaven, and as the sand which is upon the sea shore; and thy seed shall possess the gate of his enemies: And in thy seed shall all the nations of the earth be blessed; because thou hast obeyed my voice.[42]

Jehovah made the same promise to Abraham's covenant son Isaac[43] and to his son Jacob, the founder of the house of Israel.[44]

Jacob was fruitful; he did multiply.[45] So much so that Israel's exodus from Egypt saw them a multitude of hundreds of thousands if not millions.[46] Later, when Jehovah threatened to destroy all Israel for their idolatry, Moses reminded him of his promises to the patriarchs, whereupon the Lord relented.[47] Prior to his departure from among them, Moses warned Israel that their disobedience would leave them "few in number, whereas ye were as the stars of heaven for multitude."[48] From these instances emerges one clear point: the ancients regarded a numerous posterity as a very great blessing; to be denied children was to be cursed of God.

Lo, children are an heritage of the Lord: and the fruit of the womb is his reward. As arrows are in the hand of a mighty man; so are children of the youth. Happy is the man that hath his quiver full of them; they shall not be ashamed, but they shall speak with the enemies in the gate.[49]

---

[42]Genesis 22:15-18; See also *Ibid.* 17:2. Abraham 3:14; D&C 132:30.

[43]Genesis 26:4, 14.

[44]See *Ibid.* 28:3, 4; 35:11; 48:4; Exodus 32:13. A like promise is given *on a conditional basis* to all who are married for eternity in the modern temples of the Lord. Being either the literal or the adopted sons and daughters of Abraham, those faithful saints who "do the works of Abraham" will, under the patriarchal order of marriage share in his blessings. To a degree, their exaltation fulfills Jehovah's promise to Abraham—for in producing children to their own glory, they parent some of the promised posterity of Abraham as well! Each is blessed in and glorified by the other.

[45]See Genesis 47:27.

[46]See Exodus 1:7; 12:37.

[47]See Exodus 32:13.

[48]Deuteronomy 28:62; See Jeremiah 30:19.

[49]Psalm 127:3-5.

210   The foregoing passages make it clear that the commandment to multiply and replenish the earth was made binding
on the race on both sides of the flood.[50] And although it
does not appear as such in the New Testament or in the
Book of Mormon, it is restated in the Doctrine and Covenants
where the Lord declares that wives are given to men:

> . . . to multiply and replenish the earth, according to my com-
> mandment, and to fulfill the promise which was given by my Father
> before the foundation of the world, and for their exaltation in the
> eternal worlds, that they may bear the souls of men; for herein is the
> work of my Father continued, that he may be glorified.[51]

This remarkable statement greatly enlarges upon the
stated reason for childbearing as found in biblical references.
It establishes a four-fold purpose for marriage and procreation: a) to fulfill the measure of the earth's creation by bringing upon it the spirit progeny of Man,[52] b) to fulfill the Father's
promise to his spirit offspring that those who kept their first
estate could be added upon with mortal bodies and thereby
be given an opportunity to obtain eternal life,[53] c) to enable
those who did, in fact, gain eternal life to join their Father in
his work and his glory by also bringing forth spirit offspring,
and d) to assure the continuation of the never-ending work
of God.[54]

The eternities are filled with literally countless numbers
of worlds similar to our own populated by other members of
the family of Man. Enoch did not exaggerate when he exclaimed to God:

> And were it possible that man could number the particles of the
> earth, yea, millions of earths like this, it would not be a beginning to

---

[50]Joseph F. Smith declared: "The commandment has never been changed, abrogated or annulled; but it has continued in force throughout all the generations of mankind." Juvenile Instructor, Vol. 37, p. 400, July 1, 1902. See also Joseph Fielding Smith, CR, Oct. 1965, p. 29.

[51]D&C 132:63.

[52]1 Nephi 17:36; D&C 49:15, 16.

[53]Abraham 3:22-26; See Titus 1:2.

[54]D&C 132:31.

the number of thy creations; and *thy curtains are stretched out still;* and yet thou art there, and thy bosom is there; and also thou art just; thou art merciful and kind forever; . . . .[55]

Moses, after being shown only this one planet and its inhabitants, was staggered by the immensity of it all and, exclaimed, "Now, for this cause I know that man is nothing, which thing I never had supposed."[56] But the Lord did not stop with this small earth, he proceeded to show Moses "many lands" together with their inhabitants and went on to explain that his creations could not be numbered by mortal man. Similar visions of the vastness of the divine creations were granted to Abraham who wrote, "I saw those things which his hands had made, which were many; and they multiplied before mine eyes, and I could not see the end thereof."[57] Modern astronomers with a far less powerful "telescope" than was enjoyed by Abraham also indicate that there is no discernible end to the universe. Finally, the Prophet Joseph Smith, in speaking of the Only Begotten, stated:

That by him, and through him, and of him, the worlds are and were created, and the inhabitants thereof are begotten sons and daughters unto God.[58]

What does it all mean? Simply this: God's work and glory is to give life—not to prevent or destroy it. He has no inclination to practice population control. It is alien to his spirit, being of the devil who deals in death, not life. "Man is that he might have joy."[59] Joy—happiness—is magnified only as man is magnified. Those saints who share the Father's commitment to life are pleased to join him in bringing it to the unborn. Because they do the works of Abraham, they are his sons and daughters. Their posterity will be as numerous as the stars that light the heavens and the sands that border the sea.

---

[55]Moses 7:30.
[56]Ibid. 1:10.
[57]Abraham 3:12.
[58]D&C 76:24.
[59]2 Nephi 2:25.

IX

The Prophets And The Problem

For of him unto whom much is given
much is required; and he who sins
against the greater light shall receive
the greater condemnation. D&C 82:3

Contraception and abortion are sweeping across the world like a plague out of the dark ages. More and more, they are becoming medically safe, legally permissible and socially acceptable. Abortion, which involves millions of women annually, includes everything from the destruction of the fertilized ovum to the outright termination of the life of the embryo or fetus. Indeed, some abortions are virtual infanticides. Church authorities have not hesitated to employ the term murder when denouncing such acts. President George Q. Cannon said the following in 1884:

God has gathered a few people out from the nations of the earth, out of Babylon. But shall they partake of these influences? I say to you, my sisters, you teach your daughters against this accursed practice, or they will go to hell, they will be damned, they will be murderers, and the blood of innocence will be found upon them. A man that would

214   sanction such a thing in his family, or that would live with a woman guilty of such acts, shares in the crime of murder. . . . Now just as sure as it is done, and people yield to it, so sure will they be damned, they will be damned with the deepest damnation; because it will be the damnation of shedding innocent blood, for which there is no forgiveness. . . .[1]

John Taylor was no less forthright in denouncing foeticide and infanticide:

The standing law of God is, be fruitful and multiply; but these reformers are "swift to shed blood," even the blood of innocence; and with their pre-natal murders and other crimes, are slaying their thousands and tens of thousands with impunity, to say nothing of that other loathsome, disgusting, filthy institution of modern Christendom "the social evil," as well as other infamous practices. We must protest against foeticide, infanticide, and other abominable practices of Christendom being forced upon us, either in the shape of legislative enactment, judicial decision or any other adjunct of so-called civilization.[2]

In a statement especially prepared for the Relief Society Magazine in 1916, Elder Joseph Fielding Smith viewed abortion and infanticide as twin evils!

Those who attempt to pervert the ways of the Lord, and to prevent their offspring from coming into the world in obedience to this great command, are guilty of one of the most heinous crimes in the category. There is no promise of eternal salvation and exaltation for such as they, for by their acts they prove their unworthiness for exaltation and unfitness for a kingdom where the crowning glory is the continuation of the family union and eternal increase which have been promised to all those who obey the law of the Lord. *It is just as much murder to destroy life before as it is after birth*, although man-made laws may not so consider it; but there is One who does take notice and his justice and judgment is sure.[3]

---

[1]JD 26:14, 15. He was a member of the First Presidency from 1880 to his death in 1901. His statement is representative of many made by Church authorities through the years. See JD 5:91; 22:302; 23:66, 230, 231, 238; 24:11; 25:315, 316, 353, 354; 26:15.

[2]JD 20:355.

[3]RSM 3:367, 368, July 1916. When asked for a written response to the statements of Elder Smith and four other authorities who wrote on birth control in this issue, the First Presidency responded: "We give our unqualified endorsement to these articles, including that of Elder Joseph F. Smith, Jr., and commend the sentiments contained therein to members and non-members of the Church of Jesus Christ of Latter-day Saints everywhere." *Ibid.*, Vol. IV., No. 2, February, 1917, p. 68.

Because life is at issue in both contraception and abor-   215
tion, any unjustified effort to destroy it partakes of the spirit
of murder—the unlawful ending of a human life.[4] The more
"human"—the more viable—that life, the more palpable is
the act of taking it. Hence, the wrong increases as it ranges
from contraception to embrycide, to foeticide, to outright
infanticide.

It would not be just to assume that every one who has
committed these offenses is equally culpable in the sight of
God. Doubtless many women have had abortions who, had
it not been for their false traditions and ignorance of divine
law, would never have done so. The deadly teachings of
false prophets have caused many otherwise decent women
to go against their own creative instincts.[5] Their sin ought
to be judged in the dim light of their backgrounds. While
those who "murdereth against the light and knowledge of
God" cannot be forgiven under the atonement of Christ,
those lacking such knowledge—being without law—may still
obtain mercy.[6] The best example in all scripture of this
principle is that of a group of savages who, after being
converted to Christ, obtained a hope of salvation in spite
of their many murders. Speaking of their conversion, their
leader, Anti-Nephi-Lehi, said:

And I also thank my God, yea, my great God, that he hath granted
unto us that we might repent of these things, and also that he hath forgiven us of those our many sins and murders which we have committed,
and taken away the guilt from our hearts, through the merits of his Son.[7]

---

[4]The Church has no official doctrine as to when the unborn spirit enters its earthly
tabernacle. Some have taught that this occurs at "quickening." (JD 18:258.) Others, basing
their argument on 3 Nephi 1:13, have suggested that the spirit enters the body at birth.
It is possible that different spirits claim their bodies at different times. Or the spirit may
come and go much as we might visit a home under construction before finally taking
possession of it. President J. Reuben Clark speculated that the mother's own spirit may
play a significant part in the formation of her unborn child's body.

[5]The wanton killing of animals is also a sin for which men will be held accountable. See I. V., Genesis 9:11; D&C 49:21.

[6]See Alma 39:6.

[7]See *Ibid.* 24:10.

216   We can but hope that God will be equally merciful to those repentant women who, in their ignorance and often under great pressure from their husbands, lovers or families, have ended the fragile beginnings of an unborn child.

Because the gravity of the offense must be measured by the aforementioned factors, the penalties for taking or preventing life cited by the Lord's servants range from "the deepest damnation" on the one extreme to "disappointment by and by" on the other. The punishment will fit the crime. It is all sin and no amount of pharisaic reasoning will make it otherwise. But, again, some sins are more grievous than others and there are degrees of guilt in perpetrating them. It is God's prerogative to determine the individual's standing before his law. He does not judge enmasse. Each will have his day in heaven's supreme court. Justice and mercy will present their briefs and the verdict rendered will be infinitely right, being based upon one's knowledge, works, opportunities, capacities, motives and intentions. No one will have either cause or inclination to file an appeal.

There is something of a mystery in Paul's declaration that women "shall be saved in child-bearing, if they continue in faith and charity and holiness with sobriety."[8] Motherhood seems to possess a special grace of its own which serves to somewhat idemnify a woman against the loss of salvation. George Q. Cannon maintained that because of her God-ordained dependence upon man "she is not held accountable to the *same* degree that men are."[9] Yet she is accountable *as a woman:*

I say to my sisters, you expect to receive exaltation in the presence of God. Will you obtain it if you do not bring your will into subjection to the will of God? No. Will you be cast off? If you do certain things, you will. But I think the women of this Church would have to do a

[8] 1 Timothy 2:15. Asked President Joseph F. Smith: "Can she be saved without child-bearing? She indeed takes an awful risk if she wilfully disregards what is a pronounced requirement of God. How shall she plead her innocence when she is not innocent? How shall she excuse her guilt when it is fastened upon her?" *Gospel Doctrine,* 7th ed., p. 289.

[9] JD 13:207.

great many bad things before their God would cast them off entirely. The Lord may feel after them, He will bring them through circumstances such as will eventually purify them. But no woman can enter into the celestial kingdom any more than a man whose will is in opposition to the will of God.[10]

We are judged in the context of our individual lives. Obviously, the Lord's requirements for women must differ somewhat from those for men to the extent that their natures, circumstances and callings differ. Only in recognizing these differences can God be truly just.

Birth Control

In spite of all that the prophets have said, there is still division and misunderstanding among the saints over the question of birth control. That it is widely practiced for purposes of "family planning" or "spacing" cannot be denied. Thus, it is apparent that some Latter-day Saints are being influenced by the thinking and conduct of the general society. As has happened so often before in the history of Israel's associations with the "Canaanites," the chosen people have come under the influence of their faithless neighbors. Times and attitudes change. In view of the permissive spirit of our day, the following by Susa Young Gates, then editor of the Relief Society Magazine, would strike many of this generation as being overly prim and naive:

> Do you give countenance, by word or by example, to the deadly evil of so-called birth control, or limitation of offspring? These are crucial tests in this wicked day and age, and unless our lovely and beloved daughters can meet the test fairly and triumphantly they are not yet ready to bear upon their shoulders the symbolic emblems of spiritual service so long and faithfully worn by the mothers of the passing generation.[11]

Unfortunately, some, being in sympathy with the mood of the times, are seeking Church approval in following the

---

[10]JD 22:126.
[11]Susa Young Gates, RSM, June, 1921, pp. 370-371.

218 world down the well-worn path of least resistance. There have always been those whose concern was not how they might do more, but how they could do less. Pointing out that the Gospel requires a willingness to forsake all earthly interests, John Taylor said:

> Now, this is where the hardship comes in and it also accounts for this eternal rubbing and bumping. "How much can't I do, and how little can I do to retain fellowship with the Church; and how much can I act selfishly and yet be counted a disciple of Christ?[12]

However, there are many who sincerely want to do what is right but who have been confused by the conflicting counsel on "family planning" which they have received. Unfortunately, modern Israel is yet to see eye-to-eye on every principle. Like the divided branch at Corinth, we are some of Paul, some of Cephas, some of Apollos and some of Christ.[13] This is inevitable when men ignore the teachings of the prophets and turn to their worldly disciplines for the answers to life's most important questions.[14]

Wrote Elder Orson F. Whitney:

> Birth control, under God's law, is a problem that solves itself. I have no faith in the sophisms of those who reject His law, and try to substitute therefor their own vain theories for sex regulation. The eugenists may mean well, but they don't know enough to lead the world out of the wilderness.[15]

Speaking of those who deliberately "practice devices" to keep their families small, President Joseph Fielding Smith said:

> Unfortunately this evil doctrine is being taught as a virtue by many people who consider themselves cultured and highly educated. It

---

[12]JD 21:57.

[13]See I Corinthians 1:11-13.

[14]Excellent summaries of the teachings of the modern prophets on this subject are available in the various compilations of their sermons and writings. Those of Presidents Joseph F. Smith (*Gospel Doctrine*), David O. McKay (*Gospel Ideals*), and Joseph Fielding Smith (*DS*, Vol. II) are especially valuable.

[15]Orson F. Whitney, RSM 3:367, July, 1916.

has even crept in among members of the Church and has been advocated in some of the classes within the Church. It should be understood definitely that this kind of doctrine is not only not advocated by the authorities of the Church, but also is condemned by them as wickedness in the sight of the Lord.[16]

While it is true that some statements have been made by certain authorities which seem to justify artificial birth control for family planning, the writer is unaware of a single direct statement from any of the presidents of the Church supporting such conduct. To the contrary, they have consistently opposed the use of contraceptives except where the physical or mental health of mother or child was threatened. This exception would not affect five percent of all women.

Still, some maintain that the Church has taken no position on the issue and that the statements of various general authorities are simply their own opinions. This is incorrect on both counts. An official statement signed by the First Presidency of the Church was issued April 14, 1969. Then too, the pronouncements of those sustained as prophets, seers and revelators are, by definition, "the mind and will of the Lord" when they are inspired by the Holy Ghost and are in harmony with the scriptures and the teachings of the living prophet. If no counsel is to be accepted until it is issued by the First Presidency, what is the purpose of having other prophets and apostles—or, for that matter, general conferences? But aside from the right of the authorities to declare the Lord's will on all established doctrines, there is another consideration: the Lord may permit a practice which he does not condone. As in the case of divorce, God may allow his people to do something because of the hardness of their hearts which is displeasing to him and which robs them of precious blessings. If the Lord were to authorize his servants to permit the use of alcohol and tobacco, alcohol and tobacco would still be harmful to the body. Likewise, artificial birth control is spiritually, if not physically,

---

[16]DS, 2:87.

220 harmful irrespective of the "stand" of the Church. It is intrinsically wrong.

The following statement by President Joseph F. Smith has been quoted with approval by many of the general authorities:

> I regret, I think it is *a crying evil,* that there should exist a sentiment or a feeling among any members of the Church to curtail the birth of their children. I think that is a crime wherever it occurs, where husband and wife are in possession of health and vigor and are free from impurities that would be entailed upon their posterity. I believe that where people undertake to curtail or prevent the birth of their children that they are going to *reap disappointment by and by.* I have no hesitancy in saying that I believe that this is one of the greatest crimes of the world today, this evil practice.[17]

The virtual incorporation of this statement into that of the First Presidency in 1969 is evidence of the unchanging unanimity of opinion of the highest authorities of the Church:

> We seriously regret that there should exist a sentiment or feeling among any members of the Church to curtail the birth of their children. We have been commanded to multiply and replenish the earth that we may have joy and rejoicing in our posterity.
>
> Where husband and wife enjoy health and vigor and are free from impurities that would be entailed upon their posterity, it is contrary to the teachings of the Church artificially to curtail or prevent the birth of children. We believe that those who practice birth control will reap disappointment by and by.
>
> However, we feel that men must be considerate of their wives who bear the greater responsibility not only of bearing children, but of caring for them through childhood. To this end the mother's health and strength should be conserved and the husband's consideration for his wife is his first duty, and self-control a dominant factor in all their relationships.
>
> It is our further feeling that married couples should seek inspiration and wisdom from the Lord that they may exercise discretion in solving their marital problems, and that they may be permitted to rear their children in accordance with the teachings of the gospel.[18]

---

[17]*Gospel Doctrine,* 7th ed., pp. 278, 279. See also CR, October, 1965, p. 29 and RSM 4:318.

[18]Letter of First Presidency (David O. McKay, Hugh B. Brown, N. Eldon Tanner) to mission, stake and ward leaders, April 14, 1969. See "Message of the First Presidency," CR, Oct. 3, 1942, p. 12.

A comparison of these declarations suggests that the truth   221
of the matter has been established in the mouth of two
prophetic witnesses speaking more than fifty years apart.

Although the normal woman is theoretically capable of
producing thirty or more children during her childbearing
years, nature and social custom combine to reduce the actual
number she will have to considerably less than half that figure. Also, the average varies from class to class and culture
to culture. The poor tend to have more children than the
rich, backward nations out perform the technologically advanced ones, etc. Broad averages are really quite misleading.
Then too, women are not equally blessed with the physical
endurance and emotional stability motherhood requires. Some
have large families with the seeming ease of the accomplished artist while others apparently lack the skill and temperament to properly care for even two or three children.
Only the Lord can accurately measure the varying capacities
of men and women; only he knows what we are really capable of doing. Sometimes our supposed limitations are due
more to the eradicable dross in our characters than to any
functional deficiencies. In other words, the weakness is much
more of the spirit than it is of the flesh. Still, there are
women who for various legitimate reasons must limit their
offspring.

Understanding this, the Lord's servants do not presume
to suggest, much less dictate, the number of children any
given woman should have. This decision can only be made
by the couple themselves. However, to guide the saints in
the implementation of that decision, the Lord's servants have
counseled modern Israel to rely upon self-control, periodic
continence and the processes of nature rather than resorting
to the easy, undemanding, spirit-stifling use of contraceptives.
In this way, and this way only, can the saints be a light to
the world in this matter.

Of course one might follow the counsel of the prophets
and still be recreant in their duty. The unwarranted prevention of life is indefensible no matter what method is em-

222 ployed. Then how many children should a Latter-day Saint couple have—assuming that the choice is theirs to make? Brigham Young's answer would be: "It is the duty of every righteous man and woman to prepare tabernacles *for all the spirits they can.* . . ."[19] He was not alone in this belief.

Elder Rudger Clawson:

> Woman is so constituted that, ordinarily, she is capable of bearing, during the years of her greatest strength and physical vigor, from eight to ten children, and in exceptional cases a larger number than that. The law of her nature so ordered it, and God's command, while it did not specify the exact number of children allotted to woman, simply implied that she should exercise the sacred power of procreation to its utmost limit.[20]

Elder George F. Richards:

> My wife has borne to me fifteen children. Anything short of this would have been less than her duty and privilege. Had we received and obeyed the doctrine of three or four children to the home, we would have cut ourselves short of blessings more valuable to us than all the wealth of this world would be, were it ours. We might never have known in this life what our loss had been, but it would have been just as great as we now see it, and sometime we would know as we now know. Then consider the joy and value of life to others. What of our eleven children born to us in excess of the four to which such as these magazine writers would limit us? Can the value of such a mission and service be estimated? Will not these our children and their husbands, wives and children, for generations after us, if they are duly appreciative, rise up and call us blessed forever and ever?[21]

Elder Orson F. Whitney:

> I believe in large families, though I am aware, of course, that it is easier to feed, clothe, educate and rear a few children than many. But these considerations, so conclusive to some minds, have never had weight with me, contemplating as I do the eternal rather than the mere earthly phases of marriage and procreation.[22]

---

[19]JD 4:56.
[20]Rudger Clawson, RSM 3:364, July, 1916.
[21]George F. Richards, *Ibid.*, p. 365.
[22]Orson F. Whitney, *Ibid.*, p. 367.

Bishop David A. Smith:

I bear testimony of God's mercy to me. I was married in my youth and started with nothing but enough furniture to comfortably fill two little rooms which were rented, and with an income of $30 a month. I may belong to the poor and ignorant class, but I am grateful to Him to whom we must all look for final judgment, for His mercies, for my father, his family, and for the wife and nine children the Lord has given me.[23]

Elder Melvin J. Ballard:

May none of the mothers of this Church slight nor neglect those anxious ones, but open the door and give to those worthy sons and daughters of our Father the glorious privilege of coming to earth to obtain glory, honor, blessing, immortality, and eternal life in the presence of the Father, with the sanctified and the redeemed. Let not the mothers of the present nor those of the future, be swerved from the right path by any environment or circumstance that seems to mitigate against the performance of this duty. Let not poverty bar the way, for if poverty had been a consideration on the part of the mothers of the past, many of us would not be here.[24]

The ideal is one thing, man's ability to attain it another. Married couples must decide for themselves how close to that ideal they are willing and able to come. In doing so, they should call forth all of the faith and the integrity at their command. And whatever the decision, husband and wife should make it together, they should be united in it. Division on family size can lead to serious marital difficulties. It is unwise for the wife to attempt to carry the admitted burdens of motherhood without the support of her husband. She needs his cooperation and is entitled to it. If he will not give it, the responsibility for the consequences will largely be his.[25] She should not act in defiance of her husband's will in a matter which so clearly calls for mutual commitment and support.

---

[23]David A. Smith, *Ibid.*, p. 435.

[24]Hinckley, *op. cit.*, pp. 207, 208.

[25]Elder David O. McKay wrote: "Man, not woman, is the chief cause of this evil of race suicide now sweeping like a blight through the civilized nations." RSM 3:367, July, 1916.

224 However, it is as unjust for a man to deny his wife children as it would be for her to deny him the right to a vocation or to honor his duties in the priesthood. The husband who dams his wife's desire for children dams himself. He cannot be true to his calling as a son of Abraham if he denies her right to be true to her calling as a daughter of Sarah. Marriage is meant to fulfill the natures and callings of men and women, not frustrate them. Such men run the grave danger of having the "talent" taken from them as well as seeing their faithful wives given to those who have respected the unalienable right of women to have the children they desire. Every gift the Lord bestows upon us is given conditionally until we demonstrate our appreciation of it. Only then can we claim it for our own. In connection with the above masculine failing is that of castigating one's wife—or co-partner—for conceiving. Such an infantile attitude is contemptible. The burden of responsibility for the act and its consequences must be borne by both parties to it unless some form of coercion was involved.

Why Birth Control Is Practiced

Why do men and women trample the gift of parenthood under their feet? There are many reasons. Selfishness is the one most frequently cited by the prophets. This human failing is so obvious and so far-ranging in its effects on the attitudes and conduct of men and women as to make elaboration at this point unnecessary. The writer is convinced that many Latter-day Saints could and would surmount this weakness were it not for another factor: lack of understanding. Conflicting voices at almost all levels of Mormon society have given the trumpet of truth an uncertain sound. "What is right? Who are we to believe?" Such are the questions many youth are asking of their teachers and leaders today. Certainly, they cannot "govern themselves" if the "correct principles" they are taught are contradictory.

Then too, the world at large and a surprisingly large

number of those in the Church simply do not grasp their part in the great plan of salvation. Their vision is myopic when it comes to seeing beyond this brief segment of eternal time. Because their understanding is limited, their feelings are contracted and their commitments are less than total. Not all of those in the Church who are aware of the doctrinal arguments against birth control have a personal testimony of those arguments. Having ears, they hear not. The truth has not been internalized in them; it hovers above their hearts in the summits of the mind. Reason enables us to know, in part, *about* the truth, but it can never provide us *with* the truth. We cannot know any principle we do not live. As Moroni observed: "ye receive no witness until after the trial of your faith."[26] In the doing is the knowing.

Some practice birth control because they have been taught that it is wrong or unseemly to have large families. They fear man rather than God. The taunts of those who dwell in the large and spacious building of Lehi's vision are too much for them.[27] Others fear the unknown, forgetting that it does not exist for God. If, with his knowledge of the future, the Father is not afraid to send his children into this world, and they are not afraid to come, why should we fear? He fully understands that many will be born under less than optimum conditions.

Many a pioneer woman brought forth only to bury the infant somewhere along the trail west of Nauvoo. If ever women had the right to avoid childbearing, it would seem to have been those stalwart souls. Yet they did not falter. They endured what had to be endured, trusting that the important thing was not that their little ones had died, but that they had lived. Real tragedy does not lie in death, but in the denial of life. Notwithstanding its pain to the living, the Prophet Joseph Smith considered early death something of a blessing.

---

[26]Ether 12:6.
[27]I Nephi 8:26-28.

226

The Lord takes many away, even in infancy, that they may escape the envy of man, and the sorrows and evils of this present world; they were too pure, too lovely, to live on earth; therefore, if rightly considered, instead of mourning we have reason to rejoice as they are delivered from evil, and we shall soon have them again. . . . All children are redeemed by the blood of Jesus Christ, and the moment that children leave this world, they are taken to the bosom of Abraham. The only difference between the old and young dying is, one lives longer in heaven and eternal light and glory than the other, and is freed a little sooner from this miserable wicked world. Notwithstanding all this glory, we for a moment lose sight of it, and mourn the loss, but we do not mourn as those without hope.[28]

The terrible conditions under which millions of spirits enter mortality strongly suggests that they consider no circumstance too hard, no suffering too great if only they can claim a physical body and, thereby, assure themselves of that fulness of joy made possible by the resurrection.[29] Spirits will take any body.

The spirits which are reserved have to be born into the world, and the Lord will prepare some way for them to have tabernacles. Spirits must be born, even if they have to come to brothels for their fleshly coverings, and many of them will take the lowest and meanest spirit house that there is in the world, rather than do without, and will say, "Let me have a tabernacle, that I may have a chance to be perfected."[30]

Barriers

Apart from parenthood, marriage has no eternal validity. In other words, marriage is not warranted in the life to come if its benefits are limited to husband and wife. It must serve others as well; it must be productive of life. When it is not, it loses its essential reason for being. Pre-marital relations and the unwarranted use of contraceptives in marriage have two things in common: both are self-serving and both are offensive to God. When the seed of life is illicitly planted

---

[28]*TJS*, pp. 196, 197. See JD 25:375.
[29]D&C 93:33.
[30]Brigham Young, JD 3:264.

or unjustifiably destroyed, the union is despiritualized, God is shut out and the act is stripped of its sanctity. We cannot tamper with the fountain of life without offending its Source. In writing of those who favored small families, Elder David O. McKay said:

> Such parents may be sincere, even if misguided; but in most cases the desire not to have children has its birth in vanity, passion and selfishness. Such feelings are the seeds sown in early married life that produce a harvest of discord, suspicion, estrangement, and divorce. All such efforts, too, often tend to put the marriage relationship on a level with the panderer and the courtesan. They befoul the pure fountains of life with the slime of indulgence and sensuality. Such misguided couples are ever seeking but *never finding the reality for which the heart is yearning.*[31]

Men and women are permitted the privilege of sexual fulfillment because they are willing to accept its concommitant responsibilities. President J. Reuben Clark has said:

> As to sex in marriage, the necessary treatise on that for Latter-day Saints can be written in two sentences: Remember the prime purpose of sex desire is to beget children. Sex gratification must be had at that hazard. You husbands: be kind and considerate of your wives. They are not your property; they are not mere conveniences; they are your partners for time and eternity.[32]

That conjugal rights cannot be separated from conjugal responsibilities including due respect for a wife's autonomy over her own body is further attested to by President David O. McKay:

> . . . Let us instruct young people who come to us, first, young men throughout the Church, to know that a woman should be queen of her own body. The marriage covenant does not give the man the right to enslave her, or to abuse her, or to use her merely for the gratification of his passion. Your marriage ceremony does not give you that right.[33]

---

[31]RSM 3:366, July, 1916.
[32]CR, October, 1949, pp. 194, 195.
[33]CR, April, 1952, pp. 86, 87, See JD 26:314.

228   He also declared: "In the realm of wifehood, the woman should reign supreme."[34]

The Lord is a harvester of life. Contraception permits us to sow without reaping.[35] This violates the principle of justice. The use of contraceptives has been specifically denounced by Church authorities on many occasions. The following are representative statements. Wrote John A. Widtsoe:

> Birth control as generally understood implies the use of physical or chemical means to prevent conception. A large number of these devices, known as contraceptives, are on the market. None of them is certain to accomplish the purpose desired. Besides, any contraceptive is unnatural and interferes in one way or another with the physiological processes of life. All of them are in varying degrees injurious to those who use them, especially to women. That may be safely contended. The ill effects may not be felt at once, but in time will overtake the parents to their detriment.[36]

From President David O. McKay:

> Seeking the pleasures of conjugality without a willingness to assume the responsibilities of rearing a family is one of the onslaughts that now batter at the structure of the American home. Intelligence and mutual consideration should be ever-present factors in determining the coming of children to the household. When the husband and wife are healthy, and free from inherited weaknesses and disease that might be transplanted with injury to their offspring, the use of contraceptives is to be condemned.[37]

From President Joseph Fielding Smith:

> I regret that so many young couples are thinking today more of successful contraceptives than of having a posterity. They will have to answer for their sin when the proper time comes and actually may be denied the glorious celestial kingdom.[38]

---

[34]RSM, 3:367, July, 1916.

[35]Harry Emerson Fosdick called this "psychological theft."

[36]John A. Widtsoe, *Evidences and Reconciliations*, Bookcraft, Salt Lake City, Utah, 1943, Chpt. 9 "Marriage and the Family," p. 247.

[37]CR, Oct., 1943, p. 30.

[38]CR, Oct. 1, 1965, p. 29.

The use of contraceptives cannot help but detract from   229
the sacredness of the relationship.

Prevention, both by mechanical and chemical means endangers the health of women who indulge it, impairs vitality, shatters nervous energy and deteriorates the race. The moral effect of such methods of living is nothing less than disastrous. It brutalizes and makes a shame of sexual pleasure itself, and kills the sentiment of love which alone refines the act to endearment. It ministers to the gross desire for sexual promiscuity; for with a felt security, through knowledge of a preventative nature, from consequences that would expose infidelities to the marriage covenant, temptations to fornications and adulteries are greatly multiplied, and the moral tone of a community greatly lowered if not destroyed.[39]

The possibility of subtle character modifications was also recognized by Elder Widtsoe:

Moreover, since birth control roots in a species of selfishness, the spiritual life of the user of contraceptives is also weakened. Women seem to become more masculine in thought and action; men more callous and reserved; both husband and wife become more careless of each other, and increasingly indifferent to the higher duties and joys of living.[40]

Thus the practice may be both a cause and an effect of psychological or spiritual barriers between husband and wife. Some couples who remain together for reasons other than mutual devotion do not want any tangible tie to bind them together. Not really caring for one another, they avoid the ultimate testimony of married love—a child. Many an unwanted child has suffered severe emotional damage in being rejected by one or both parents who viewed it as a living reminder of the despised mate.

On the other hand, there may not be any deep-seated antipathy between husband and wife, they may be simply bored with each other and, therefore, reluctant to further cement the marriage with a child. Needless to say, boredom

---

[39]Elder B. H. Roberts *The Improvement Era,* 31:184, January, 1928. Entire article merits careful study.

[40]Widtsoe, *op. cit.,* p. 248.

230   is the sure sign of a dying—if not dead—romance. Love and boredom are as antithetical as faith and doubt. The practice of contraception is increasing along with the rise in marital disharmony, desertion, separation, and divorce. While a causal relationship is yet to be established for these facts, it appears that those marriages in which the risk of unwanted children has been all but eliminated via contraception and/or abortion are characterized by instability.

> The principal reason for marriage is to rear a family. Failure to do so is one of the conditions that causes love to wilt and eventually to die.[41]

A marriage is no stronger than the spiritual, emotional, and physical ties which bind it together. As society cuts and eliminates more and more of these ties, we can anticipate a steady decline in the duration and quality of more and more marriages.

Something precious is lost when a couple build a contraceptive wall between themselves. The act becomes a contradiction. For how can the ultimate expression of marital love be damned at the very moment of its consummation? Indeed, in its completeness, consummation is not a thing of the moment—it is eternal. Only when an immortal soul lies in its mother's arms has there been a perfect consummation. It is the willingness of husband and wife to allow for this possibility which hallows the act.[42]

When the pure love of Christ flows between a man and his wife who somewhat understand the mystery of "one flesh," they do not want any walls, any barriers to stand between them.[43] They desire complete consummation. Anything,

---

[41]David O. McKay, CR, October, 1943, p. 31.

[42]The sexual relationship is justified even though the wife is past the childbearing years or the couple are incapable of having children. We are judged not only by what we do, but also by what we would do if circumstances permitted. As King Benjamin explained, when the needy come to us for succor we should say *in our hearts:* "I give not because I have not, but if I had I would give." Mosiah 4:24. The Lord intended that women should rest from the labors of childbirth. In doing so, they are not expected to dam their emotional needs.

[43]See Ephesians 5:31-33.

whether tangible or intangible, whether of the mind or of the body which might frustrate that goal is cast aside. They consider their full acceptance of both the privileges and the responsibilities of their union to be an act of faith and, therefore, an act of love. Such love leaps walls. It risks. It does not doubt. It does not fear. Indeed, it *wants* to prove itself by the sacrifices it is willing to make and the uncertainties it is prepared to face.

The Spirit of Restraint

If the law of Christ was less demanding, it would be more popular with the masses. But this cannot be, its function is to make saints of natural men and women. This process involves sacrifice and self-denial. The metaphor Jesus employed in making this point was the cross.

If any man will come after me, let him deny himself, and take up his cross and follow me. And now for a man to take up his cross, is to deny himself all ungodliness, and every worldly lust, and keep my commandments. Break not my commandments for to save your lifes; for whosoever will save his life in this world, shall lose it in the world to come.[44]

The issue is ever the same: man's will versus the will of the Lord. Practicing self-denial is not the natural thing to do. The natural thing is to cater to one's appetites and passions. The saint must consciously resist that propensity. Keeping the commandments thus becomes a trial of the will. We must rule all *things*, not be ruled by them. Said Brigham Young:

You cannot inherit eternal life, unless your appetites are brought in subjection to the spirit that lives within you, the spirit which our Father in heaven gave. I mean the Father of your spirits, of those spirits which he has put into these tabernacles. The tabernacle must be brought into subjection to the spirit perfectly, or your bodies cannot be raised to inherit eternal life; if they do come forth, they must dwell in a lower

---

[44]I.V., Matthew 16:25-27.

232 kingdom. Seek diligently, until you bring all in subjection to the law of Christ.[45]

The sex drive must be controlled by the will of the spirit as much as wealth, power, or any other thing. Being married no more justifies unrestrained sexual activity than being rich justifies extravagance. Indeed, our ability to control the rights, privileges, and means we enjoy is at the very crux of the issue of salvation. Temperance is as essential in the marital relationship as it is in any other phase of life. Marriage, too, has its proper bounds and limitations.

While it is true that we poor mortals are weak, it is not the Lord's intention that we should remain so or that we should use our weaknesses as an excuse for living beneath our divine potential. Consider these words of the Lord to Moroni:

I give unto men weakness that they may be humble; and my grace is sufficient for all men that humble themselves before me; for if they humble themselves before me, and have faith in me, then will I make weak things become strong unto them.[46]

Who can doubt this? No man or woman has achieved sanctification without the strengthening arm of the Almighty.

When Paul besought the Lord to deliver him from what was apparently a physical weakness of some kind, he was told: "My grace is sufficient for thee; for my strength is made perfect in weakness."[47] The humble apostle accepted his "thorn" and, apparently carried it to the grave—not with moanings and groanings, but triumphantly:

Most gladly therefore will I rather glory in my infirmities, that the power of Christ may rest upon me. Therefore I take pleasure in infirmities, in reproaches, in necessities, in persecutions, in distresses for Christ's sake: for when I am weak, then am I strong.[48]

---

[45]Quoted by David O. McKay, CR, April 6, 1947, p. 120.
[46]Ether 12:27.
[47]2 Corinthians 12:9.
[48]Ibid., 12:9, 10.

The Savior promised the Twelve that he would not for-   **233**
sake them. He knows that we cannot live the divine ideal
without his support. Indeed, lacking it, every commandment
may seem a "thorn in the flesh" to someone. The Master
has not left his own either comfortless or powerless. If, to
use Paul's metaphor, Christ is formed in us via the sanctifying influence of the Holy Ghost, we are endowed with the
same spiritual power which enabled Jesus to overcome the
world, the flesh, and the devil.[49] Nephi observed: "the Lord
giveth no commandments unto the children of men, save
he shall prepare a way for them that they may accomplish
the thing which he commandeth them."[50] This includes the
commandment to multiply and replenish the earth. With
God's help we can do what we ought to do. The world is
forced to go its own way because the Lord's way is an impossible way without his sustaining power. That power can
be ours if we are not of little faith.

> Gospel doctrine should make every Latter-day Saint married couple
> eager for the privilege and obligations of parenthood. And they should
> have the faith and trust that the Lord will provide the means for obeying
> his law.[51]

It is often argued that the more a couple love one another, the more difficult it is to avoid sexual intimacy. If
this is true, there must be a great deal of love in our sex
obsessed world today! However, the converse is the case:
sex is most imperative when love is least present. Physical
intimacy has become a substitute for genuine devotion. The
rampant hedonism of our day is both a cause and a result of
the withdrawal of the Spirit of God from the world. As it
diminishes, men and women will inevitably look more and
more to the physical order for comfort and satisfaction. Since
the spirit and the body are the soul of man, when the spirit
is stifled and its needs denied, the flesh will assume domi-

---

[49]Galatians 4:19; John 15:1-8.
[50]1 Nephi 3:7.
[51]Widtsoe, *op. cit.*, p. 251.

234   nance. This condition is analogous to that of the person who, in losing his sight, concentrates on improving his ability to touch, hear, and smell. Knowing this, Satan tries to push us to one extreme or the other: fanatical asceticism or blatant animality. Yes, we will cling to something—if not love, then lust, if not spirit, then flesh, if not God, then the devil.

Will power is really spirit power. Our ability to govern ourselves in righteousness is equal to the degree of mastery which the spirit enjoys over its earthly tabernacle. The more strength and nourishment the spirit receives from the Spirit of the Lord, the greater our will power. Jesus was able to overcome every temptation because he was filled with the Spirit. We previously noted that since God is love, the Spirit of God is the spirit of love. Therefore, in receiving the Spirit, we are also receiving the pure love of Christ. This love not only motivates those possessing it to keep the commandment to multiply, it also enables them to exercise self-control in doing so. Therefore, the husband who loves his wife with the pure love of Christ will never impose himself on her. Their relations will be by mutual consent and with regard for her health and well-being.

Since the natural consequences of intercourse are more immediate and more lasting for the wife than for her husband, it is for her to decide when she is prepared to accept them. There is a due time for everything; only she can know when the time to bear a child has come. When it is born, she should be allowed an adequate period to renew her body and regain her strength before relations are resumed and before entering upon another pregnancy. Said Elder Orson F. Whitney:

> During certain periods—those of gestation and lactation—the wife and mother should be comparatively free to give her strength to her offspring; and if this involves some self-denial on the part of the husband and father, so much the better for all concerned.[52]

---

[52]RSM 3:367, July 1916. See JD 13:207, 208.

Both husband and wife must exercise self-control if 235
this is to be done without recourse to some form of contraception other than that provided by the menstrual cycle. This
may appear unfair to those women who are subject to ir-
regular cycles. However, the admitted inequities of nature's
method of birth control are, presumably, to be borne along
with all of the rest of life's inequities until a better day
comes. In all likelihood, menstrual irregularities were unknown in the beginning and came about over a period of
time through the violation of God's laws of health and
hygiene. If so, the sins of the mothers of past ages have been
visited on their daughters living today. But again, are we to
free ourselves of the natural consequences of the race's past
sins by resorting to new sins? Or is there a better way?
Paul's way was to go to the Lord with his weakness and obtain the strength to transcend it.

One reason many are called and few are chosen is that
they fail the test—which is to live celestial principles in a
telestial setting. Insofar as circumstances permit, we are
expected to do the eternally *natural* thing under *unnatural*
conditions. Just as a kite rises only as it is pulled against
the wind, so do we achieve the end for which the commandments are but the means, only by resisting the path
of least resistance—the way of the world. However, we can
take heart from the fact that those things which call for
sacrifice and sheer grit in mortality will be accomplished with
ease and unmitigated joy in eternity. But first we must
demonstrate our love of righteousness by practicing it in
adversity. Doing the easy and the convenient thing proves
nothing, for it does not call for effort, self-denial or any
strength beyond our own. Only after we have been tried
successfully in the refining fires of human weakness and
worldly opposition can we abide the eternal burnings of
celestial glory—for "our God is a consuming fire."[53]

---

[53]Hebrews 11:29; See TJS, pp. 347, 367.

236   **A Missionary Calling**

As mortals, we stand at a junction of eternity. As Latter-day Saints, we can do the seemingly impossible: we can simultaneously travel the three main highways forming that junction—the way of the living, the way of the dead, and the way of the unborn. We travel the highway of the living when we take the Gospel of Jesus Christ to the nations and gather the scattered sheep of Israel into the fold of the Church and kingdom on earth. We travel the highway of the dead when we search out their records and perform the ordinances necessary for their salvation. And we travel the highway of the unborn when we bring them into our families where they can be raised in the nurture and admonition of the Lord. This enables us to practice prevention rather than cure, for we gather some of the Father's choice sons and daughters into the kingdom *before* they are lost and scattered among the nations. President Brigham Young taught:

> . . . there are multitudes of pure and holy spirits waiting to take tabernacles, now what is our duty?—to prepare tabernacles for them; to take a course that will not tend to drive those spirits into the families of the wicked, where they will be trained in wickedness, debauchery, and every species of crime. It is the duty of every righteous man and woman to prepare tabernacles for all the spirits they can. . . .[54]

The same view was expressed by President Wilford Woodruff:

> Another word of the Lord to me is that, it is the duty of these young men here in the land of Zion to take the daughters of Zion to wife, and prepare tabernacles for the spirits of men, which are the children of our Father in heaven. They are waiting for tabernacles, they are ordained to come here, and they ought to be born in the land of Zion instead of Babylon.[55]

---

[54]JD 4:56.

[55]Wilford Woodruff. JD 18:129. See *Evidences and Reconciliations*, p. 251.

And by President Joseph Fielding Smith:

If these iniquitous practices find their place in our hearts and we are guilty, then when we arrive on the other side—and discover that we have deprived ourselves of eternal blessings and are accused by those who were assigned to come to us, because, as President Young has said, they were forced to take bodies in the families of the wicked— how will we feel? Moreover, *may we not lose our own salvation if we violate this divine law?*[56]

The situation of the unborn is comparable to that of passengers on a sinking ship. The more souls a rescue vessel can find, the fewer will drown or be left adrift in lifeboats or forced to cling to flotsam in the cold and deadly waters of the open sea. It is the failure to really *hear* the testimonies of the modern prophets that causes some to be remiss in having more children. But those saints blessed with spiritual acuity will bring as many souls aboard the good ship Zion as they possibly can. They will eagerly "throw out the life line."

Doing so is another way of fulfilling the admonition of Brigham Young as reemphasized by President David O. McKay: "Every member a missionary." What better way to honor that charge than to assure the unborn of a safe and righteous harbor upon their earthly landfall. It is written that great shall be our joy if we save one soul in the kingdom of God. Would not that joy be even greater if that soul were our own child? On the other hand, what sorrow we will know if that soul comes unto its own and its own receives it not!

Now I wish to ask a question: How will a young married couple feel when they come to the judgment and then discover that there were certain spirits assigned to them and they refused to have them? Moreover, what will be their punishment when they discover that they have failed to keep a solemn covenant and spirits awaiting this mortal life were forced to come here elsewhere when they were assigned to this particular couple.[57]

---

[56]DS 2:88. Italcs original
[57]Joseph Fielding Smith, *CR*, Oct. 1965, p. 29.

238   Those who come to understand something of the love
that is in God and who share in its selfless wonder, can no
more resist its will than they can live apart from its source.
Like Enoch, whose heart under the influence of the Holy
Spirit "swelled wide as eternity," they will suffer the little
children to come unto them as often and as long as human
circumstances guided by the intelligence of heaven will
permit.

President Stephen L. Richards in a sensitive and pene-
trating observation said:

> To warn of a great danger I must speak of it more specifically.
> I do so most reverently. If it shall please the Lord to send to your
> home a goodly number of children, I hope, I pray, you will not deny
> them entrance. If you should, it would cause you infinite sorrow and
> remorse. One has said that he could wish his worst enemy no more
> hell than this, that in the life to come someone might approach him
> and say, "I might have come down into the land of America and
> done good beyond computation, but if I came at all I had to come
> through your home and you were not man enough or woman enough
> to receive me. You broke down the frail footway on which I must
> cross and then you thought you had done a clever thing."[58]

Some feel that their deepest hurts were inflicted by the
children they brought into the world, and no one can deny
that many parents have suffered profound disappointments in
this regard. However, no matter how painful such wounds,
they are only mortal and will pass away with every other
mortal thing. Life is meant to be bitter-sweet. Those who
attempt to have it otherwise, will find its ending the bitterest
of all. Contrasting the faithless with those who bring forth
unto God, Bishop David A. Smith wrote:

> For as the first grow more selfish and more covetous, which often
> causes the severing of the marriage bond or the entering into it for the
> mere sake of form, the latter class become more self-sacrificing, their
> hearts become more tender, and they possess a greater love and sympathy
> for the children of God. Their lives are not void with emptiness for they

---

[58]Stephen L. Richards, *CR*, Oct., 1941, p. 108. See *CR*, Oct., 1942, p. 12 and Oct.,
1951, pp. 112, 113.

are living for others. Their lives are filled with joy and happiness, for they know that they are trying to fulfill the purpose of their creation. Their sorrows are not the sorrows filled with bitterness, but sorrows which tend to mellow them in the eyes of God.[59]

Lasting sorrow does not stem from the acts of others, but from our failings toward ourselves. The saddest words of tongue or pen pertain to those things that might have eternally been. No, it is not the children parents received that will forever cause them pain—it is the missing child who waited for a claiming that never came.

Blessed is the man and blessed is the woman to whom no sin is imputed in the marriage relation, but who carefully observe the law of their natures, and keep the commandments of God. To them the future will bring no regrets, and they will not be troubled by an accusing conscience or keen and abiding anguish of the soul.[60]

Conclusion

Elder John A. Widtsoe wrote: "As a rule, women who have large families are healthy throughout life . . . Large families are the most genuinely happy. That is the verdict of human experience."[61] The writer, whose mother bore ten children, fully concurs. While statistical proof may not be available on this point, there is certainly no real evidence to the contrary. No one can seriously suggest that the smaller the family, the happier, the less lonely, and the less selfish the child.

Those who are endowed with a patriarchal or matriarchal spirit need children. George Reynolds was the father of thirty-two children by three wives. At the death of his first child at sixteen months, he wrote: "Home seems very lonely without a baby."[62] We need each other. The universe is vast and awesome. How cold and forbidding it would be

---

[59]RSM 3:435, Aug. 1916.
[60]Elder Rudger Clawson, RSM, 3:364, July, 1916.
[61]Widtsoe, op. cit., pp. 246, 248.
[62]Journal of George Reynolds, Vol. IV, p. 264.

240   without friends and loved ones. And life is uncertain. Death may thin the shallow ranks of the small family and leave the parents "without the ministrations of loved ones to smooth their pathway down to the grave."[63]

While "man proposes, God disposes." Those who wish to pre-determine the time and number of their offspring are assuming several things: a) that they will not be separated by death or other circumstances, b) that they can conceive a child any time they choose to do so, c) that their children will not fall victim to disease or accidental death and, d) that God will always be willing to send them one of his children. These assumptions are not warranted by the nature of mortality. The creation of life is essentially a spiritual enterprise. It is for the flesh to be submissive to the spirit, not the spirit to the flesh.

I know it is supposed by some that the power of increase is inherent in us and in all living things, and in all plants, but I do not view it in that light. I view the temporal organism as the instrument and not the creator itself; it is only the instrument by which it is worked out and accomplished; that the principle of life and eternal increase pertains not to the flesh nor to the grosser elements of this earth, but it is the spiritual power that has emanated from a nobler sphere that has come out from God, or that had its exitence previously in a first estate.[64]

The Old Testament notion that God could cause a woman to be barren is considered a naivete by our sophisticated generation. Those who tempt the Lord by expecting him to wait upon their convenience may find that their ancient fathers and mothers were not so naive after all. More than one couple who delayed having a family has learned, to their bitter regret, that they delayed too long. Now, they would give all that they have, all that has crowded life out of their lives, in exchange for one child they could call their own.

---

[63]Rudger Clawson, RSM, 3:364, July, 1916.
[64]Erastus Snow, JD 26:218.

Melvin J. Ballard, who was the youngest of eleven chil- **241**
dren born to a mother whose sacrifices for her family won
her their undying gratitude, declared:

> . . . All the honor and glory that can come to men or women by
> the development of their talents, the homage and the praise they may
> receive from an applauding world, worshipping at their shrine of genius,
> is but a dim thing whose luster shall fade in comparison to the high
> honor, the eternal glory, the ever-enduring happiness that shall come to
> the woman who fulfills the first great duty and mission that devolves
> upon her to become the mother of the sons and daughters of God.[65]

When this brief day draws to its close and we take a
parting look at our material wealth, our honors, our worldly
pleasures and successes—at all those things that once mat-
tered so very much—we will find them mute and unfeeling
at our passing. For the most part, one's demise provokes
little more than a comment at someone's breakfast table. It
remains for those dearest to us to truly lament our passing.
Only they can preserve our name and our presence in the
land. Only they will continue to care long after we have
vanished from their sight. Children are the work and the glory
of the Saints—their immortality and eternal life.

> The Lord has told us that it is the duty of every husband and
> wife to obey the command given to Adam to multiply and replenish
> the earth, so that the legions of choice spirits waiting for their taber-
> nacles of flesh may come here and move forward under God's great
> design to become perfect souls, for without these fleshly tabernacles
> they cannot progress to their God-planned destiny. Thus, every husband
> and wife should become a father and mother in Israel to children born
> under the holy, eternal covenant.
>
> By bringing these choice spirits to earth, each father and each
> mother assume towards the tabernacled spirit and towards the Lord him-
> self by having taken advantage of the opportunity He offered, an obliga-
> tion of the most sacred kind, because the fate of that spirit in the
> eternities to come, the blessings or punishments which shall await it in
> the hereafter, depend, in great part, upon the care, the teachings, the
> training which the parents shall give to that spirit.

---

[65]Hinckley, *op. cit.*, pp. 203-204.

No parent can escape that obligation and that responsibility, and for the proper meeting thereof, the Lord will hold us to a strict accountability. No loftier duty than this can be assumed by mortals.[66]

[66]The First Presidency, CR, October 3, 1942, p. 12. (Heber J. Grant, J. Reuben Clark, Jr., David O. McKay)

X

A House Divided

And if a house be divided against itself, that house cannot stand.
Mark 3:25.

When a marriage begins with great expectations, the failure to realize them is a matter of keen disappointment. It could not be otherwise. Joy and sorrow have a common origin. The home is potentially the source of our greatest happiness and, therefore, our greatest pain. A soul-satisfying home life bespeaks an inner peace with God and man. The strength derived therefrom enables one to face the world with confidence and equanimity. We can labor with serenity in hell itself if only we can return to heaven at the end of the day. Home should be that heaven. Indeed, the glory of one's home is prophetic of the glory of one's heaven in the life to come.

Here is where heaven must have its beginning—where its foundation must be laid, not only for our present happiness, but for its eternal

244   perpetuity. . . . Seek to make your heaven in your home; seek to develop its perfections there; seek to develop its truthfulness there. Why? Simply because you cannot make it anywhere else. It is not possible, because home is the nursery where all the constituent principles of heavenly bliss and glory are to be developed. Why, then, think of finding them in your wanderings over the face of the earth, when home is the only place where they are to be found, and where they must be developed.[1]

When those principles are developed, all else is placed in right perspective. For the home is the center of life, not something peripheral to it. All that we do and are outside of it is secondary in importance to what we do and are within its gates. For this reason, "No other success can compensate for failure in the home."[2] When this failure becomes excessive, familial antagonisms and dissensions erupt into outright warfare. Too often the end result is not repentance and peace but family disorganization via desertion, separation or divorce.

In spite of the great amount of time and energy expended on research into the causes of marital failure, very few of the presumed experts in the field ever get beyond the primary and secondary symptoms associated with the failure. Economic problems, sexual incompatibility, cultural and religious differences, emotional and social immaturity, etc., etc.—all of which describe without explaining—are commonly cited as causes of divorce and family breakdown. However, the ultimate cause lies beneath and beyond them all in the very heart, the immortal nature of the individual himself. As well might we argue that the reason a ship ran aground and sank with all hands was because the helmsman got drunk in order to blot out bad news from home as to argue that the popular "causes" of marital disharmony are in fact, the inevitable causes. While one man might do as the distraught helmsman did, another would not have so reacted. It was *the man*, not the provocation, that was to blame. God wills that man should act upon things and that things should be acted upon.[3]

---

[1] Amasa Lyman, JD 7:343, 345.
[2] President David O. McKay, CR, April 4, 1964, p. 5.
[3] See 2 Nephi 2:26; Helaman 14:30.

We are meant to rule circumstances; circumstances   245
should not rule us. As Cassius observed, "The fault, dear
Brutus, is not in our stars, but in ourselves, that we are
underlings."[4] Men rule the stars, the stars do not rule men.
If circumstances inevitably dictate the course of human action,
freedom is an illusion. When we allow factors external to
ourselves to rule us, we do so because we are either weak,
wilfull, ignorant or inept.

No, it is not the things external to us which are the
ultimate causes of marital disharmony. Like the winds which
sweep the surface of the sea into stormy unrest, they do not
last forever nor can they significantly affect its on-going tides
or intrude upon the quiet of its depths. But shallow hearts,
like shallow waters, are easily upturned and divided. The
heart of all of our problems continues to be the heart of
man.[5] Then, should the family ever be divided? Should the
home ever be abandoned? Is divorce ever justifiable? Let us
consider the Savior's teachings relative to these questions.

What God Has Joined

In fulfilling the Law of Moses, Jesus revived principles
long obscured beneath an overburden of rabbinic interpreta-
tion. No one was better qualified to do this than he, for he
was Jehovah, the giver of the Law.[6] Knowing that the "letter"
of the scribes had killed the spirit of the commandments,
Jesus breathed life back into them by restoring their lost
import.

The statement in the Law upon which the Jews based
their justification of divorce is as follows:

When a man hath taken a wife, and married her, and it come to
pass that she find no favor in his eyes, because he hath found some uncleanness in her: then let him write her a bill of divorcement, and give
it in her hand, and send her out of his house. And when she is departed

---

[4]*Julius Caesar*, Act I, scene 2.
[5]Mark 7:18-23.
[6]See 3 Nephi 15:4, 5; John 8:58; I Corinthians 10:4.

246 out of his house, she may go and be another's man's wife. And if the latter husband hate her, and write her a bill of divorcement, and giveth it in her hand, and sendeth her out of his house; or if the latter husband die, which took her to be his wife; Her former husband, which sent her away, may not take her again to be his wife, after that she is defiled; for that is abomination before the Lord: and thou shalt not cause the land to sin, which the Lord thy God giveth thee for an inheritance.[7]

The ambiguity of the phrase, "some uncleanness in her," led to much debate among the various rabbinical schools, of which those of Hillel and Shammai were especially prominent. While Hillel maintained that husbands had the right to put away their wives for even trivial faults, Shammai insisted that only adultery was a defensible cause. The Pharisees sought to embroil Jesus in the issue:

The Pharisees also came unto him, tempting him, and saying unto him, Is it lawful for a man to put away his wife *for every cause?* And he answered and said unto them, Have ye not read, that he which made them at the beginning made them male and female, And said, For this cause shall a man leave father and mother and shall cleave to his wife: and they twain shall be one flesh? Wherefore they are no more twain, but one flesh. What therefore God hath joined together, let not man put asunder. They said unto him, Why did Moses then command to give a writing of divorcement, and to put her away?[8] He saith unto them, Moses because of the hardness of your hearts suffered you to put away your wives: but from the beginning it was not so. And I say unto you, Whosoever shall put away his wife, *except it be for fornication*, and shall marry another, committeth adultery: and whoso marrieth her which is put away doth commit adultery.[9]

---

[7]Deuteronomy 24:1-4.

[8]The following is an example of a certificate of divorce: "I N. have put away, dismissed, and expelled thee N. who heretofore wast my wife. But now I have dismissed thee, so that thou art free, and in thy own power, to marry whosoever shall please thee; and let no man hinder thee. And let this be thee a bill of rejection from me according to the Law of Moses and Israel.

'Reuben, the son of Jacob, witness.

'Eliezer, the son of Gilead, witness. . . .' "

See Dummelow, J. R., *A Commentary on the Holy Bible by Various Writers.* New York: Macmillan. 1946. pp. 688.

[9]Matthew 19:3-9. Adultery was defined as illicit sexual intercourse involving either betrothed or married persons. Under Levitical law, the penalty for this sin was death. Levit. 20:10. Consequently, when the ancient Israelites "put away" their wives it was presumedly for reasons other than immorality. However, since the death penalty was not in vogue among the Jews in Jesus' day, an aggrieved husband could only free himself of an unfaithful wife by issuing her a bill of divorce. See Deuteronomy 22:13-28; Matthew 1:18.

Note that before answering their specific query, Jesus 247
dealt with the transcending principle behind it. The incarnated Jehovah was not to be ensnared in myopic rationalizations over legal technicalities; he was far more concerned with the nature of marriage than the grounds for divorce. Therefore, he looked beyond things as they were to the truth of things as they were meant to be. He did this by recalling the first marriage on earth, that of Adam and Eve—two immortal beings. Having been performed by the Most High, it was no mere social contract, but an unbreakable union. Contracts are limited agreements between two or more parties who forever remain separate and distinct from one another; true marriage is the deathless bonding of two harmonious personalities. Thus Jesus concluded: "What therefore *God* hath joined together, let not man put asunder." In truth when a man and a woman are "joined together" by the powers of heaven, man *cannot* put them asunder.

However, in this world, men marry and are given in marriage by other men; God is not a party to their actions. Therefore, man can—and does—terminate those marital arrangements of his own devising. Different societies frame different laws pertaining to the intimate association of the sexes. Such arrangements are legal and moral by human standards; the children born of these covenants are legitimate. To this extent, the words of Hebrews are applicable, "Marriage is honorable in all, and the [marriage] bed undefiled. . . ."[10] However, if God is not a party to these unions, the contracting parties have no lasting claim either on one another or on any children produced by them. They will be "put asunder" either by divorce or death.

Orson Pratt contrasted the marriages of this world with those contracted under the authority of the priesthood:

Where man usurps authority to officiate in the ordinance of God, and joins together the sexes in marriage, such unions are illegal in the sight of God, though they may be legal according to the laws and govern-

---

[10]Hebrews 13:4.

ments of men . . . Point out to us a husband and wife that God has joined together from the second century of the christian era until the nineteenth, if any can. Such a phenomenon cannot be found among Christians or Jews, Mahometans, or Pagans. . . . Marriages, then, among all nations, though legal according to the laws of men, have been illegal according to the laws, authority, and institutions of Heaven. All the children born during that long period, though legitimate according to the customs and laws of nations, are illegitimate according to the order and authority of Heaven. Those things which are performed by the authority of man, God will overthrow and destroy, and they will be void and of no effect in the day of the resurrection. All things ordained of God and performed and sealed by his authority, will remain after the resurrection. . . .[11]

We cannot make the Lord an *ex post facto* member of the wedding. If he did not perform the ceremony (via his authorized servants on earth), it is a purely man-made affair subject to man-made attitudes and laws. This was the case with the marital arrangements of the Sadducees who, because they erred—"not knowing the scriptures, nor the power of God"—ridiculed both eternal marriage and the resurrection which made it possible.[12] Of all man-made alliances Jesus said:

The *children* of *this* world [in contradistinction to those not of *this* world] marry, and are given in marriage. But they [among those of *this* world] which shall be accounted worthy to obtain that [immortal] world, and the resurrection from the dead, neither marry nor are given in marriage: Neither can they die anymore: for they are equal unto the angels [who are also immortal but unmarried]; and are the *children* of God [not his mature sons and daughters]; being the children of the resurrection.[13]

Jesus Repudiates Divorce

Jesus cited the union of Adam and Eve as the perfect example of God's will for every marriage—the divine prototype. In light of this ideal, what conceivable reason would

---

[11]Orson Pratt, *The Seer*, pp. 47, 48. See DS, 2:81 and JD 16:173-177, 256; 17:151-153; 18:47-51.

[12]See Matthew 22:23-28; Luke 20:27-33.

[13]Luke 20:34-36. See D&C 132:8-17.

there be for entertaining the possibility of divorce? Divorce, like death, stems from the absence of the life-sustaining qualities inherent in God. A marriage whose builder and maker is the Lord must be everlasting since he is everlasting. Divorce is as alien to the nature of a marriage in the Lord as death is to the nature of a glorified, resurrected being. The violation of the *principle* of marriage via the *practice* of divorce does not invalidate God's original intent in the least. Marriage is what the Lord designed it to be, not what men make it. God's "cause" in uniting the male and the female transcended "every cause" men might advance for putting them asunder. For although divorce was an accepted practice long before the days of Jesus, yet, as he pointed out to the Pharisees who sought to justify it by appealing to Moses, "from the beginning it was not so." The Lord God never willed divorce anymore than he willed any other negative thing. He builds for life, not for death—for eternity, not for time. The Lord does not plan failure although he does plan *for* failure.

Being legalists, the Pharisees assumed that anything the Law allowed could be done with impunity. Jesus' suggestion that one could be law-abiding and still stand condemned before God was a startling departure from traditional rabbinic thought. Like so many others, the Pharisees mistook permission for condonation. They failed to appreciate the fact that the Lord had accommodated his law to the imperfections of his people. Thus, putting away one's wife was technically "lawful" but morally wrong. It did not originate with Jehovah and his law, but with man and his weakness. In rejecting their ritual offerings, the Lord strongly denounced the practice of divorce among the Jews of the fifth century B.C.:

Because the Lord was witness to the covenant between you and the wife of your youth, to whom you have been faithless, though she is your companion and your wife by covenant. Has not the one God made and sustained for us the spirit of life? And what does he desire? Godly offspring. So take heed to yourselves, and let none be faithless to the

250 wife of his youth. *"For I hate divorce,"* says the Lord the God of Israel, and covering one's garments with violence, says the Lord of hosts. So take heed to yourselves and do not be faithless."[14]

Marriage is the very foundation of God's everlasting labors wherein he continues to bring to pass the organized existence of the family of mankind.[15] If marriage is but a temporary expedient, then the family is equally transitory. And if the family has no enduring validity, then God himself is void of lasting purpose and significance. Divorce is antithetical to the very work and glory of God. True, Moses permitted his people to practice divorce but, as Jesus observed, he did so because of "the *hardness* of your hearts." The Lord permits divorce, but he does not condone divorce.

While those who obtain a civil divorce and (if applicable) a cancellation of sealings are free to remarry, the issue of quilt or innocence is another matter. President Joseph Fielding Smith has declared:

If all mankind would live in strict obedience to the gospel, and in that love which is begotten by the Spirit of the Lord, all marriages would be eternal, divorce would be unknown. Divorce is not part of the gospel plan and has been introduced because of the hardness of heart and unbelief of the people. . . . There never could be a divorce in this Church if the husband and wife were keeping the commandments of God. . . . When divorce comes to those who are married in the temple, it has come because they have violated the covenants and the obligations they have taken upon themselves to be true to each other, true to God, true to the Church. If they will continue to live in that faithfulness, if they will have love in their hearts for each other, respect each other's rights and not one attempt to take an advantage unduly of the other but have the proper consideration, there will be no failures. . . . Marriage according to the law of the Church is the most holy and sacred ordinance. It will bring to the husband and the wife, if they abide in their covenants, the fulness of exaltation in the kingdom of God. When the covenant is broken, it will bring *eternal misery to the guilty party,* for we will all have to answer for our deeds done while in the flesh. It is an ordinance that cannot be trifled with, and the

---

[14]Malachi 2:14-16. Revised Standard Version.
[15]See Moses 1:39; D&C 132:63.

covenants made in the temple cannot be broken without dire punishment to the one who is guilty.[16]

Scriptural Grounds for Divorce

Some scholars maintain that Jesus did not allow for divorce for any cause whatsoever. They point out that Matthew's qualifying phrase, "saving for the cause of fornication" is unsupported either by Mark, Luke or Paul.[17] However, a study of all pertinent passages suggests that Matthew's "exception" is in reality only a more comprehensive statement of the Savior's views on the subject.[18]

Matthew	Mark	Luke	Paul
But I say unto you, That whosoever shall put away his wife saving for the cause of fornication, causeth her to commit adultery: and whosoever shall marry her that is divorced committeth adultery.[19]	And he saith unto them, Whosoever shall put away his wife, and marry another, committeth adultery against her. And if a woman shall put away her husband, and be married to another, she committeth adultery.[20]	Whosoever putteth away his wife, and marrieth another, committeth adultery: and whosoever marrieth her that is put away from her husband committeth adultery.[21]	And unto the married I command, yet not I, but the Lord, Let not the wife depart from her husband; But and if she depart, let her remain unmarried, or be reconciled to her husband: and let not the husband put away his wife.[22]

[16]DS, 2:80-84. Italics original. See also CR, April, 1961, pp. 48-50.

[17]Scholars theorize that Matthew's exception is an interpolation designed to make Jesus' teaching more palatable to the later church. However, while neither Luke, Paul nor, possibly, Mark were present when the Savior gave these instructions, Matthew was an ear-witness to them. Not only this, of the four, only Matthew was one of the Twelve. Then too, the absence of material from one account does not necessarily invalidate its presence in another. Textual variations are very common and may stem from a given Gospel writer's desire to emphasize a particular aspect of the Lord's teachings.

[18]He included the disputed passages in his restatement of the sermon on the mount to the Nephites, and in a revelation to Joseph Smith. See 3 Nephi 12:32; D&C 42:74-77.

[19]Matthew 5:32. See Ibid., 19:9; D&C 42:74, 75.

[20]Mark 10:11, 12.

[21]Luke 16:18. Luke, who is noted for his compassionate interest in womankind, stigmatized both husbands while remaining silent as to the wife's culpability.

[22]1 Corinthians 7:10, 11.

252   In considering these passages, we must remember that Jesus came to fulfill the law as he had given it—not as it was being interpreted by the Pharisees. Under the law, adultery was punishable by death; divorce was automatic. However, the prescribed penalty was not enforced in that day. It was therefore, unnecessary for Jesus to specify adultery as a grounds for divorce—no one disputed it.

But were there other acceptable grounds? Jesus' answer was yes, fornication. But was not fornication in marriage adultery? It was. Consequently, the Aramaic term Jesus used did not refer to infidelity in marriage but to infidelity before marriage. The King James translators, unlike their modern counterparts, correctly selected the specific term, fornication, rather than the imprecise term, unchastity or unfaithfulness, to convey the Lord's meaning. That Jesus did regard fornication and adultery as two separate and distinct forms of infidelity is affirmed not only by Matthew but also in a latter-day revelation to Joseph Smith:

> Behold, verily I say unto you, that whatever persons among you, having put away their companions for the cause of *fornication*, or in other words, if they shall testify before you in all lowliness of heart that this is the case, ye shall not cast them out from among you; But if ye shall find that any persons have left their companions for the sake of *adultery*, and they themselves are the offenders, *and their companions are living*, they shall be cast out from among you.[23]

It is apparent that adultery and fornication do not have interchangeable meanings in this passage. Putting away their companions (whether husband or wife) "for the cause of fornication" is in contradistinction to leaving their companions "for the sake of adultery."

Whereas the Jews regarded the issuance of a bill of divorce the end of a marriage, Jesus maintained that its dissolution could, in God's eyes, only result from fornication or adultery. These sins constitute spiritual divorce. In other words, unchastity, not legal action, is the essence of divorce.

---

[23]D&C 42:74, 75. See also 3 Nephi 12:32.

Adultery was an act of divorce because it violated the union   253
of man and woman after the fact of marriage. On the
other hand, fornication—pre-marital unchastity—was also an
act of divorce because it defiled a potential union before it
existed.[24] Thus, illicit sex, either before or after marriage, is
a sin against marriage. The Law recognized this fact and
permitted a husband to disown a wife if he discovered that
she was not a virgin at the time of marriage.[25]

> Then they shall bring out the damsel to the door of her father's
> house, and the men of her city shall stone her with stones that she die:
> because she hath wrought folly in Israel, to play the whore in her father's
> house: so shalt thou put evil away from among you.[26]

In allowing a man to put away his wife "for the cause
of fornication," Jesus was simply unholding the Law of Moses.
He himself had insisted that "not one jot or one tittle shall
in nowise pass from the law, till all be fulfilled."[27] He never
opposed the law's demands, only the hypocrisy of its
practitioners. For example, he did not deny that, under the
law, an adulteress should be stoned, but he did challenge
her accusers to find a man innocent enought to lead out in
the deed.[28] Jesus exposed the poor woman's judges for the
hypocrites they were. To accuse her was to accuse themselves; they knew this. Those who were so anxious to uphold
the law's claim on the adulteress, turned from it fearing its
claim on themselves. Even as mankind had to wait four
millennia for perfect mercy to be incarnated, so must it yet
wait a season for perfect justice to descend from heaven.
Still, though muted, that justice once walked the earth

---

[24]This is implicit in the Law's requirement that the seducer of an unbetrothed
virgin marry her and "not put her away all his days." Deuteronomy 22:29.

[25]See Deuteronomy 22:13-21.

[26]Deuteronomy 22:21. The validity of this principle is further supported by a
modern revelation to the effect that the plural wives of Joseph Smith "who are not
pure, and have said they were pure, shall be destroyed, saith the Lord God." D&C
132:52.

[27]Matthew 5:18.

[28]See John 8:7; Deuteronomy 22:22.

254 between those extremes which so often assume its throne and presume to speak in its behalf. For in upholding the law pertaining to adultery, and in declaring fornication the only other acceptable basis for divorce, Jesus rejected both Shammai and Hillel—taking a position between their two extremes.

Adultery Via Divorce

Jesus shocked friend and foe alike in maintaining that, from God's viewpoint, adultery was a consequence as well as a cause of divorce. Chief responsibility for the offense rested with the one who struck the fatal blow against the original union. A man was justified in divorcing a wife who, in committing fornication or adultery, had—in effect— divorced him. She struck the blow with her own hand. Her huband's bill of divorce was, therefore, nothing more than the legal death certificate attesting to the marriage's demise. On the other hand, the husband who put away a faithful wife struck the fatal blow by virtually forcing her into an adulterous second alliance. Consequently, any marriage he contracted thereafter would be an offense against his abandoned wife.[29] In summation, adultery was committed by: a) the woman who remarried during her first husband's lifetime,[30] b) the man who married a divorced woman and, c) the husband who unjustifiably divorced a wife and then married someone else.

Jesus' teaching on this subject has been deemed harsh and repressive by some. Indeed, the initial reaction of his own disciples was that it was better to remain unmarried rather than be so bound to a wife.[31] However, the Savior of men

---

[29]It was not the taking of another wife, but the unwarranted "putting away" of one which constituted adultery. Polygamy was practiced among the Jews both before and after Jesus' day. He never condemned the principle as such. The ancient patriarchs practiced plural marriage by divine command. See Romans 7:1-3; 1 Corinthians 7:39; D&C 132:34-39, 61, 62.

[30]Adultery was not a *fait accompli* until the separation ended in remarriage. The sin lay in the adulteration of the original union, not in separation as such. See I Corinthians 7:11.

[31]See Matthew 19:10.

was also the champion of women. In affirming his Father's will, Jesus asserted the right of women to be secure as wives and mothers and, implicitly, the right of children to be cared for by their own parents. No longer were wives to be considered mere property which could be discarded and exchanged at at the whim of their husbands. To appreciate the Lord's position, we must be mindful of the status of Jewish women at that time. The majority were fairly well-treated by their husbands, most of whom prized and honored a good wife. The family was all-important so that, morally speaking, the Jewish nation had no peers among the surrounding gentile nations. Still, there were injustices. For example, whereas a married woman would be branded an adulteress for becoming involved with any man—married or not—a married man went uncondemned so long as he restricted his assignations to unmarried women.[32]

Then too, under the Law, only the husband could issue a bill of divorce, a wife was helpless to free herself.[33] Ordinarily, this certificate freed the wife to remarry. However, in Jesus' mind this did not alter the fact that her doing so violated the original union. In every instance where Jesus employed the term, adultery, it was in connection with an unauthorized third person becoming involved in the "one flesh" relationship of a man and his wife.[34] It was the betrayal of God's intent "from the beginning" that marriage should be an unbroken bond between a man and a woman which Jesus denounced. Therefore, all parties to the action were tainted by it: the first husband for unjustly casting his

---

[32]See John 8:1-11. Note that although the adulterous pair were caught "in the very act," only the woman was brought to judgment.

[33]It is generally thought that Mark's version allows either mate to initiate the divorce action because he adapted the Savior's teachings to the Greco-Roman situation of his readers in which women did exercise that privilege. For example, Herodias divorced her husband, Herod Philip in Rome in order to marry his half-brother, Herod Antipas.

[34]Plural marriage does not violate the principle of "one flesh." The nature of eternal marriage is such that while a woman may be sealed to but one man, a man may be sealed to several women. The relationship of Christ (the head) to the Church (the body) exemplifies this truth. For while there is but one Bridegroom, one Beloved Son, there are many brides and many sons of God. See Matthew 25:1; Ephesians 5:23, 24; Hebrews 2:10; 3 John 3:1-3. See JD 6:356; 13:39.

256

wife aside, the wife for marrying another while her husband yet lived, and the second husband for taking another man's wife. Thus the shadow of betrayal fell across both subsequent marriages.

The issue was not law, but reality. Adultery contaminates the union of husband and wife via the unsanctioned introduction into it of a third party. It is the pollution of the marital relationship through the admixture of an alien, divisive personality. Viewed in this light, the question of culpability is extraneous to the issue. Jesus was concerned with the spiritual implications of adultery, not its legal definition.

Indeed, there are circumstances in which one might be virtually forced to enter into an adulterous, though legal, relationship. For example, necessity imposed remarriage on female Jewish divorcees who lacked the economic means to support themselves and their children.[35] This is why Jesus maintained that "putting away one's wife" for reasons other than her own infidelity would "*cause her* to commit adultery." Worse still, failing to obtain a second mate, many destitute women resorted to beggary or prostitution for survival. Is it any wonder Jesus repudiated the notion that a man could capriciously abandon a wife?

Still, a woman's plight did not alter the *fact* that remarriage during her husband's lifetime partook of the spirit of adultery against the original union. It might be justified by both God and man, but it *was* a reality. For example, the transgression of Adam was imposed upon him by the necessity of remaining with Eve so "that man might be." It was justified. However, he *did* disobey a commandment and he *did* fall. The fact of the matter was one thing, the guilt or innocence stemming from the fact another. Jesus' teaching is clear: the intimate relationship of man and woman is meant to be an integral part of their unbreakable union. It is adultery to defile that union. Consequently, both pre-

---

[35]An abandoned wife is as justified in seeking a second husband as an orphan is in seeking foster parents. Being "the weaker vessel," she does not sin in remarrying if she was wrongfully put aside or if her husband is deceased. See Romans 7:1-3, I Corinthians 7:8, 9, 27, 28.

marital and marital unchastity differ only in degree, not kind. For this reason, the Church makes no practical distinction between them.

It should be stressed that because the sealing power of the priesthood includes the divine authority to bind and to loose, to seal and to unseal, adultery is not imputed to the innocent victims of divorce who have been freed to remarry by that authority. Sin is not impugned to one who is justified by the Lord in either marrying or remarrying.[36] However, guilt does attach itself to one who, having been sealed by the authority of the Priesthood, obtains a civil divorce and then remarries without a prior cancellation of sealings:

> I think I can say here safely and truthfully that no judge in this world in any court of the land can annul a marriage for time and all eternity. He may separate the husband and wife by legal enactments so far as this world is concerned, but he cannot separate that husband and wife so far as the next world is concerned. Only the President of the Church has authority to cancel sealings, and when the man and his wife lose their faith and go to the courts and get a separation, and then go out and marry according to the laws of the land, they are not culpable before the law of the land, but they are before the kingdom of God and what the Savior says here in this revelation [Matt. 19:9] is absolutely true: . . . .[37]

Spiritual Infidelity

Recognizing the dual nature of man, Jesus emphasized the dual nature of the commandments.[38] For example, Jesus taught that adultery was spiritual as well as physical in character.

> Ye have heard that it was said by them of old time, Thou shalt not commit adultery: But I say unto you, That whosoever looketh on a woman to lust after her hath committed adultery with her already in his heart.[39]

---

[36]See D&C 132:44, 61-63.
[37]Joseph Fielding Smith, CR, April, 1961, p. 50.
[38]Matthew 5:21-48.
[39]Ibid., 5:27, 28.

258   Obviously, then, infidelity is not limited to one's overt behavior, any division of mind or heart is a degree of infidelity.[40] When such division is deep and long-lasting where one's mate—or one's God—is concerned, it is, in effect, the spiritual counterpart of adultery.

It is for this reason that the prophets defined ancient Israel's worship of other gods as fornication and adultery. In a particularly moving account of Jehovah's first claiming of Israel, Ezekiel writes of how the Lord brought life and salvation to her:

> Now when I passed by thee, and looked upon thee, behold, thy time was the time of love; and I spread my skirt over thee, and covered thy nakedness; yea, I sware unto thee, and entered into a covenant with thee, saith the Lord God, and thou becamest mine.[41]

Thereafter Israel "played the harlot" as it were, "upon every high mountain and under every green tree."[42] She "committed fornication with the Egyptians"[43]and "adultery with stones and with stocks."[44]

Such treachery violates the mind to mind, heart to heart bond between husband and wife much as unchastity violates their flesh to flesh union. It is profound alienation of affections—spiritual infidelity—a hydra-headed creature of many guises. It usually expresses itself in oblique rather than direct ways. For example, whereas one could take life with a gun, the deed might be accomplished more subtly by employing ridicule, mental torture, gossip, falsehoods, etc.[45] There are numerous ways of destroying a human being which do not require the shedding of blood. Jesus was murdered before he was crucified.

---

[40]For an excellent summary of the dimensions of infidelity, see Spencer W. Kimball, CR, October 6, 1962, pp. 56-60.

[41]Ezekiel 16:8. See entire chapter.

[42]Jeremiah 3:6.

[43]Ezekiel 16:26.

[44]Jeremiah 3:9. See also Isaiah 1:21; Hosea 2; D&C 88:94.

[45]See Matthew 5:21, 22; Alma 36:14.

> Yet each man kills the thing he loves,
> By each let this be heard,
> Some do it with a bitter look,
> Some with a flattering word,
> The coward does it with a kiss,
> The brave man with a sword![46]

So too, infidelity can be expressed in outright adultery or by less obvious methods which may not only elude the conscience, but actually cause the faithless one to feel self-vindicated: "After all, is it anything more than just due for my companion's inadequacies and offenses?" Perhaps so. Men and women do fail one another; offenses do come. The vital issue is how we respond to those offenses. Infidelity is the hypocrite's way, not the Lord's way. Better an honest sword, than a deceptive kiss. In a summation of Israel's spiritual infidelity, Jehovah lamented:

Surely as a wife treacherously departeth from her husband, so have ye dealt treacherously with me, O house of Israel, saith the Lord.[47]

Love not only serves to seal up a man and a woman in a valid union, it seals *out* everything and everyone alien to that union. Jesus told the Twelve: "If a man love me, he *will* keep my words. . . ."[48] Love is its own imperative. We cannot love the Lord and not keep his commandments. Whether toward God or one's mate, infidelity always stems from the fact that—for whatever reason—commitment of heart and mind have been weighed in the balances and found wanting.[49]

Husbands may express their alienation by failing to properly provide for their families, by undue attention to their vocations or hobbies, by desertion, coldness, drunkenness, or brutality, by indifference to their calling as fathers and spiritual leaders in the home, by a general unwillingness to guide, sustain and support their wives in their labors, etc.

---

[46]Oscar Wilde, "The Ballad of Reading Gaol." *The Pocketbook of Verse*, p. 306.
[47]Jeremiah 3:20.
[48]John 14:22, 24.
[49]See D&C 64:34.

260   Wives are inclined to reveal their disaffection by either careless or obsessive homemaking, by either refusing to bear
and properly care for children or by excessive attention to
them, by denial of conjugal rights,[50] by a flirtatious spirit,
by fault-finding and derision—especially before children—or
by unjustifiably pursuing a career or some other time-con-
suming interest outside of the home, etc. There is much
overlapping of these factors of alienation between men and
women; neither sex has a corner on the market. Note too,
that infidelity can be reflected in extremes. Too much of one
thing, too little of another; always an imbalance; always a
distortion of values. Thus men violate God's commandment
given through Adam to watch over, bless and sustain their
wives, and women, in turn, fail to obey the commandment
given to Eve and her daughters to center their lives and affections in their husbands, their children and their homes.
It is all infidelity, regardless of the guise it may wear. As
such it partakes of a divided heart, double-mindedness—
marital duplicity.

Planned hypocrisy is sometimes advocated as a cure for
those marriages characterized by monotony and boredom.[51]
The question is, should one feign the fruits of love?[52] Should
a wife resort to feminine wiles? Should she view her husband
as a fortress to be overthrown by woman's ancient weapons?
Should she practice guile as a means of manipulating him?
In other words, should she *use* herself in ways which will
enable her to *use* him? Advocates of this devious approach
to human relationships are very popular today. Manipulative
propaganda is not new; sophistry had its beginnings with
Satan in the pre-mortal world. It was his chief weapon in
the war in heaven and remains a favorite tool of liars everywhere. False prophets of marital happiness find many "silly
women" who much prefer the easy lie to the hard truth. And
the truth is that manipulative techniques have and always

---

[50]See 1 Corinthians 7:3-5.

[51]How many Christians experience this sort of "marriage" to Christ!

[52]The heart justifies or condemns our actions. A false offering is rejected by God
even though it outwardly meets all of the requirements of a true one. See Moroni 7:5-10.

will be used in the absence of sincere devotion. Artificial affection—like artificial fruit—may, at first glance, appear genuine, but it is only illusory. It is devoid of life, and, consequently, cannot nourish the soul. With time, it gathers dust and is eventually discarded.

Love has its own instinct. Not even a puppy has to be taught how to express it. Wives who feel that they must learn certain "techniques" before they can effectively relate to their husbands apparently do not realize how close to the spirit of harlotry they have moved.[53] Famous courtesans were skilled in the nuances of sexual love, yet they knew little or nothing of love itself. A wife who must be instructed in the "proper technique" for speaking, responding, reacting and otherwise relating to her husband is a pathetic caricature of a woman in love. If her husband is beguiled by such behavior, he is either very naive, very self-centered or very stupid . . . probably all three.

Through Isaiah, Jehovah chastised those who "draweth nigh unto me with their mouth, and honoreth me with their lips; but their heart is far from me."[54] No sin drew sharper or more frequent rebuke from Jesus than that of hypocrisy. Feigned love, loyalty or righteousness was an abomination in his sight.[55] This disease of the spirit followed him throughout his ministry. It challenged him, misunderstood him, rejected him, ridiculed him, betrayed him, kissed him, denied him, lied about him, struck him, spat upon him, judged him, flogged him, washed its hands of him, and, when it could do no more, crucified him.

There can be no marriage in the Lord if the parties to it are lacking in personal integrity. Guileful behavior may temporarily serve one's purposes, but it will fail in the end. Integrity—wholeness of character—should manifest itself in all that we do. A true disciple of Jesus Christ will act with

---

[53]Such matters as personal grooming, personality development, homemaking skills, etc. are both justifiable and desirable and are not to be confused with these deceptive practices.

[54]See Matthew 15:8; Isaiah 29:13; Joseph Smith 2:19.

[55]See Matthew 23.

262   integrity toward his country, his church, his employer, his neighbor, his family or his dog. The virtue—or lack of it—of others will not dictate his conduct. He will strive to be true—as God is true—although every one else is false.[56]

Personal integrity is the key to resolving those dilemmas associated with particularly stressful circumstances. For example, how should we conduct ourselves when oppressed? Do we owe others our fealty when they do not fully respect our rights as human beings? Is it wrong to protect one's self with a measure of guile when conditions not of our making nor to our liking are imposed upon us? Specifically, how should a wife act toward an abusive, unworthy husband? Is it a case of fighting fire with fire, of an eye for an eye, or is there a better way of dealing with the situation?

As in most things, Jesus' approach to life is our best guide. The humble, compassionate and generous deeds of Jesus have been duplicated in the lives of many noble people. The Christ-like thing has been done time and again—but not consistently. It is not so much what Jesus did which sets him apart from others as it is the consistency with which he did it. His disciples lacked his consistency because they lacked his integrity. No circumstance caused him to compromise his standards. He overcame the world because he was true when it was false. So too, those who would emulate the Master must strive to maintain their integrity in all circumstances—good and bad. Right conduct is not meant to be a matter of convenience, but a way of life. And it is bought with a price: self-denial, sacrifice, persecution, rejection, misunderstanding, etc. A hallmark of the true disciple is his ability to do right in the midst of wrong, to accept punishment without rancor—not because he is guilty, *but in spite of being innocent.*

Consider the counsel of the apostle Peter to the Church in his day.

For this is thankworthy, if a man for conscience toward God endure grief, *suffering wrongfully.* For what glory is it, if, when ye be buffeted

---
[56]See Romans 3:4.

for your faults, ye shall take it patiently? but if, when ye do well, and suffer for it, ye take it patiently, this is acceptable with God. For even hereunto were ye called: because Christ also suffered for us, leaving us an example, that ye should follow his steps. Who did no sin, neither was guile found in his mouth; Who when he was reviled, reviled not again; when he suffered, he threatened not; but committed himself to him that judgeth righteously: Who his own self bare our sins in his own body on the tree, that we, being dead to sins, should live unto righteousness; by whose stripes ye were healed. For ye were as sheep going astray; but are now returned unto the Shepherd and Bishop of your souls.[57]

Men and women who would become one with Christ must do so in all things. We cannot expect to share in his glory if we are unwilling to share in his pain.[58] Commitment to Christ saves us from some trials only to bring others upon us. No one can be in the world while not of it and escape persecution.[59] Is Christ to be crucified and his prophets stoned while the saints go unscathed?

A woman who has entered into a covenant with Christ is a saint first and a wife second. Her covenant with the Lord, not her marriage vows, should be the ultimate determinant of her conduct. Indeed, she is a better wife because of her covenant. She can be even more faithful in adversity, not less so. She can be armed with a spiritual power which will enable her to transcend adverse situations. If anyone had the right to be disloyal, it would be a slave whose servitude was imposed upon him. Yet the apostle Paul counseled those slaves who had become free men in Christ to use their new-found hope as an incentive for even more faithful service to their masters.

Servants, be obedient to them that are your masters according to the flesh, with fear and trembling, in singleness of your heart, *as unto Christ; Not with eyeservice,* as menpleasers; but as the servants of Christ, doing the will of God from the heart; With good will doing service as to the Lord, and not to men: Knowing that whatsoever good

---

[57]I Peter 2:19-25. See JD 22:102; 25:325.
[58]See Romans 8:17, 35-39.
[59]See Matthew 10:34-36.

264 thing any man doeth, the same shall he receive of the Lord, whether he be bond or free.[60]

In other words, they were no longer merely slaves, they were *Christian* slaves—men and women who served an earthly master well because their heavenly Master asked it of them. They did not do it to please men, but to please God. Their integrity as saints would not allow them to behave in any way but Christ's way. So too, the wife whose husband is less than he ought to be cannot be untrue to him without dishonoring her Lord and herself. She will sustain her husband in truth—without guile—because she cannot dishonor herself as a saint.

The Sword of Truth

Life does not always allow for clear choices between good and evil. In some instances, the issue is not doing what is right, but knowing what is right. Many a poor soul has been impaled on the horns of this dilemma. The best thing to do in any given situation can only be determined after all of its nuances and ramifications have been considered. Even then, the final decision may be wrong. Fortunately, humanity is still made of clay; we have not yet been cast in the bronze of immortality. The Potter can still correct any flaws stemming from our sins and weaknesses if we will permit him to do so.[61] He is the truth which will eventually free us of our mistakes and their temporal consequences if we will but approach him in all humility and honesty of heart.

Pretense—maintaining appearances for appearances sake—meant nothing to Jesus. He was a realist. Although he taught that divorce was contrary to the will of heaven, He

---

[60]Ephesians 6:5-8. Brigham Young said that "the woman that bears wrong . . . patiently . . . will be crowned with a man far above her husband. . . ." JD 17:160. John Taylor said: "When the books are opened, every one will find his proper mate. . . ." JD 1:232.

[61]See Jeremiah 18:1-6; Romans 9:21; JD 2:151.

nevertheless allowed for it under certain circumstances. God   **265**
permits divorce in fact; he does not condone it *in principle.*
Forbidding divorce on any grounds whatsoever is both un-
scriptural and immoral. The Lord would not have given the
Church the authority to bind and to *loose* if such were the
case.[62] What hypocrisy to claim that thieves and murderers
may repent and enter heaven but that those who err in
choosing a mate must be condemned to a lifetime of marital
hell. Is a woman the prisoner of her husband regardless of
how he may abuse her just so long as he does not commit
physical adultery? Such a restricted view would allow the
practice of all manner of soul-destroying tyrannies with seeming impunity. Human judgment is fallible—especially when
we are young and inexperienced. Mistakes are made.
Nothing is gained by perpetuating a relationship which is
hopelessly wrong. Truth is *divisive.* Christ came, not with
the olive branch of universal peace, but with the sword of
truth.[63] Peace follows the truth, it cannot precede it. An
enduring relationship—whether with God or man—cannot
be coerced; it must be achieved without compulsory means—
being founded upon the natural harmony of its component
parts.

In most instances, those who have committed themselves
to Christ can achieve that harmony if only they will be
patient and long-suffering, which is to say, if only they will
love deeply enough, long enough. Actually most couples
are far more alike than they care to admit. More often than
not, they criticize weaknesses in their mate which they,
themselves, possess, but resent. Thus each becomes a scape-
goat for the other. It is a futile enterprise: both are sent
bleating into the wilderness carrying the mate's sins and,
therefore, carrying his or her own.[64] Many marriages could
be saved if only the parties to them would develop a greater
sense of honesty and humility and then season these qualities
with an active sense of humor.

---

[62]Matthew 16:19; 18:18; D&C 132:45, 46.
[63]Ibid 10:34-38; Luke 14:26, JD 1:234.
[64]Leviticus 16:1-10.

266   They owe this to their children. For marriage is a covenant with the unborn. The obligations of parenthood are inherent in those conjugal associations that make it possible. There is no way under heaven for parents to divorce themselves from their responsibilities toward the children they bring into the world. Their stewardship cannot be blithely handed over to someone else. Many parents are much too cavalier in this regard. The sins committed by children in consequence of parental failure will be upon the heads of the parents, not their surrogates.[65] Who can measure the harm done when parental selfishness robs children of the guidance and affection to which they are entitled? Characteristically, the very young are quick to forgive; it is hard for them to understand why their parents are lacking in this quality. Children should no more be required to choose between their father and mother than the saints should be asked to choose between one prophet and another. It is designed that children should serve a marriage and, in return, be served by it. They justify both its existence and its perpetuation. They should not be robbed of their childhood. They should not be driven into the world of adult realities before the due time. Nor should they be obliged to lay the foundation of their own marriages on the insecurities of a broken home. The home belongs to the family. Like a ship, it should be abandoned only when and if the safety and shelter it affords its passengers is outweighed by the dangers of remaining aboard.

    Although divorce compounds the hurts of parents and children alike, in a given situation it must be weighed against the damage the marriage itself is producing. The spiritual and emotional scarring which comes with living in a home characterized by nameless obscenities, insecurities, strife, brutality, drunkenness, etc.—or even by the subtle, but pervasive, atmosphere of restrained hatred and infidelity—can be far worse than that resulting from a swift severing of an unholy alliance. Children can endure a great deal if they feel that they are loved. If they do not, it makes little difference

---

[65]D&C 68:25.

whether the loneliness of being unloved is experienced with or without one or both parents. Most children are blessed with an emotional resiliency and a truth-accepting disposition beyond that of older people. When provided with an honest statement of the facts, the young are inclined to accept them. Idealistically, every home should be a sample of heaven on earth. Realistically, few are. Most marriages can survive and most families can be relatively happy with something less than heaven. Divorce is unjustified in these instances. But where a home bespeaks, not heaven—or even earth—but hell itself, it is not *home* and should be cast into the bottomless pit along with the devil and his angels.

Divorce is becoming increasingly a phenomenon of the middle-aged, as well as the very young. The passing of the last child into adulthood seems to expose a weakness, an emptiness in the marital relationship of a growing number of couples. For too many, the tie that binds is not love, but duty —especially duty toward children. When, presumably, that duty has been discharged, many couples are no longer willing to remain together. Certainly children can do much to cement and sustain a marriage. Without them, many marriages would be discarded before the parties to them had time to successfully adjust for the long voyage. However, it is not children, but the bond between husband and wife as such which is the ultimate basis of a lasting marriage. If that bond is non-existent or seriously flawed, children usually do little more than patch over the cracks of parental division. Indeed, children may become unwitting pawns in a marital chess match; or, being privy to the truth, they may also enter the "war game" and play one parent against the other. The principle of divide and conquer has many applications.

The nature of rule, command or leadership imposes obligations on those in authority that are above and beyond those reciprocal duties incumbent upon their subjects or followers. Unequal power produces unequal responsibilities. it is a matter of *noblesse oblige:* the more influential the person, or the greater their knowledge, or the more dependent

268

others are upon them, the more essential it is for them to honor their trust. For example, God bestows the priesthood with an oath and a covenant "which he cannot break, neither can it be moved."[66] His very integrity as God is bound up in his oath. Paul said: "Let God be true, but every man a liar."[67] Though men are free to be faithful or unfaithful to their covenants, a similar choice does not exist for God. Again, the earth faithfully fulfills the measure of her creation in spite of the despoilations of her ungrateful children. And the roots of a tree remain steadfast when its branches flail at the wind. So too, a government is expected to uphold constitutional law even though some citizens commit acts of sedition. Likewise, parental responsibility does not end simply because juvenile delinquency begins. Children leave parents, parents should not disown children. God does not forsake men; men forsake him. A disgruntled citizen may leave his country for a cause that would not warrant his country sending him into exile. People apostatize from the Church for more numerous reasons than those for which they might be excommunicated. Thus, the dependent person is freer to end a relationship than the one he or she is dependent upon.

Consequently, a husband, having accepted the role of guide and protector of his wife, is obligated to be more patient and long-suffering with her than she might choose to be with him. In practical terms, this means that a wife is at greater liberty to leave her husband than he is to leave her. A man is not justified in abandoning his wife unless she first breaks the marriage covenant through some serious act of disloyalty. Human weaknesses and imperfections should not be equated with infidelity—virtually the only legitimate ground for a husband initiating divorce proceedings.

As God hates putting away, husbands among this people can put their wives away only for causes mentioned in the holy writ; but

---

[66]D&C 84:40.
[67]Romans 3:4.

wives, on the other hand may claim freedom and support on other and more numerous grounds.[68]

While a woman may obtain her freedom on more numerous grounds than could her mate, her culpability in doing so is another matter. She should be very sure that circumstances warranted her action since she, in leaving him, must bear the greater responsibility for the divorce itself.

Therefore, it behooves a woman to be very sure that she is not using divorce as an escape from the frustration of her own unrealistic expectations.

John A. Widtsoe recounted an incident in the life of President Young which bears on this point:

> The day journal of Brigham Young records that one day a sister came to him and said: "My husband is not good to me. I want a divorce." The journal goes on further to say that President Young talked with her about an hour, from ten to eleven in the morning. The journal gives the exact time. Then, when they had finished, he turned to the woman, and he said: "Sister, I have heard your story. I am not going to give you a divorce." As you know, Brigham Young was a friend to the cause of women. He felt that they had the first right of choice. "I will not give you a divorce," he said. "Go home and be good to your husband, and don't expect heaven on earth."
> There is a tremendous lesson in that last phrase: "Don't expect heaven on earth."[69]

More often than not, those who demand heaven on earth do not find it in this life or qualify for it in the life to come.

However, when a woman deems her situation unbearable, she has her God-given agency. She should not be accused of sin in ending a hopeless marriage. Indeed, divorce may be an act of repentance. Although Paul admonished the Christian slave to be honorable in his servitude, the apostle did not deny him the right to free himself if the op-

---

[68]Moses Thatcher, JD 26:314. President David O. McKay observed: "We have too many divorces in the Church, and men, I think we are to blame for most of them—not all, but most of them." CR, October 10, 1959, p. 89. "For a man to seek for a divorce is almost unheard of, the liberty upon this point rests with the woman. . . ." George Q. Cannon, as quoted in *The Mormon Question in Its Economic Aspects*, 1886, p. 59.

[69]CR, Oct. 5, 1947, p. 153.

270 portunity arose.[70] By analogy, we should be loyal citizens so long as the state protects us in our unalienable rights. When the state ceases to do so, we may continue to give it our loyalty, but it has no right to *demand* that loyalty.[71] God has denied no one the right to revolt against tyranny. Nowhere has he said that continual submission to bondage and oppression is required of us if we are to escape the onus of sin. To so submit may earn heaven's praise, but refusing to do so will not call down heaven's censure.[72]

What is important is that however we act, it is with integrity. Whether we remain a slave, an abused wife, or an oppressed citizen, or whether we renounce our former fealty and strike for freedom—our conduct, right or wrong, should be honorable. A divided heart—double-mindedness—can only produce feigned love, loyalty and obedience. Such hypocrisy robs us of integrity without freeing us from servitude. All are betrayed in that wretched state: the hated master, the compromised slave, and the Lord.

Therefore, other than outright fornication or adultery, what other circumstances might warrant divorce? President David O. McKay cited some of the more obvious ones:

Unfaithfulness on the part of either or both, habitual drunkenness, physical violence, long imprisonment that disgraces the wife and family, the union of an innocent girl to a reprobate—in these and perhaps other cases there may be circumstances which make the continuance of the marriage state a greater evil than divorce. But these are extreme cases—they are the mistakes, the calamities in the realm of marriage.[73]

That there are limits to what a woman is expected to endure was also the contention of Elder Moses Thatcher:

The allegiance of a wife in this Church is not due to an unfaithful, deceiving or cruel husband. And he who regards his wife as the

---

[70]See 1 Corinthians 7:21, 22. The entire letter to Philemon is concerned with the fate of a run-away slave, Onesimus, whom Paul converted while he, himself, was a prisoner.

[71]See D&C 134:5.

[72]Although we are expected to patiently endure the first instance of physical abuse, such restraint in connection with further offenses—while pleasing to God—is not demanded by him. See D&C 98:28-30.

[73]CR, April 8, 1945, p. 141. See CR, April 5, 1952, p. 86; DS 2:82.

creature of his sinful pleasure, made and given to gratify his fallen nature is unworthy of a wife or to be the father of children.[74]

If a marriage is dragging a woman down to the point where her very salvation is in jeopardy, divorce may be her only recourse. It is one thing to go to hell to save sinners and quite another to remain there with them. Jesus did the former, not the latter.

How often is it the case among us, that women desirous of salvation are compelled to leave their husbands that become drunken, that become apostates, that become careless and indifferent, that do something or other that forfeits their standing in the Church of Christ? And then what is to become of such women? According to our faith no woman should be connected with a man who cannot save her in the Celestial Kingdom of God. What I mean by this is: if a man apostatizes and breaks covenants and loses his standing in the Church of Christ, he is not in a fit condition to save himself, much less to lead his wife aright. He cannot lead her in the path of exaltation, because he has turned aside from that path; he has gone into another path. If she follow him, she will follow him to destruction; she will take the downward road. She will never find, while following him, and he in that condition, the path of salvation.[75]

Many converts left their fathers, mothers, wives, husbands and even children for the Gospel's sake. This is not a desirable sacrifice, but it is one which circumstance sometimes makes necessary.

Many women in our community have left their husbands; many men have left their wives and children; young boys have left their parents and brothers and sisters, and young girls have come away, and left all. They had friends, homes, plenty, parents, brothers and sisters; yet when the spirit of the Gospel came upon them they were so enamored with it, and it gave such light, knowledge and intelligence, that they were willing to forsake all, and follow with the Latter-day Saints for life eternal. This is the case with quite a portion of our community. We all, then, started for life and salvation, and we still have no other object.[76]

---

[74]JD 26:315.
[75]George Q. Cannon, JD 25:368. Joseph F. Smith said, "it is the duty of the woman to follow the man in Christ, not out of him." JD 16:247. See *Ibid.*, 4:165; 24:171.
[76]JD 18:236.

272   Such sacrifices are not wrong, for in speaking of those who had "forsaken all" Jesus said:

> And every one that hath forsaken houses, or brethren, or sisters, or father, or mother, or wife, or children, or lands, for my name's sake, shall receive a hundredfold, and shall inherit everlasting life.[77]

President Joseph F. Smith recognized the fact that not all marriages should be perpetuated.

> If a man and woman should be joined together who are incompatible to each other it would be a mercy to them to be separated that they might have a chance to find other spirits that will be congenial to them. We may bind on earth and it will be bound in Heaven, and loose on earth and it will be loosed in Heaven.[78]

Incompatibility is a valid ground for divorce *if* it stems from a basic and unalterable disharmony of natures. Its heights and depths must be honestly surveyed, however, lest acute differences be confused with chronic ones or a passing rude blast be taken for a prevailing wind.[79] But if the incompatibility is profound and unchangeable, it should be faced. Remaining with a false religion will not transform it into a true one. We can only repent of it by apostatizing from it. When *fundamentally* dissimilar natures are joined together, time and truth will eventually sever them apart. No false alliance can endure.

Forgiveness and Divorce

However, before taking the drastic step of divorce, one should make very certain that it is a false alliance. Those who err in the decision to marry, can err in the decision to divorce. Therefore, when threatening differences arise in a marriage, the Lord's counsel should be followed:

---

[77]Matthew 19:29.

[78]*Box Elder News*, Jan. 28, 1915. p. 4. Because of the alienation between his wife and himself, Martin Harris was instructed to: "Leave thy house and home, except when thou shalt desire to see thy family. . . ." D&C 19:36. The Harris' were subsequently divorced.

[79]See CR, April 6, 1971, p. 133.

Moreover if thy brother shall trespass against thee, go and tell him his fault between thee and him alone: if he shall hear thee, thou hast gained thy brother. But if he will not hear thee, then take with thee one or two more, that in the mouth of two or three witnesses every word may be established. And if he shall neglect to hear them, tell it unto the church: but if he neglect to hear the church, let him be unto thee as an heathen man and a publican. Verily I say unto you, Whatsoever ye shall bind on earth shall be bound in heaven: and whatsoever ye shall loose on earth shall be loosed in heaven.[80]

Obviously, one can be loosed from a mate (or an enemy) and still love them and, therefore, forgive them their trespasses. Neither love nor forgiveness necessitates the continuation of a relationship which can only produce further harm.

But we do not love to associate with our enemies, and I do not think the Lord requires us to do it. If He does He will have to reveal it, for I cannot find it anywhere revealed. . . . We should keep ourselves aloof from the wicked; the dividing line should be distinctly drawn between God and Belial, between Christ and the world, between truth and error, and between right and wrong. . . . Now, here is the law of God upon the subject; it is the word of the Lord: "Come out from among them and be ye separate, and touch not the unclean thing." What affinity can we have for them? Let them alone, let them go their own way. Help them to all the happiness that it is possible for them to obtain in this world; for it will be all that they will ever get, unless they repent of their sins, and forsake their wicked ways.[81]

The essence of forgiveness is the absence of punitive action for *past* offenses. Forgiveness does not necessarily restore former trust or require the resumption of former relationships. An employer may refuse to file charges against a dishonest worker and yet not retain him in his employ. A woman may forgive her husband for his repeated acts of brutality against her and still divorce him. The Prodigal Son was accepted back, but he did not regain the inheritance which he had squandered.[82] Perfect forgiveness includes the

---

[80]Matthew 18:15-18. See D&C 42:88-93; 64:8-12.

[81]Joseph F. Smith, JD 23:285, 286.

[82]See Luke 15:3. The ring and the fatted calf are symbolic of heaven's love, not of its blessings.

274

blotting out of past offenses so that it is as though they had never happened.[83] This is known as the remission of sins and is possible only through the atonement of Christ. So that while the remission of sins is an aspect of the forgiveness of sins, the two are not always synonymous. Mortals are expected to forgive the offenses of others, but only God can fully remit sin so that it does not jeopardize one's *future* relationship with Him.

Witholding punishment is the first mile of forgiveness required of every would-be saint. The second mile is walked when the offender is welcomed back as a friend and a brother. This, however, is as dependent upon his repentance as it is upon the injured party's forgiveness. To the degree that circumstances will permit, the spirit of remission should enliven every act of forgiveness. The best robe, a ring on the finger, the fatted calf—these are three tokens of God's awesome love for us, three reminders of the grand objective of human contrition and divine compassion.

Therefore, before legally declaring one's mate to be "as an heathen man and a publican", there should be a mutually-agreed-upon separation to allow tempers to cool, emotions to calm and truth to prevail. God himself delays his judgment of mankind until the last possible moment. He, too, has been obliged to separate himself from his children. However, he is doing everything possible—even to sacrificing his Beloved Son—to effect a reconciliation. Can we do less? How patient Jehovah has been with *his* errant wife! Every reproof has been followed by assurances of deathless devotion.

Can a woman forget her sucking child, that she should not have compassion on the son of her womb? yea, they may forget, yet will I not forget thee. Behold, I have graven thee upon the palms of my hands; thy walls are continually before me.[84]

Although Israel sinned against Jehovah, yet he has not given her a bill of divorcement.

[83]See Isaiah 1:18; Psalm 103:12; D&C 58:42; Mormon 9:3-6.
[84]Isaiah 49:15, 16.

Thus saith the Lord, Where is the bill of your mother's divorcement, whom I have put away? or which of my creditors is it to whom I have sold you? Behold, for your iniquities have ye sold yourselves, and for your transgressions is your mother put away.[85]

While men and women may be justified in divorcing an unfaithful mate, they are not required to do so. Mercy can season justice. Indeed, the whole tenor of the plan of salvation is that it must do so. Even when it comes to the treatment of an adulterous mate, the Lord is our Shepherd, pointing the way and setting an example others may follow:

They say, If a man put away his wife, and she go from him, and become another man's, shall he return unto her again? shall not that land be greatly polluted? but thou hast played the harlot with many lovers; yet return again to me, saith the Lord.[86]

It is because Jehovah loves Israel with a pure love that he is able to be so long-suffering. Infidelity is a shattering assault against married love. Those who can find it in their hearts to forgive an unfaithful, but repentant, mate are to be commended. Truly, theirs is a "work of faith, and labor of love, and patience of hope."[87]

Faith, hope and charity are inseparable companions; if one is lost, all are lost. The Gospel is a message of reconciliation to God and our fellow man via "these three."[88] We are false disciples of the Master if we do not do all in our power to fulfill the Gospel's goal in our own lives. We must put off the natural man and become as little children, being meek and of a gentle disposition even as Jesus declared himself to be.[89] This produces a paradox: we become less inclined to judge or to forsake others and yet more qualified to do so. The Lord chastises those he loves, but he does not abandon

---

[85]Isaiah 50:1.

[86]Jeremiah 3:1.

[87]I Thessalonians 1:3.

[88]See I Corinthians 13:13.

Paul counseled against hasty divorce in pointing out that the believing mate might save the unbelieving one. See I Corinthians 7:12-16; D&C 74.

[89]See Matthew 11:29; 18:1-5; Mosiah 3:19.

them.[90] Only when his children fully reject his love does he lose hope for their salvation.[91] So too, while some are forced to make judgment, they should first make certain that the beam is out of their own eye. It is not wrong to judge, but it is wrong to judge wrongfully.[92]

Divorce is an act of judgment. Those who cry out for mercy for their own sins and short-comings are miserable hypocrites if they then demand justice for the sins and failings of others.[93] We shall, indeed, be judged as we judge. Consequently, the decision to divorce should not be based upon minor irritations, frustrations and differences. We are all poor, finite creatures, struggling with varying degrees of understanding and success for a place in the sun. We marry fallible, imperfect human beings, we are unjustified in forsaking them simply because they prove to be a bit more imperfect than we bargained for. Neither trivial differences nor the loss of physical beauty, health, wealth, status, or any other features of marriage's first blooming justify divorce. Time's wrinkles must be accepted as part of life's wholeness. Nor can we smooth away the years with a new relationship at the expense of the old. A true marriage is "rooted and grounded" in God. As long as the parties to it are joined to him, they will be joined to one another.

> We men of the priesthood who have knelt at the sacred altar and on that altar clasped the hand of a sainted companion and have entered an eternal triangle, not a companionship of two, but of three—the husband, the wife, and God—the most sacred triangle man and woman can become a part of. But my heart sinks in despair when I witness so many who have and are withdrawing that hand from one another. They don't do that until they first divorce God from that triangle, and after divorcing God, it is practically impossible for them to stay together side by side.[94]

---

[90]Hebrews 12:6, 7; D&C 101:4, 5.

[91]See 2 Nephi 33:9; D&C 1:33.

[92]See D&C 107:30, 31; Matthew 7:1-5. The Inspired Revision of Matthew 7:2 reads, "Judge not unrighteously, that ye be not judged; but judge righteous judgment."

[93]See Matthew 18:21-35. D&C 64:8-12.

[94]Matthew Cowley, CR, October 3, 1952, p. 27.

When all is said and done, the overriding justification for ending what was meant to be an everlasting union is the inability of husband and wife to achieve a viable degree of oneness of heart and mind with God—and with themselves. Hardness of heart (the want of love) and blindness of mind (the want of truth) are the essential causes of virtually all inter-personal estrangement. Because of them, many of our Heavenly Father's children will be "divorced" from his presence forever. Because of them, relatively few men and women will create that holy bond which is the key to eternal life and exaltation. There does come that moment when judgment must be laid "to the line, and righteousness to the plummet."[95]

---

[95]Isaiah 28:18.

XI

Woman And The Priesthood

Woman is co-eternal in her being with that Father who gave her organized existence as one of his daughters.[1] He holds her in equal esteem with his sons, for "God is no respector of persons."[2] Heaven knows but one aristocracy and that is the aristocracy of righteousness. "Behold, the Lord esteemeth all flesh in one; he that is righteous is favored of God."[3] The basic laws by which the blessings of heaven are obtained apply with equal force to both sexes. The woman who fills the measure of her creation is as approved, successful and happy as any man can hope to be. Woman is spirit of man's spirit and bone of his bone. To the extent that she shares a common origin and divinity with him, she is one with him.

[1]D&C 93:29; TJS pp. 352, 353.
[2]Acts 10:34; D&C 1:35; 38:26.
[3]1 Nephi 17:35.

280   Thus, the sexes were created relatively equal and should remain so as both grow and develop toward perfection.[4] However, the preservation of this equality is assured only when men and women share a mutual commitment to God and to one another. For their equality is not sameness. Indeed, the divine potential possessed by each sex is made possible by their very dissimilarities. It is the blending of these complementary natures which transforms the melodies of existence into a symphony of life. The "harmony of the spheres" is not limited to those worlds which brighten the universe. That harmony is made possible by the greater harmony which exists between those men and women—those persons—by whom and for whom those worlds exist.

Gifts of the Spirit

As a person, a woman can enter into a valid covenant with Jesus Christ thereby obtaining a remission of her sins and a hope of salvation in the celestial kingdom. The gift of the Holy Ghost can be hers together with one or more of the gifts of the Spirit.[5] These gifts are freely given to all who earnestly seek them according to their faith and diligence—subject only to the discretion of the Holy Ghost.

For example, the gift of prophecy—of inspired utterances—have been enjoyed by many women. One such woman was Miriam, the sister of Moses.[6] Another was Deborah, one of the judges in ancient Israel.[7] And Huldah, who lived in the days of Isaiah.[8] A fourth was Anna, the aged widow from the tribe of Asher, who was present when Mary and Joseph

---

[4]Obviously, the sexes cannot be absolutely equal as such while still being different. "Equality" is an almost meaningless term except where God and his law are concerned. Said President J. Reuben Clark: "Now, I am trying to get out of all this only the one fundamental thought—we were not all equal at the beginning; we were not all equal at the Grand Council; we have never been all equal at any time since, and apparently we never shall be." CR, October, 1956, p. 84.

[5]See 1 Corinthians 12; D&C 46; Moroni 10.

[6]See Exodus 15:20.

[7]See Judges 4, 5.

[8]See 2 Kings 22:14; 2 Chronicles 34:22.

brought their infant son to the temple. She thereafter "spake of him to all that looked for redemption in Jerusalem."[9] Heber C. Kimball declared that when the saints are truly united "the same Spirit and power will rest upon our sisters as it did upon Mary, Elizabeth, and Anna, and thousands of others."[10] Indeed, many women in modern Israel have enjoyed the gift of revelation and prophecy.

Oh, Ye Latter-day Saints, you talk about revelation and wonder if there is any revelation. Why bless your souls, say nothing about the apostles and elders around me, these mountains contain thousands upon thousands of devoted women, holy women, who are filled with the inspiration of Almighty God, and these sons and daughters partake of the inspiration of their mothers, as well as of their fathers. . . .[11]

That the gifts of the Spirit were to be enjoyed by women as well as men was the clear teaching of Joseph Smith. In meeting with the "Female Relief Society" he "gave a lecture on the priesthood, showing how the sisters would come in possession of the privileges, blessings and gifts of the priesthood, and that the signs should follow them, such as healing the sick, casting our devils, etc., and that they might attain unto these blessings by a virtuous life, and conversation, and diligence in keeping all the commandments. . . ."[12] In that lecture the Prophet defended the idea that women could bless the sick and otherwise call upon the Spirit. In her synopsis of his remarks, Eliza R. Snow wrote:

No matter who believeth, these signs, such as healing the sick, casting out devils, etc., should follow all that believe, whether male or female. He asked the Society if they could not see by this sweeping promise, that wherein they are ordained, if it is the privilege of those set apart to administer in that authority, which is conferred on them; and if the sisters should have faith to heal the sick, let all hold their tongues, and let everything roll on. . . .

[9]Luke 2:36-38.
[10]JD 5:87. See also 5:34. Speaking of the hymn, "O My Father," Wilford Woodruff said: "That hymn is a revelation, though it was given unto us by a woman, Sister Eliza R. Snow." Millennial Star, 56:229, April 9, 1894.
[11]Wilford Woodruff, "Deseret Weekly," 45:545. October 9, 1892.
[12]History of the Church, 4:602. See "Woman's Exponent," 7:91, November 15, 1878.

282

Respecting females administering for the healing of the sick, he further remarked, there could be no evil in it, if God gave his sanction by healing; that there could be no more sin in any female laying hands on and praying for the sick, than in wetting the face with water; it is no sin for anybody to administer that has faith, or if the sick have faith to be healed by their administration.[13]

This teaching was confirmed by Brigham Young:

It is the privilege of a mother to have faith and to administer to her child; this she can do herself, as well as sending for the Elders to have the benefit of their faith.[14]

In 1852, Elder Ezra T. Benson told the saints: "The priests in Christendom warn their flocks not to believe in 'Mormonism'; and yet you sisters have power to heal the sick, by the laying on of hands, which they cannot do."[15]

However, it must be emphasized that the priesthood presides and has been specifically commissioned to bless the sick and afflicted members of the Church. It is in the *absence* of the priesthood that women are justified in independently exercising their own faith in seeking a healing blessing from the Lord.

When your husbands are absent you sisters should ask God's blessing that he should lead you in the paths of life, and further, you should lay hands on your sick children and rebuke diseases in faith and power, and God will be near you. . . .[16]

. It should be noted that such ministrations are properly confined to children and other women; only the priesthood is authorized to bless all:

As I say, there are occasions when perhaps it would be wise for a woman to lay her hands upon a child, or upon one another sometimes, and there have been appointments made for our sisters, some good

---

[13]TJS 224, 225. See also 229.

[14]Brigham Young, JD 13:155. See 18:71.

[15]Millennial Star, 15:130. While a female may annoint with oil and lay on hands in the prayer of faith, she cannot do so in the name of or by the authority of the Holy Priesthood, anymore than an unordained male could do so.

[16]John Taylor, "Woman's Exponent," 5:148-9.

women, to anoint and bless others of their sex who expect to go through times of great personal trial, travail and "labor;" so that is all right, so far as it goes. But when women go around and declare that they have been set apart to administer to the sick and take the place that is given to the elders of the Church by revelation as declared through James of old, and through the Prophet Joseph in modern times, that is an assumption of authority and contrary to scripture, which is that when people are sick they shall call for the elders of the Church and they shall pray over and officially lay hands on them.

It is the prayer of faith that saves the sick . . . So can people out of the Church, and so they have done. Having faith in God, they have asked God in the name of Jesus Christ to heal the sick by the laying on of their hands, and some of them have got well, and a good many others have died, like it is with all of us.[17]

Thus, faith should be an ever-ready source of divine support for every man, woman and child.

While most women today have ready access to the ministrations of the priesthood, their pioneer sisters were often left to manage for themselves while their men-folk were away, sometimes for months and years. Consequently, those women relied upon the gifts of the Spirit—especially healing —in caring for their families. This is doubtless one reason why these gifts were, comparatively speaking, so common among them. However, there has never been a time when the wives and mothers of the Church needed the aid of the Holy Ghost more than today. Indeed, the lack of such gifts as faith, wisdom, knowledge and discernment, etc., can only diminish the ability of fathers and mothers to guide their children in this perilous period. For these *are* the last days —the days of "wickedness and vengeance" when the saints are going to need all of the divine assistance they can get. Who can say with certainty what the future will bring?[18] It is not impossible that some of the women of the Church may yet, like their pioneer counterparts, be called upon to round up their shoulders and carry some of the burdens normally borne by their fathers and husbands. It is a wise woman who

---

[17]Charles W. Penrose, CR, April 6, 1921, p. 199.
[18]See JD 3:15.

284   magnifies her own spiritual potential by earnestly seeking after the "best gifts."[19]

Woman's "Priesthood"

Since women have enjoyed so many spiritual gifts and played such significant parts in the unfolding drama of the Lord's people, two questions arise. The first has to do with the fact that comparatively little scripture is directly concerned with them. Men dominate both ancient and modern revelation. There are a few stories—notably in the Old Testament—in which women figure prominently, but other than these, references to them are quite spotty. There are a number of reasons for this. For one thing, scripture is the work of men; although quoted, women had no direct part in producing the various books. But more importantly, the very nature and purpose of scripture dictates its male orientation. For its central theme is the salvation of mankind, and the chief responsibility for declaring it devolves upon men rather than women. This, because man has been designated the direct and immediate respresentative of the Lord on earth.

As we have seen, this does not mean that women are denied direct personal revelation or the gifts of the Spirit. But it does mean that there is a proper channel of authority reaching back to God which makes for the orderly management of human affairs. It remains for the priesthood to convey to women those commandments of the Lord which are appropriate to their callings. Grave harm has been done to women when certain passages of scripture have been misapplied to them. Some pertain to men alone while others pertain to women alone. For example, the Lord's instruction to the man, Adam, differed from those given to the woman, Eve. The general tendency to make a blanket application of all scripture to both sexes is based upon a misunderstanding of their respective roles.[20]

---

[19]D&C 46:8.

[20]The law of Moses, Jesus' teachings on divorce and Peter and Paul's writings on marriage, distinguish between the sexes as to their duties and responsibilities. Said Brigham Young: "When we speak of law and of the transgression of law, we refer to the law of God to man." JD 8:222.

Heaven, itself, bears witness to the proper roles of men and women. God does not send his daughters on errands to this world until it is time for them to acquire mortal bodies. And when they set them aside in death, they do not venture forth again until the resurrection.[21] Claims of females, such as the Virgin Mary, appearing from heaven with messages for a church or for the world are false. The voice of the priesthood is a male voice; nowhere in all scripture is there record of any female being heard speaking in behalf of God. The Lord does not send women to do the work of men; it is not for women to receive instructions for the Church and kingdom and priesthood of God.[22] The message of salvation is a priesthood message delivered by male messengers to male prophets. It is all under the direction of the Godhead— three male deities. It is revealed through the instrumentality of the Holy Ghost, an unembodied spirit man. It is validated by the atoning sacrifice of the *Son* of God and it is the responsibility of men to take the good news of salvation into all the world.[23] Woman's primary role is in the home just as man's is in the fields—the world. Each has proper labors to perform and a proper place in which to perform them. If women do the work of men and men do the work of women the result is confusion, strife, insecurity and a loss of basic identities.

The second question is: "Why can't women *hold* the priesthood?" In other words, why can't women exercise the same prerogatives and perform the same ordinances granted to men?[24] The answer lies in the character of the priesthood itself. In an ultimate sense, priesthood is the sum of all divine authority and power as it exists in the Most High. Only the Gods have absolute priesthood; men receive it line upon line in connection with their various offices and callings.

---

[21]However, disembodied female spirits may appear to living persons—usually family members—in order to comfort and inform them on personal matters.

[22]They may receive personal revelation for themselves and their own families.

[23]Women are permitted to serve as missionaries under the direction of the priesthood. They serve at their own request and only after reaching legal age.

[24]See CR, October 4, 1963, p. 29.

286 These positions define the proper bounds and limitations of their activity. Should a man attempt to either exceed or avoid his responsibilities, he would jeopardize his own salvation. Legal authority is, therefore, central to priesthood:

> The question, "What is priesthood?" has often been asked me. I answer, it is the rule and government of God, whether on earth, or in the heavens; and it is the only legitimate power, the only authority that is acknowledged by Him to rule and regulate the affairs of His kingdom. When every wrong thing shall be put right, and all usurpers shall be put down, when he whose right it is to reign shall take the dominion, then nothing but the Priesthood will bear rule; it alone will sway the sceptre of authority in heaven and on earth, for this is the legitimacy of God.[25]

It is the unique responsibility of men to act as God's agents or legal administrators in representing him on earth. Only those called as was Aaron have the right to declare God's will to men and to commit *him* to covenants with them.[26] It is this authority which a woman cannot "hold."[27] Her "priesthood" callings are not elder, bishop, seventy or apostle—but wife, mother, teacher and comforter. These are at least as important and demanding as any of those exercised by men.[28] In honoring these callings, she becomes a true "helpmeet" of "Adam" in his labors in the field. She does this, not by sharing his immediate burdens and responsibilities, but by freeing him to labor with an eye single to God even as she should be freed of those concerns which would prevent her from having an eye single to her husband. Woman's God-ordained "callings" are uniquely adapted to

---

[25]John Taylor, JD 1:224. See CR, Oct. 4, 1963, p. 29.

[26]Hebrews 5:1-10.

[27]Said President Charles W. Penrose: "Sisters have said to me sometimes, 'But, I hold the priesthood with my husband.' 'Well,' I asked, 'what office do you hold in the priesthood?' Then they could not say much more. The sisters are not ordained to any office in the Priesthood and there is authority in the Church which they cannot exercise; it does not belong to them; they cannot do that properly any more than they can change themselves into a man." CR, April 6, 1921, p. 198. See *Ibid.*, p. 24.

[28]Pres. J. Reuben Clark said that wives and mothers possess "a function as divinely called, as eternally important in its place as the Priesthood itself." RSM, 33:801, December, 1946.

and reflective of her feminine qualifications. It is in magnifying them that she magnifies her "priesthood" and her husband's priesthood.

> Do they hold the priesthood? Yes, in connection with their hus-
> bands and they are one with their husbands, but the husband is the head.
> And women are so constituted that they are much better prepared to
> feel after the welfare of families than men are. They can sympathize
> with the sisters, for they are one with them. I remember a certain lady
> said to me in talking about some things, "You never was a grandmother."
> "No." said I, "I never was? I never had that experience." "Well, then,
> you cannot enter into the feelings of a grandmother." No, and I never
> was a wife, and therefore I could not enter into the feelings of a wife.
> But a wife can enter into a wife's feelings and into a mothers' feelings
> and they can sympathize with the sisters, and pour in the oil and wine
> and they can teach the sisters correct principles, teach them cleanliness,
> kindness and sisterly sympathetic feelings. They are doing this to a great
> extent, therefore I say God bless the sisters. They are one with us in
> seeking to promote the welfare of Israel.[29]

A woman should no more covet the duties of her husband than he should covet the office and calling of his appointed leaders. It is for each to do his or her part as that
part is designated by the Lord. Like Alma, we should feel to
say: "Now, seeing that I know these things, why should I
desire more than to perform the work to which I have been
called?"[30]

The spirit of envy and competition is alien to the Spirit
of Christ. It is especially inappropriate where the priesthood
is concerned. It is, perhaps, a greater sin for a woman to
covet a man's priesthood than it would be for her to covet
anything else. And there is no need for her to do so. Eternal
marriage unites their "priesthoods" in one, making them a
shared blessing.

For priesthood is not only a divine power of attorney
by which men on earth act, lead and rule in God's behalf, it
it also the means by which all things are organized and
controlled. If the sick are healed, if the dead are raised, if

[29]John Taylor, JD 20:359. See JD 17:119; 22:316.
[30]Alma 29:6.

288

mountains are moved, if the winds are stilled or life is begotten, it is by virtue of this power. To the extent that anyone organizes or controls matter, he or she is drawing upon
the *principle* of priesthood.[31] However, it is *only* when such
things are done in harmony with and by the direct authority
of the Lord that they can be said to be acts of the Holy
Priesthood. The Spirit of the Lord pervades the universe and
is the "power of God" by which he organizes, controls and
sustains all things.[32] Consequently, every existing form of
life must acknowledge that it is "in him we live, and move,
and have our being."[33]

Both men and devils can and do use their God-given
agency to control the elements, but they do not exercise the
priesthood in doing so. Still, they employ a degree of its
power in everything they do—whether good or evil. The distinction is, that while the priesthood is infinite and eternal,
the power of men and devils is finite and temporal. Men
grow in the *principle* of priesthood only as they grow in its
attributes, powers and authorities so that the epitome of
priesthood is God. He has shared a small portion of his power
with all men. How they use it will determine how much
priesthood they will possess in eternity.

In nothing is the complimentary relationship of priesthood men and women more wonderfully manifest than in
the organizing and perfecting of an intelligence. The first
phase of this greatest of miracles is carried out by our Eternal Parents whose efforts constitute the pattern to be followed by their mortal counterparts. In doing so, each has
both a leading and a supporting role to play in the eternal
drama. Thus, while priesthood men share in the begetting of
life, they cannot *bear* it. Only women have the power to
bring the conception to fruition and actually organize a body

---

[31]Speaking of woman's power to organize matter into tabernacles suitable for the
Father's spirit progeny, J. Reuben Clark said: "This was her calling; this was her blessing,
bestowed by the Priesthood." RSM, 33:801, December, 1946.

[32]D&C 88:13.

[33]Acts 17:25, 28.

for its waiting spirit.[34] Men do not *hold* this aspect of divine authority.

Similarly, while women may assist,[35] the actual begetting of spiritual life is the immediate responsibility of the priesthood. In other words, the rebirth by which any soul becomes a son or a daughter of Christ, is the direct result of the labors performed by priesthood men in connection with the saving ordinances of the Gospel. Thus Paul could speak of: "My little children, of whom *I travail in birth* again until Christ be formed in you."[36]

And so, woman and the priesthood work together. She bestows bodies of flesh and bones upon her sons and daughters which enable them to obtain a fulness of joy. And the priesthood, in turn, provides the means by which these souls are born again into the family of God. More than that, the priesthood which initiated the process by which life is organized, will perfect the joint creative labor of man and woman. For by virtue of the keys of the resurrection, the priesthood will redeem those tabernacles of clay, which the women of the earth prepared for their children, and clothe them with immortal glory![37]

How can any woman with understanding feel that her calling is beneath her?[38] The wise wife and mother in Israel is grateful for her vital role in the plan of salvation. She honors her husband in his station, no matter how humble it may be. She teaches her children the dignity of work no matter how menial it may appear to others. She knows that "Well done, thou good and faithful servant" is for door-

---

[34]For a sensitive description of the mother's role in organizing life, see President J. Reuben Clark, RSM 33:801, December, 1946.

[35]Indeed, their part is vital! "Thus to the full stature of manhood and womanhood, mother guides, incites, entreats, instructs, directs, on occasion commands, the soul for which she built the earthly home, in its march onward to exaltation. God gives the soul its destiny, but mother leads it along the way." J. Reuben Clark, RSM, 33:803.

[36]Galatians 4:19.

[37]See JD 6:275; 15:137; 25:34.

[38]"From that day, when Eve thus placed first among her blessings the power to bear children, the greatest glory of true womanhood has been motherhood." J. Reuben Clark, RSM, 33:801.

290   keepers as well as for prophets. Being lowly in heart, she does not fill her sons with notions of high office—the devil's disease—but simply with the desire to act well their part. How a woman regards her own calling directly influences how she will look upon those of her husband and sons. The wives and mothers among the saints do have priesthood. They have been given a work to do. Its faithful performance will be rewarded beyond their fondest dreams.

Now, brethren, the man that honors his Priesthood, the woman that honors her Priesthood, will receive an everlasting inheritance in the kingdom of God; but it will not be until this earth is purified and sanctified, and ready to be offered up to the Father. But we can go to work now and live as near as we can like the family of heaven, that we may secure to ourselves the blessings of heaven and of earth, of time and of eternity, and life everlasting in the presence of the Father and the Son. This is what we want to do. Remember it, brethren and sisters, and try to live worthy of the vocation of your high calling. You are called to be Saints—just think of and realize it, for the greatest honor and privilege that can be conferred upon a human being is to have the privilege of being a Saint. The honor of the kings and queens of the earth fades into insignificance when compared with the title of a Saint. You may possess earthly power, and rule with an iron hand, but that power is nothing, it will soon be broken and pass away; but the power of those who live and honor the Priesthood will increase forever and ever.[39]

A Mother In Israel

Whether born under the covenant or gathered out of the world, a faithful mother in Israel has become a daughter of Abraham via the new and everlasting covenant of the Gospel.[40] In doing so, her heart is turned to her ancient fathers as theirs is turned to her.[41] She has obeyed the counsel of Isaiah:

Hearken to me, ye that follow after righteousness, ye that seek the Lord: look unto the rock whence ye are hewn, and to the hole of the

[39]Brigham Young, JD 17:119, 120.
[40]See Abraham 2:10.
[41]See D&C 98:16.

pit whence ye are digged. Look unto Abraham your father and unto   **291**
Sarah that bare you: for I called him alone, and blessed him, and increased him.[42]

The Holy Ghost has become her companion, guiding
and directing her in all that she does. Her children are begotten unto the Lord and are, themselves, blessed with his
Spirit even from the womb.

Never cease a day of your life to have the Holy Ghost resting
upon you. Fathers, never cease to pray that your wives may enjoy this
blessing, that their infants may be endowed with the Holy Ghost, from
their mother's womb.[43]

The advantage of being so endowed stems from the fact
that a child's education begins before it is born:

I consider that the mother has a greater influence over her posterity
than any other person can have. And the question has arisen some time:
"When does this education begin?" Our prophets have said, "When the
spirit life from God enters into the tabernacle." The condition of the
mother at that time will have its effect upon the fruit of her womb; and
from the birth of the child, and all through life, the teachings and the
example of the mother govern and control, in a great measure, that
child, and her influence is felt by it through time and eternity.[44]

As Christ is the vine and his saints the branches, so are
parents the vine and their children the branches. If the
vine is filled with the Spirit, that lifepower can then flow
from them to their offspring.

When wives become one with their husbands, when there is no
evil interruption, children will be begotten, born and reared under
greatly improved influences. The Holy Ghost will rest upon and dwell
with the parents, and their offspring will be mighty and godlike. I
would not give much for a man nor a woman that does not enjoy the
fellowship of the Father, of the Son, and of the Holy Ghost. If I do not
have the Holy Ghost, I shall not produce the fruit that is designed by

---

[42]Isaiah 51:1, 2.

[43]Brigham Young, JD 1:69. See also 4:277; 9:37; 11:215.

[44]Durham, G. Homer. *The Discourses of Wilford Woodruff* [Bookcraft, Salt Lake
City, 1946], p. 269.

292   the holy order of matrimony. Mary, the mother of Jesus, was a pure woman, and was ordained and designed to bear the Son of God, because no woman in her sins was worthy of performing that work. How long will it be before we will have children filled with the Holy Ghost from their birth, who will grow up steadfast in the truth, even sons and daughters of God?[45]

A celestially-oriented home is a temple of temples, in which, as President Stephen L. Richards explained, parents "are called to officiate in a transcendentally beautiful and vital service."

As a priest and priestess in the temple of the home, it is their high privilege to receive the spirit children of our Eternal Father into mortality; then to nurture, train, and lead these chosen ones coming to their home back into the eternal presence whence they came. It takes but a moment to say this sentence; it takes a lifetime to fill the mission of parenthood. It is a glorious mission when it is accepted and fulfilled. It is a tragic experience when it is resented. Women of the kingdom find the supreme joy of their lives in their families despite the sacrifices and self-denial entailed in their care and training. They are taught, and they believe that the highest blessings of heaven will be realized through the projection of their homes into eternity.[46]

If a woman is saved in child-bearing, she is exalted in child-guidance. From time immemorial, the dominant role of the mother in the moral and spiritual development of the child has been both recognized and honored.

It is the mother's influence that is most effective in moulding the mind of the child for good or for evil. If she treat lightly the things of God, it is more than likely her children will be inclined to do the same, and the Lord will not hold her guiltless when he comes to make up his jewels; he will disown all such when he comes to claim his own, and will say, Go hence, I never knew you.[47]

President Young's views were shared by President Joseph F. Smith:

---

[45]Heber C. Kimball, JD 4:277.
[46]CR, October 5, 1952, p. 100.
[47]Brigham Young, JD 18:263.

The influence of women is far more potent than [that] of man. The influence of the mother is far more deep and lasting than any that can possibly be exerted; that of the father is nothing like equal to it.[48]

She is the most influential person in the child's life not only because she is with the child more than anyone else, but more importantly, because she is with the child *in a special way*. She is no hireling servant, she is the true shepherd.[49] She was once prepared to lay down her life for her little lamb. That lamb should not be forced to follow a stranger. The Good Shepherd of all mankind has set the example for motherhood. He has ever sought to gather his sheep to *himself*. He never willed to be separated from his flock. When circumstances required, faithful servants were appointed to watch over them in his absence.

Mother belongs at home during the formative years of her child's life. No amount of sophisticated reasoning can free her of the obligation to *be available* whenever she is needed. And she is needed *when* she is needed, not simply when she chooses to be available. The popular argument that it is the quality of the relationship, not the amount of time involved in it which is most important is, to say the least, specious. Motherhood is not an either-or proposition. One might as well argue that a hundred calories of good nourishing food is more important to good health than two thousand calories made up of starches. Starvation on the one hand versus malnutrition on the other hardly makes for a satisfactory choice in either case!

There is a "due time" for everything. A mother cannot teach her little ones the lessons of life they need to learn in infancy and childhood if she is absent from them during the bulk of their waking hours. If they are to be learned quickly and well, these lessons must be taught in the natural context of each day's events. It is in the ongoing relationships associated with a child's early development that

[48]Joseph F. Smith, Young Woman's Journal 3:143.
[49]See John 10:12.

294 provides a mother with the *natural* teaching aids she needs to train up her child in the way it should go. An hour or so at night spent with a child may seem to be sufficient for its well-being, but it cannot replace the moment to moment association God intended that human mothers should provide their small children. A price will be paid—by the parents and by the malnourished child. We are only now beginning to appreciate the psychological damage hidden neglect has inflicted on children in this culture. The moral and spiritual harm done them while perhaps less rapid in its manifestation is potentially of even greater duration and effect.

In the early days of the Church, every prophet beginning with Joseph Smith warned the Saints against allowing their children to be taught by gentile unbelievers. Eventually, this counsel was ignored and others were allowed to educate them. Now conditions have worsened to the point where some Latter-day Saints are foolishly entrusting even their very young children to public agencies.[50]

> This divine service of motherhood can be rendered only by mothers. It may not be passed to others. Nurses cannot do it; public nurseries cannot do it; hired help cannot do it—only mother, aided as much as may be by the loving hands of father, brothers, and sisters, can give the full needed measure of watchful care. The mother who entrusts her child to the care of others, that she may do non-motherly work, whether for gold, for fame, or for civic service, should remember that "a child left to himself bringeth his mother to shame." (Prov. 29:15.)[51]

If we turn our children over to the care of those who know not God, what a precious opportunity to mold that tender clay is lost! For while others can provide a child's basic physical and psychological needs, *they cannot nourish its spirit.* Children do not live—cannot live—by bread alone! They will never grow up without sin unto salvation until they receive that special endowment of love, guidance and example which only a true mother and a true father in

---

[50]See CR, October 4, 1963, pp. 34-40; October 7, 1951, pp. 110-112.
[51]The First Presidency, CR, October 3, 1942, p. 12.

Israel can offer. Loving the Lord with all one's heart requires consecration—not tithing. A tithe of a mother's time and attention is not enough; she must—insofar as she can—practice consecration toward her little ones if she, and they, are to be free of the blood and the sins of this generation.[52]

A mother in Israel knows that she is the first and the most important teacher her child will ever have. The infant clay, being soft and pliable, will never again be quite so responsive to the hands of any mortal potter. Home is the greatest school of all, and mother its greatest teacher. Thus the primary responsibility for the basic education of a child rests with her. The following statement by President Young is representative of the views of all of the prophets of the Lord:

It depends in a great degree upon the mother, as to what children receive, in early age, of principle of every description, pertaining to all that can be learned by the human family. . . . I can see mothers pay attention to everything under heaven, *but* the training up of their children in the way they should go, and they will even make it appear obligatory on the father to take care of the child at a year old. . . . I will tell you the truth as you will find it in eternity. If your children do not receive impressions of true piety, virtue, tenderness, and every principle of the holy Gospel, you may be assured that their sins will not be required at the hands of the father, but of the mother. Lay it to heart, ye mothers, for it will unavoidably be so. The duty of the mother is to watch over her children, and give them their early education, for impressions received in infancy are lasting. You know, yourselves, by experience, that the impressions you have received in the dawn of your mortal existence, bear, to this day, with the greatest weight upon your mind. It is the experience of people generally, that what they imbibe from their mothers in infancy, is the most lasting upon the mind through life. This is natural, it is reasonable, it is right. I do not suppose you can find one person among five hundred, who does not think his mother to be the best woman that ever lived. This is right, it is planted in the human heart. The child reposes implicit confidence in the mother, you behold in him a natural attachment, no matter what her appearance may be, that makes him think his mother is the best and handsomest mother in the world. I speak for myself. Children have all confidence in their mothers; and if mothers would take proper pains,

---

[52]D&C 68:25.

296 they can instil into the hearts of their children what they please. You
will, no doubt, recollect reading, in the Book of Mormon, of two thousand young men, who were brought up to believe that, if they put their
whole trust in God, and served Him, no power would overcome them.
You also recollect reading of them going out to fight, and so bold were
they, and so mighty their faith, that it was impossible for their enemies
to slay them. This power and faith they obtained through the teachings
of their mothers. The character of a person is formed through life, to a
greater or less degree, by the teachings of the mother. The traits of
early impressions that she gives the child, will be characteristic points
in his character through every avenue of his mortal existence.[53]

"But few women have a realizing sense of the immortal,
invisible, and powerful influence they exert in their sphere."[54]
The greatest social tragedy of our times may well prove to be
the exodus of millions of women from that sphere into the
world of men. They, and those who abet them, will have to
answer for their crimes against their children and their children's children. What does it profit any man or any woman
to gain all that the world has to offer, if they do so at the
expense of the souls of the innocent?

A child's first world is primarily its mother's world. She
is all things to her offspring, acting as both father and mother
much of the time. The practical fact of the matter was summed
up by President J. Reuben Clark:

Now, brethren, at best we are somewhat clumsy at leading and
directing our children. We are away from home, of necessity, a great
part of the time, our thoughts are along other lines, we have to battle
for our existence, for the livelihood of our families. Those of us who
hold Church positions are absent in the evenings, in addition to the days
that we spend getting our livelihood. I repeat, we are a little bit clumsy.
And so to the sisters of the Church, the mothers of the Church, they
whom the Lord has designed and planned should be the immediate instrumentality of perpetuating the race and of bringing spirits to this
earth, providing bodies of them, to them we must primarily look for the
rearing of our children.[55]

---

[53]Brigham Young, JD 1:66, 67. The entire discourse is worthy of careful study. See
also 15:12.
[54]Brigham Young, JD 8:62.
[55]CR, Oct. 6, 1951, p. 58.

However, as the years pass and life's basic lessons are learned, it is designed that the weight of responsibility should shift more and more to the father. His role as provider and protector is expanded to more directly include that of educator and guide pertaining to the world beyond the hearth. Addressing himself to the sisters, President Young counseled:

Teach your children; for you are their guardians, to act as father and mother to them until they are out of your care. The teachings and examples of our mothers have formed, to a great extent, our characters and directed our lives. This is their right, when they act by the power of the Priesthood, to direct the child until it is of a proper age, and then hand it over to the husband and father, and into the hands of God, with such faith and such love of virtue and truth, and with such love of God and its parents, that that child can never suppose that it is out of the hand and from under the control of the parent. Do not call it "mine." Let your maxim be, "This is not mine," whether you have one child or a dozen. "It is not mine, but the Lord has seen fit to let me bear the souls of the children of men. It is from my Father and God, and I will do my duty and hand it over to him," and have that faith that the child can never wring itself out of the hands of a good father and mother—can never stray away,—no, never. That is the privilege of mothers. It is you who guide the affections and feelings of the child. It is the mothers, after all, that rule the nations of the earth. They form, dictate, and direct the minds of statesmen, and the feelings, course, life, notions, and sentiments of the great and the small, of kings, rulers, governors, and of the people in general.[56]

A mother in Israel is a missionary in the best sense of the word. Her influence not only extends to her own family, but to all of those who will be blessed through her by virtue of the faithful lives of her children.[57] When both she and her husband have done all that they could do for their children by way of helping them grow up righteous men and women, the burden of responsibility shifts to them.

Let us do our duty to our children, train them in the way they should go, give them the benefit of our experience, teach them true principles and do all we can for them, and when they reach years of

---

[56]Brigham Young, JD 9:38. See 1:246.
[57]See JD 11:338.

298 maturity, if they walk in evil ways, we may mourn and bewail their follies, but we shall be guiltless before God so far as they are concerned.[58]

All such parents can take comfort in these words by President Young:

Let the father and mother, who are members of this Church and kingdom, take a righteous course, and strive with all their might never to do a wrong, but to do good all their lives; if they have one child or one hundred children, if they conduct themselves towards them as they should, binding them to the Lord by their faith and prayers, I care not where those children go, they are bound up to their parents by an everlasting tie, and no power of earth or hell can separate them from their parents in eternity; they will return again to the fountain from whence they sprang.[59]

A true mother in Israel is like no other mother on earth! She loves the Lord with all of her heart, might, mind and strength. She loves her children *as herself*—for they *are* herself. She is filled with intelligence. The Spirit of God, of revelation, accompanies her in her daily labors. She knows by that Spirit how to love, to teach, and to guide her children in the nurture and admonition of the Lord. Being an Israelite, she knows that she is an exile from Zion who is obliged to raise her children in Babylon. Consequently, she endeavors to infuse her children with the spirit of Zion, of the pure in heart. She teaches them the ways of the Lord as opposed to the ways of the world. She helps them interpret that world in the light of God's word and to correctly choose between temporal wrong and eternal right. Her example is as the thunders of Sinai. Her precepts are written upon the tablets of her heart in imperishable letters of truth. Therefore, her children know by word, by deed and by Spirit that she is a prophetess to her own. Trained up by such a mother, and sustained by a father of like character, what justification would any child have for departing from the ways of righteousness all of his days?

---

[58]Brigham Young, JD 14:287.
[59]Brigham Young, JD 11:215; TJS, 321.

Motherhood is near to divinity. It is the highest, holiest service to be assumed by mankind. It places her who honors its holy calling and service next to the angels. To you mothers in Israel we say God bless and protect you, and give you the strength and courage, the faith and knowledge, the holy love and consecration to duty, that shall enable you to fill to the fullest measure the sacred calling which is yours.[60]

Adam, Where Goest Thou?

Adam's transgression caused him to experience a new emotion—fear. That fear caused him to hide himself from the presence of the Lord.[61] Most of his sons have done the same. Man, who was given stewardship over all things, has largely abdicated his responsibilities toward womankind, brute creation and the earth itself. The question God addressed to his son some six thousand years ago might well be repeated today: "Where goest thou?"[62] Indeed, where is "Adam" going? The answer is to be found in the many mansions of eternity: he is going in all directions. However, those men who do the works of father Adam will follow him into the very presence of God where they will be crowned with glory and eternal lives. They will have progressed from a state of dependency, of sonship, to that of patriarchal rule over their own posterity.[63]

But before they can be granted such dominion, they must prove their fitness by being faithful over a few things. Such is the lesson of the parable of the talents.[64] Among the "few things" the Lord has entrusted to the care of the men of modern Israel, the most important are: their own bodies, the Holy Priesthood, the Gospel of Jesus Christ—with its principles, ordinances and gifts—and their sisters, daughters, wives and children. The men of the priesthood will stand or fall in terms of their stewardships over these "talents."

---

[60]The First Presidency, CR, October 3, 1942, pp. 12-13.
[61]See Genesis 3:10.
[62]Moses 4:15.
[63]See JD 3:266; 11:262.
[64]Matthew 25:14-30.

Your wives are given to you as a stewardship to improve upon in building up and establishing the kingdom of God, and your children are given to you as a stewardship. Where did their spirits come from? Did they come from you? No; they came from God. Who is the Father of those spirits? God, and he will require them of you, and those spirits have also got to give an account to their Father from whom they came; they have got to render up an account. Thus you see, that you have to render an account of your wives and children, of your substance, and everything that pertains to this earth, and you cannot avoid it, without suffering a loss.[65]

For the priesthood is magnified through these talents more than any others. Unfortunately, too many holders of the priesthood do just that—they only hold it, they do little or nothing with it. They bury it. Priesthood must be fully exercised to be fully magnified. To do this, it must infuse every facet of life. Or, more correctly, every facet of life must be correlated with and by the priesthood. Clearly, priesthood is not priesthood any more than love is love until and unless it is given form and expression. The priesthood, like love, must have an object. God is love because he loves *something*. So too, the priesthood is priesthood only when it is acting upon or responding to some material reality—be it organizing an earth, carrying the gospel to the nations, ministering to the sick or counseling an errant child. In other words, potential priesthood does not become actual priesthood until it is directed toward some object or purpose. It is the failure to so employ it that constitutes the "slothful servant."

Initially, the responsibility for carrying out God's will is a male responsibility. Failure to do so is fundamentally a male failure. A woman's ability to faithfully serve the Lord depends upon the treatment she receives from her father, brothers, husband and other males. If they have been righteous in their conduct toward her, she is obliged to respond in kind. On the other hand, if they have betrayed their stewardships, she will be thrown into confusion and disorder. Bad leaders make for rebellious and disorganized followers.

---

[65]Heber C. Kimball, JD 4:252. See JD 25:162-63.

When we are provided with proper guidance and protection, we have no cause to sin—the guilt becomes our own.

The behavior of a parent, husband, leader or ruler does influence the conduct of a child, wife, follower or subject. If the fountainhead is pure, there is good reason to expect the waters flowing from it to be pure as well. At least any impurity subsequently found in those waters will not be attributable to that fountainhead. However, if it is impure, how can its waters be uncontaminated? It is for this reason that Christ, the fountainhead of eternal life, is a living indictment of those who claim discipleship under him, yet are, themselves, impure. And it is for this reason that those who have been made impure by the sins and traditions of their fathers will be saved.[66] Scripture is primarily designed to instruct God's stewards in their stewardships. When fathers, husbands, prophets and priests are pure before the Lord, noble children, faithful wives and a righteous Israel will stand beside them.

Had Adam failed to honor his stewardship, Eve would have been denied the guidance, support and protection her Father intended she should have. Priesthood and manhood are inseparably connected in the Father and those sons who become like him. A whole man is a fatherhood man even as a whole woman is a motherhood woman. The man who does not magnify his priesthood in the home throws an unnatural burden on the motherhood of his wife. A chain reaction results: the sins of the father are visited on his wife and children. Had Christ failed to fulfill his stewardship, his apostles and prophets could not have effectively fulfilled theirs. In large measure, the success of the lesser is dependent upon the fidelity of the greater. The failure of fatherhood is the chief reason for the failure of motherhood.[67] Similarly, delinquent children are more often than not the product of parents who—for whatever reasons—failed to magnify their callings as such.

---

[66]See 2 Nephi 4:5-9; Jeremiah 31:29, 30.

[67]See JD 4:155.

302

> Show me disobedient children, and I will show you disobedient
> parents, the world over. Where there are disobedient and rebellious
> children in the midst of Israel, tell me who their father and mother are,
> and I will point out to you disobedient, rebellious, disaffected parents;
> and if there is a woman in any family whose children dishonour their
> father, I will show you a woman that dishonours her husband and shows
> him disrespect, from which the children take their example.[68]

Priesthood is the authority and power to organize, sustain, direct, redeem and sanctify. These operations are as valid in terms of the home as they are in terms of a planet or a galaxy. The microcosm is, ultimately, the macrocosm: This is why those who prove faithful over a few things will be made rulers over many things. Many are called and few are chosen to retain the priesthood in eternity because their hearts are set upon the things of the world rather than upon the work and the glory of that God they purport to represent.[69] A true priesthood father is like no other father on earth. His children recognize the difference between him and other men. His priesthood is a light to his family and, therefore to the world. Men and women can provide all of the essential ingredients of good parenthood as defined by social scientists without being members of the Church. Both the gospel and the holy priesthood must *make* a difference for there to *be* a difference!

A "good" husband respects his wife's right to her own identity. He is pleased when she expresses her feminine desires, interests and ways. Insofar as he can, he helps her carry her daily burdens. He is courteous, considerate and appreciative. He knows that she has needs which leap the walls of home and go bounding off across the fields. The inner woman is a young girl—a blithe spirit. She cannot *live* without sunshine, flowers and spring winds. Nor can any really happy marriage. But in addition to these vital things, a priesthood husband blesses his family with spiritual guidance and power. He is the vehicle through which sancti-

---

[68]Elder Erastus Snow. JD 5:291.
[69]See D&C 121:34-40.

fication comes to his companion. Paul compared the role   303
of such a husband to his wife with that of Christ to the
Church:

> Husbands, love your wives, even as Christ also loved the church, and
> gave himself for it; That he might sanctify and cleanse it with the wash-
> ing of water by the word, That he might present it to himself a glorious
> church, not having spot, or wrinkle, or any such thing; but that it should
> be holy and without blemish. So ought men to love their wives as their
> own bodies. He that loveth his wife loveth himself. For no man ever
> yet hated his own flesh; but nourisheth and cherisheth it, even as the
> Lord the church: For we are members of his body, of his flesh, and of
> his bones. For this cause shall a man leave his father and mother, and
> shall be joined unto his wife, and they two shall be one flesh. This is a
> great mystery: but I speak concerning Christ and the church. Neverthe-
> less let every one of you in particular so love his wife even as himself;
> and the wife see that she reverance her husband.[70]

Jesus personified the true man, the true husband. Being
filled with the Spirit, he could minister in Spirit and in truth.
The Christ-like man will emulate him and strive to lift his
family to God. Said Lorenzo Snow:

> The men who are sitting here this day ought to be, when in the
> presence of their families, filled with the Holy Ghost, to administer the
> word of life to them as it is administered in this stand from sabbath to
> sabbath. When they kneel down in the presence of their wives and chil-
> dren they ought to be inspired by the gift and power of the Holy
> Ghost, that the husband may be such a man as a good wife will honor,
> and that the gift and power of God may be upon them continually. They
> ought to be one in their families, that the Holy Ghost might descend
> upon them, and they ought to live so that the wife through prayer may
> become sanctified, that she may see the necessity of sanctifying herself
> in the presence of her husband, and in the presence of her children,
> that they may be one together, in order that the man and the wife may
> be pure element, suitable to occupy a place in the establishment and
> formation of the kingdom of God, that they may breathe a pure spirit
> and impart pure instruction to their children, and their children's chil-
> dren.[71]

---

[70]Ephesians 5:25-33.
[71]JD 4:155.

304   *Holy* men are men filled with the *Holy* Ghost. Good husbands and fathers become holy husbands and fathers as they honor their covenants and magnify their priesthood—in themselves, their homes, the Church and the world at large.

The Lord's Army

The men of the priesthood are the Lord's army.[72] It has won mighty victories and suffered stinging defeats during the course of its operations on this planet. Its ranks have known patriots of the noblest order and traitors of the deepest dye—on the one hand, Enoch and Daniel, on the other, Cain and Judas. Jesus Christ is its commander-in-chief, the Great High Priest under whom all of the faithful prophets and apostles have served since the beginning of time. In these last days, Joseph Smith was appointed its first and chief officer. It remained for him to organize anew the army of Israel. This, he did and it has been engaged in continuous battle with the forces of error ever since. But while "the enemy is combined," a comparable unity of purpose has not characterized the Lord's army.[73] It was this weakness which explains the expulsion of the saints from Missouri beginning with the mobbings of July, 1833.[74]

It soon became obvious that modern Israel was not yet worthy to claim its promised land and establish its holy city. Before the saints could "build up the waste places of Zion," they needed to "be taught more perfectly, and have experience, and know more prfectly concerning their duty, and the things which I require at their hands."[75] The Lord's army had to become as holy as the priesthood they bore.

But first let my army become very great, and let it be sanctified before me, that it may become fair as the sun, and clear as the moon, and that her banners may be terrible unto all nations; That the kingdoms

---

[72]See JD 18:273.
[73]See D&C 38:12.
[74]See D&C 101:1-9, 75; 103:1-10; 105:1-10.
[75]D&C 105:10.

of this world may be constrained to acknowledge that the kingdom of Zion is in very deed the kingdom of our God and his Christ; therefore, let us become subject unto her laws.[76]

This recognition of and allegiance to the kingdom of God will come about through the faith and diligence of those men comprising the army of Israel. Faith is the key to power. Only as men exercise it in conjunction with their authority does the priesthood become a living force. Men deceive themselves if they suppose that the fulness of the priesthood is obtained by the mere act of ordination. The awesome power of Enoch and Melchizedek was predicated upon their faith in and devotion to the Lord.

For God having sworn unto Enoch and unto his seed with an oath by himself; that every one being ordained after this order and calling should have power, *by faith*, to break mountains, to divide the seas, to dry up waters, to turn them out of their course; To put at defiance the armies of nations, to divide the earth, to break every band, to stand in the presence of God; to do all things according to his will, according to his command, subdue principalities and powers; and this by the will of the Son of God which was from before the foundation of the world. And men *having this faith*, coming up unto this order of God, were translated and taken up into heaven.[77]

That faith is an imperative where the priesthood is concerned is also attested to by Moroni:

. . . O Lord, thy righteous will be done, for I know that thou workest unto the children of men according to their faith; For the brother of Jared said unto the mountain Zerin, Remove—and it was removed. And if he had not had faith it would not have moved; wherefore thou workest after men have faith. For thus didst thou manifest thyself unto thy disciples; for after they had faith, and did speak in thy name, thou didst show thyself unto them in great power.[78]

---

[76]D&C 105:31, 32. Said Orson Pratt: "Do you suppose that the Lord will suffer any unclean thing to be in that army? Not at all, for his angels and he himself are to go before us. God will not dwell in the midst of a people who will not sanctify themselves before him." JD 15:363.

[77]I.V., Genesis 14:30-32.

[78]Ether 12:29-31. See Moses 7:13; D&C 45:66-70.

306 God is no respecter of persons. It was as necessary for Jesus to have faith in order for him to fulfill his missions as it was for Joseph Smith or any other servant of the Lord. Such faith is both a cause and a result of obedience to the principles of life and salvation. It is the spirit of the priesthood, filling it with life and power. It distinguishes between the many who are called and the few who are chosen. Those, like Jesus, who perfect this faith do not simply *hold* the priesthood or exercise the priesthood—they *are* the priesthood. Can God be distinguished from his attributes? Are they not as one? Can any man become as God unless he internalizes the Holy Priesthood which has been bestowed upon him? Those who are never chosen fail to do this. They view the priesthood as a thing wholly apart from themselves. Thus, they act in its authority, but not in its power. Being double-minded, having a divided loyalty, "they do not learn this one lesson":

> That the rights of the priesthood are inseparably connected with the powers of heaven, and that the powers of heaven cannot be controlled nor handled only upon the principles of righteousness.[79]

It is the inseparable connection between the powers of heaven and the authority of the priesthood which justifies a man in assuming presidency over his family and fellow saints. Even then it remains for them to give him their sustaining vote. However, true saints will follow the leadership of a righteous man. What a compelling thing is love! What a power is faith! What a comfort is humility! How marvelously were these divine qualities combined in Jesus, the Great High Priest of us all!

The husband, the father, the teacher, the leader whose soul is knit to the Master's as a branch is joined to the vine need never apply coercion. The magnetism of his own virtue, like a mighty sun, will draw men, women and children to him in everlasting orbits of loyalty and devotion. He will

---

[79]D&C 121:36.

rule the only way a man can rule: by an affinity of hearts and minds. Having magnified his Priesthood, he is magnified by it. It is sealed upon him with this promise:

The Holy Ghost shall be thy constant companion, and thy scepter an unchanging scepter of righteousness and truth; and thy dominion shall be an everlasting dominion, and without compulsory means it shall flow unto thee forever and ever.[80]

---

[80]D&C 121:46. See JD 20:258-63.

EPILOGUE

The Lord's course is one eternal round.[1] Within its encompassing orbit, the paths of all men twist and turn and likewise end where they began. Pertaining to this world, it all began in Eden when Adam offered his first sacrifice—his own spiritual life—a sacrifice made on behalf of his wife as well as the untold billions of spirits awaiting fleshly tabernacles. He willingly accompanied the Woman into exile from the presence of the Lord.

While it was foreordained and central to a grand theological design, Adam's sacrifice, like that of the Lamb of God, was no less real, no less painful. Adam did not possess the hindsight with which we now so glibly philosophize about his fatal decision.

When he accepted the forbidden fruit from his wife's hand and joined her in mortality, she incurred a debt of gratitude toward the Priesthood which she acknowledged by her humble acceptance of God's judgment upon her. And in honoring her husband as her temporal lord, in placing her womanly affections upon him alone, and in becoming the mother of all living, she laid down her life for others as Adam had laid down his life for her.

Those women who do the works of Eve become, in fact, her eternal daughters. In emulating their ancient mother, they help to lift whatever curses and limitations the Fall has inflicted upon them.

Man and woman find salvation together. They must close the circle of eternal progression if they are to regain the presence of God. Therefore, symbolically speaking, they must return to Eden. The garden is still there, waiting for them; it remains in that spiritual sphere in which it was created.[2] But Satan will not be on hand to threaten them with sin

---

[1]D&C 3:2.
[2]Moses 3:9. JD 14:231.

310   and death. And the cherubim will be gone; no sword will bar the way to the tree of life. Nor will there be any forbidden fruit; the tree of knowledge will have become an immortal ornament of the garden of the Lord.[3]

And Eve, with perfect understanding and unmitigated love, will share the fruits of Eternal Life with him who was faithful to her unto death. All debts will be fully paid— Woman's debt to the Priesthood for its efforts in her behalf, and the Priesthood's debt to Woman for her indispensible part in its eternal labor: the immortality and eternal life of man.

> And then the priesthood will wish to proclaim their debt to these their helpmeets without whom the Priesthood could not have worked out their destiny. And the Priesthood shall bow in reverence and love unbounded before these mothers who did the service the Priesthood could not do, and thank and praise them for bearing their children. . . .[4]

Woman and the Priesthood will enter the presence of the Father to go no more out. They will return, not the child-like innocents they once were, but as mature, resurrected beings filled with light, truth, and glory. Legions of earthly sons and daughters will accompany them and, with songs of everlasting joy, be reunited before the blazing throne of the Eternal Patriarch. The family of Man will be home.

The original triangular and linear relationships of God, man and woman will be perfected and augmented by a celestial circle.

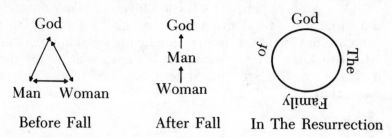

Before Fall	After Fall	In The Resurrection

---

[3]Revelation 2:7; 22:2; Psalms 1:3; Proverbs 3:18.
[4]J. Reuben Clark, RSM, 33:804.

Husband and wife, exalted parents in their own right, will 311
continue to honor their Heavenly Father and Mother in that
everlasting land of promise—the triangle. And Woman,
although a reigning majesty, will nevertheless continue to
acknowledge the Priesthood of her divine companion even as
he continues to obey the Gods who made his own exaltation
possible—the line. This Patriarchal Order will produce a
perfect union, not of persons, but of hearts, minds and glories
—the circle.

Thus, all everlasting associations (as represented by the
three symbols) will blend into the one, perfect order of Heaven!

Husbands, wives, fathers, mothers, sisters, brothers, children—all will be encompassed within the love of God.[5] Pride,
jealousy, covetousness, competition, and their many companions will have been banished forever. Curses, real and
imaginary, will be no more. Perfection will cleave to perfection with a resultant fulness of joy becoming the equal
endowment of every faithful man and woman. Possessing the
power of eternal lives, they will beget a posterity as vast as
the stars of heaven or the sands upon the seashore. Their
family will be their kingdom—theirs to love, to bless, and to
rule under the Most High God worlds without end.[6]

---

[5]See D&C 6:20.
[6]See D&C 76:56, 59; 132:19, 20.

INDEX

A.

Abel first righteous mortal born on earth, 173.

Abortion an equalizing factor of modern marriages, legalizing of, 69; Church authorities have not hesitated to employ term murder in denouncing, 213; that which is involved in, 213; and infanticide viewed as twin evils, 214.

Abraham instructed to take second wife, 175; and Sarah both of Semitic origin as descendants of Shem, 179; the great promise to, 208; granted vision of vastness of divine creations, 211.

Absalom murders Ammon for violation of his sister, 137; banished by father, David, 137.

Abstractions always victims of rationalization, 111.

Acceptance of perversion demanded, social and legal, 140.

Adam to be alone, not good for, 36; Michael became known as, 36; taught correct principles, 36; names Eve - the mother of all living, 41; made lord of all creation, 41; becomes steward of Eve by divine appointment, 41; "fell that man might be," 42; was not deceived, 42; taught plan of salvation, 52; Eve honors Father by accepting rule of, 53; blesses God for good news of divine pardon, 207; Where Goest Thou?, 299.

Adam and Eve met as total strangers, 40; experienced innocence in Garden of Eden, 41; fall signalled coming of age for, 54; mated in spirit before mated in flesh, 85.

Adam's love thwarts Satan's designs, 5; transgression affected all creation, 43.

Adoption bears witness of parental drive, widespread, 191.

Adulterous mate, Lord points way to treatment of an, 275.

Adultery produces devastation when it occurs in marriage, 133; no, if every man was pure of heart, 134; Pharisees sought to embroil Jesus in issue of, 246; and fornication do not have interchangeable meanings, 252; was an act of divorce, 253; Jesus' employment of the term, 255; Jesus concerned with spiritual implications of, 256.

Affection should grow between husband and wife, mutual, 84; artificial, may appear genuine but it is only illusory, 261.

Agency, man endowed with moral, 21; moral, vital to work of God, 22; of women equal to that of man, 58.

Allegiance when out of harmony with God, we owe no one, 50; to Kingdom of God will come through faith and diligence of army of Israel, 305.

Alma describes spiritual nature of man, 66; denounces hypocrisy of Zoramites, 111; tells Corianton of abomination of adultery, 144.

Ammon and Tamar, 136; seduces virginal half-sister Tamar, 136.

Animals were denizens of the Garden, 37.

Anthropomorphic nature of God negated, 10.

Apostasy cited as reason for restoration, 13.

Arabs, Ishmael became patriarch to 100 million, 178.

Army of the Lord, men of priesthood are the, 304.

Athanasian creed might have been written by Plato, 11.

Authoritarian marriages still dominate the world, variations of, 71.

Authority of husbands and churches being challenged today, 48; proper channel of, reaching back to God, 284.

tinuation of harmful relationship, 273; what a compelling thing is, 306.

Lovers must change before love can die, 87.

Loves but does not abandon them, the Lord chastizes those he, 276.

Loyalties threatened, mankind's, 7.

Loyalty passes from father to husband, woman's, 51.

Lucifer seeks to rob God of his family on earth, 5; motivated by a desire to be independent of all authority, 47; God himself could not save, 161.

Lucifer's successful beguilement of woman, 45.

Lyman Amasa, quoted on home as place where heaven has its beginning, 243.

M.

Malachi's prophecy fulfilled with coming of Elijah, 76.

Male-imposed bondage, woman no longer will accept, 26; women justified in denouncing, exploitation, 29; determines sex of unborn child, 40; initially the responsibility for carrying out God's will is a, responsibility, 300.

Maleness and femaleness make for very real differences, 38.

Males have abetted women as co-producers of economic wealth, 27.

Man, origin of man is destiny of, 4; did not theorize God into existence, 10; and woman originate in God, 15; and Woman, 15; the eternal nature of, 20; and woman endowed by attributes of divine parents, 20; continues to know more about environment than self, 20; did not originate in chaotic darkness, 35; is both male and female, 36; was complete with woman before him, 37; and woman are equal before the Lord, 38; has autonomy-free will, 38; also a products of woman, 40; obliged to labor for his substance, 43; destined to know many thorns and thistles, 43; to "rule over" woman a dictum often misinterpreted, 44; stands between woman and God, 52; puts curse on woman by his own failures, 60; woman needs, to be fulfilled as a woman, 61; advances only with help of God, 97; designated the direct representative of

the Lord on earth, 284; true saints will follow leadership of a righteous, 306.

Manipulative propaganda is not new as sophistry had its beginnings with Satan, 260.

Mankind robbed of truth about self, 11; should repent of its selfishness, 205.

Man's origin not on this small planet, 1; diversity accounts for failure of social sciences, 19; wide range of, characteristics, 21; stewardship over women initially founded on divine authority and worthiness, 50; natural results of, offenses are everywhere apparent, 204.

Man-made church has right to speak for God, no, 48.

Marital enterprise mirrors spiritual predispositions of parties to it, every, 65.

Marriage and family not chance inventions, 5; learned of, in first estate, 5; world needs to preserve ideals of, 7; divine foundation of, destroyed, 12; jeopardy caused by false theology, 13; modern, in danger, 13; women leave home to escape, 26; patriarchal order of, 48; Paul alludes to new and everlasting covenant of, 48; principle of, is of God, 65; has its degrees of glory, 65; A, in the Lord, 65; worldly, caters only to wants, 66; true, patriarchal in nature, 72; legal, being replaced by "arrangements," 70; A, in the Lord, 74; Brigham Young quoted on, relation, 74; eternal only when contracted under law of God, 75; of a true union can be of life-long devotion, 87; relationship spiritually consummated is foundation for celestial union, 89; importance of selecting, partner, 89; should take place in presence of two witnesses: the mind and the heart, 90; is an act of faith, 90; should be within one's means, 93; celibate life more rewarding than loveless, 96; true, is patriarchal in order, 97; in the Lord is God-ordained, 102; in assuming, perogatives without its obligations we are thieves and robbers, 146; alone endows with key for entering into sexual relationship, 146; is honorable in all, 146; becomes the unique sum of two lives, 148; all expressions of intimate affection should begin with, 157; fourfold purpose of, and procreation, 210;

only genuine, can sweeten what must be a bitter and tenuous union, 131.

Repentant couple may have a rewarding and happy life together, the truly, 150.

Restoration, apostasy cited as reason for, 13.

Restraint, The Spirit of, 231.

Resurrection, love will be total when perfected in, 85.

Revelation, women not denied personal, 284.

Richards, George F., quoted on number of children his wife bore him (15), 222.

Richards, Stephen L, describes a priest and priestess in the temple of the home, 292; on providing home for a goodly number of children, 238.

Rigdon, Sidney, testifies of risen Christ, 2.

Right conduct not meant to be a matter of convenience, 262.

Righteous principles, men and women can cope with change when committed to, 24.

Righteousness is an acquired state, 155; heaven only knows aristocracy of, 279.

Roberts, Brigham H., discussed moral effect of contraceptives, 229.

Rod of iron, word of Lord described as a, 112.

Romney, Marion G., quoted on receiving the Holy Ghost, 77; quoted on making life's decision by guidance of Holy Spirit, 89.

S.

Sacrifice for others is true discipleship, 31; law of, introduced to Adam, 52.

Sadducees ridiculed both eternal marriage and the resurrection, 248.

Salvation, come to Christ for, 61; hope of, given savages who are converted to Christ, 215.

Samuel warned against physical appearance of Eliab, 94; Hannah's prayers answered in bearing of, 186.

Santification, Brigham Young quoted on, VIII.

Sarah, the Matriarch of Israel, 174; childless for ninety years, 175; conflicts between, and Hagar, 176; complains to Abraham about Hagar, 176; gives birth to Isaac, 178.

Satan a home-wrecker without peer, 5; man turns to, inspired gods of wood and stone, 10; leads man to pillage and assaults against haven's rule, 36; informs Adam and Eve of nakedness, 55; dupes women into believing they are brides of Christ, 61; endeavors to get men to abuse priesthood power and authority, 72; a product of ruthless envy, 94; leads unwary carefully "down to hell," 109; assaults integrity of male and female natures, 141; inspired Cain with thought of murder, 173; influenced Adam's children against father, 203; repeats successes of the antediluvian period, 203.

Satan's efforts to pervert sex drive aimed at frustrating plan of salvation, 202; campaign to destroy family of God, VII.

Saul's daughter, Michael, was given to David, 38.

Savior quoted on "where your heart is," 24; personifie~ all that is divine and noble, 102.

Savior's mother had several children, 62.

Science achievements do not necessitate surrender of moral values, 7; man will not practice his, within bounds of morality and humility, 204.

Scientists and educators support moral disintegration, 127.

Scripture dictates its male orientation, very nature of, 284; some, applies to women and some to men, 284.

Scriptural grounds for divorce, 251.

Sealed to worthy husband commits self to his law, woman, 48.

Sealing power of priesthood necessary for eternal union, 76; demonstrated love for God and for each other justifies, to eternal life, 83.

Second world began under same divine junction to multiply upon the earth, 208.

Seek first kingdom of God applies equally to men and women, command to, 32.

Self-control, periodic continance and nature, modern Israel counseled to rely on, 221; husband and wife should exercise, 235.

Self-denial not popular thing to do, practicing, 231.

Selfish factors enter cause of working mothers, 26.

Selfishness a reason for birth control, 234.

Self-fulfillment only achieved as we voluntarily surrender it, 31.